SPSS MADE SIMPLE

OTHER TITLES OF RELATED INTEREST IN SOCIOLOGY

Research Methods and Statistics

Computer Software for the Social Sciences

SPSS MADE SIMPLE
SECOND EDITION

JOHN HEDDERSON
County of Los Angeles
Internal Services Department
Urban Research Section

MELINDA FISHER
University of Texas at El Paso
Department of Sociology

Wadsworth Publishing Company
Belmont, California
A Division of Wadsworth, Inc.

Editor: Serina Beauparlant
Editorial Associate: Marla Nowick
Production: Stacey C. Sawyer
Design: Al Burkhardt
Print Buyer: Randy Hurst
Copy Editor: Patterson Lamb
Chapter 1 Illustration: Bob Haydock
Cover: Al Burkhardt
Signing Representative: Tamy Stenquist
Compositor: G&S Typesetters, Inc.

 This book is printed on acid-free recycled paper.

SPSS^x, SPSS, and SCSS are the trademarks of SPSS Inc. for proprietary software.

Printed in the United States of America

1 2 3 4 5 6 7 8 9 10—97 96 95 94 93

ISBN 0-534-19992-5

Library of Congress Cataloging in Publication Data

Hedderson, John.
  SPSS made simple / John Hedderson, Melinda Fisher.
    p. cm.
  Rev. ed. of: SPSS^x made simple. c1987.
  Includes bibliographical references and index.
  ISBN 0-534-19992-5
  1. SPSS (Computer file) 2. Social sciences—Statistical methods—Computer programs. I. Fisher, Melinda. II. Hedderson, John. SPSS^x made simple. III. Title.
HA32.H43 1993
005.3'29—dc20   92-41434
                                             CIP

PREFACE

After twelve years of teaching SPSS, I am convinced that SPSS is not easy for the average college student to learn. I am also convinced that the program manuals are not easy to teach from. Students who are experienced with statistics and programming or students with a high aptitude for this type of work will learn SPSS easily. The rest suffer. Typically, my students have scant training in statistics or programming and have average or less-than-average aptitude for this work. Often they are not comfortable with mathematics, computers, and "that sort of thing." I wrote *SPSS Made Simple* to help this type of student and his or her instructor.

Organization

As the title implies, my book does not attempt to present all the intricacies and capacities of SPSS. In Part 1, I have tried to put in only what is essential for a student with little background in statistics and no background in programming to do successful analyses with SPSS. Being able to produce interesting output quickly is a tremendous morale booster. In Part 1 of the text, my objectives are

- to minimize student errors
- to teach the student to think in terms of coding data into cases, variables, and formatted records

- to introduce the student to basic data file cleaning through the LIST command
- to introduce the student to univariate analysis through the use of the FRE-QUENCIES command
- to teach the student how to focus on subsets of his or her cases using the SELECT IF command
- to teach the student how to transform variables and create new variables with the commands, RECODE, COMPUTE, and IF
- to introduce the student to bivariate analysis through the commands CROSSTABS, MEANS, CORR, and PLOT
- to show the student how to compare data files from different years using the JOIN command.

Part 2 covers multivariate statistical techniques that, in themselves, are not simple. Although I present simple approaches to using SPSS to produce analyses, my discussion of the meaning of the statistics is unavoidably more challenging and less complete than the discussion in Part 1. Part 2 includes chapters on using data from the Bureau of the Census and on using SPSS/PC+.

Advantageous Features

Throughout this book I have tried to proceed step-by-step without making implicit leaps in logic or sneaking in new terms without definitions.

A single topic, the correlates of happiness, is used for examples throughout the text to illustrate the various procedures as they are introduced. This extended example elaborates chapter by chapter how happiness corresponds with gender, education, income, health, marital status, and parenthood.

An easily conducted research project is incorporated into the text. This project gives the student the experience of being involved in an analysis from data collection to final product.

Data from a National Opinion Research Center General Social Survey is available from Wadsworth Publishing Company to instructors who adopt the book, so that analyses paralleling those in the text can be done as exercises.

Each chapter has Review Questions with answers that enable the students to test their comprehension of the chapter. Each chapter also has Assignment Questions with answers provided only to the instructor to test the students' comprehension.

Outputs discussed in the nucleus of the manual are simplified to facilitate the learning of key statistics. At the end of each chapter, there are replications of SPSS outputs; these enable the student to see the context in which the statistics appear and provide the instructor the option of discussing additional statistics.

A glossary of examples enables the student to look up quickly command keywords and specifications.

Finally and very significantly, this manuscript condenses into one book the most essential material covered in several expensive SPSS manuals.

Acknowledgments

Anyone who has worked on a textbook appreciates that the end product is a collective effort. That is why, outside the preface, I use the plural "we" in my writing, even though I was originally the sole author. This project began in the summer of 1983 as a text for SPSS. The draft manuscripts produced in subsequent summers benefited from the labor of many people, and the first edition of this book was published in 1987. Melinda Fisher joined work on the second edition as a contributing author.

Special thanks go to the questioning students who sought clarification and examples and applications in their classes.

The Wadsworth team assisting me with this edition has been exceptionally well by Serina Beauparlant and Marla Nowick. My first communication with Wadsworth was through marketing representatives Nancy Tandberg and Tamy Stenquist, who have shared their thoughts over the years on textbooks, education, and the cosmos while ably representing Wadsworth up and down the Continental Divide from Anchorage to El Paso.

I also benefited from the patient work of the Department of Sociology and Anthropology staff at the University of Texas at El Paso, especially Bea Ogaz and Irene Casas, who weathered the production of ever longer manuscripts, including the one that disabled the department's best printer. (In 1989 I left El Paso to join the County of Los Angeles, ISD, Urban Research Section.)

Invaluable service was done by the guinea pigs who "volunteered" at my behest to serve as test readers. Their willingness to plunge through material admittedly less entrancing than a best-selling novel and point out confusing pages and errors have been invaluable. Foremost among these have been my daughter Shanti, my brother Mark, and my friends Gregory Van Boom and Sarah Ray.

My colleague at UTEP Howard Daudistel served as a more statistically sophisticated reader and adviser. Roland Padilla of the University of Texas at El Paso, computer center, created the NORC90 file used throughout the text.

I appreciate the numerous constructive comments of the following reviewers whose work improved this book substantially: Ken Berry, Colorado State University; David Chilson, Bowling Green State University; Scott Feld,

State University of New York at Stony Brook; Larry Felice, Baylor University; Richard Harris, University of Texas at San Antonio; Jeff Jacques, Florida A&M; David Marshall, Texas Woman's University; and Dave Thissen, University of Kansas.

Finally, I am most grateful for the patience and support of my wife Janine Twomey.

Note to the Student

SPSS is a computer program for doing statistical analyses. A program is a set of instructions to the computer. This manual will show you how to use SPSS. The SPSS acronym stands for the Statistical Package for the Social Sciences. Pronounce each letter of the acronym separately—S-P-S-S.

If you are unfamiliar with statistics or computers, you may be a little nervous—perhaps very nervous. Relax. You do not have to be a genius to do statistical analysis or to use a computer. Step by step, this book will explain how to do statistical analyses with SPSS. After studying it, you still will not be an expert on statistics or computers. You will, however, be able to do the procedures used most often in academic, government, and business work.

The SPSS material is most easily learned by studying examples. We will study happiness as a learning example using data gathered from a sample survey of the United States. In particular, we will study how happiness is affected by gender, education, income, health, marital status, and parenthood. We challenge you to venture a guess right now as to which of these variables will be most strongly associated with happiness.

We start with an introduction for beginners. The rest of Part 1 proceeds gradually through basic statistical analyses. Part 2 introduces some of the more sophisticated statistical procedures of SPSS. Part 2 also covers how to use tapes from the U.S. Bureau of the Census and how to use SPSS/PC+, a version of SPSS designed for use on personal computers.

CONTENTS

PART <u>1</u>

LEARNING THE BASICS

If you have never used a computer or the SPSS program before, Part 1 is the place to begin. Part 1, consisting of seven chapters, discusses using computers, preparing data files for computers, saving and retrieving SPSS system files, and using the most basic SPSS commands. If you have experience using SPSS, you can go directly to the chapters that discuss whatever commands you need more information about.

- In Chapter 1 you are introduced to computers and SPSS.
- In Chapter 2 you learn to code data for computer analysis and to save and retrieve SPSS system files.
- In Chapter 3 you learn to examine your data for errors and to obtain the distribution of cases by variable categories.
- In Chapter 4 you learn to transform variables into new categories, to compute new variables, and to label your output clearly.
- In Chapter 5 you learn to use the command CROSSTABS to examine the association between two variables. You also learn to use control variables with CROSSTABS.
- In Chapter 6 you learn to use the command MEANS to compare group means on variables.
- In Chapter 7 you learn to use the commands CORR and PLOT, two more ways of examining the association between two variables.
- In Chapter 8 you learn to compare data from two years in different files. This process uses the ADD command.

Part 1 also provides practice in using an SPSS system file. As an example, we use the National Opinion Research Center's 1990 General Social Survey, discussed in Appendix B. The text examples focus on the characteristics of respondents that are associated with happiness. However, the file contains many other variables covering a broad range of attitudes and background information.

Part 1 also provides class assignments that involve gathering and coding data, using the Happiness Questionnaire in Appendix C. This research project involves collecting information about people and their level of happiness. You will be instructed chapter by chapter on how to treat the information you collect so it can be analyzed with SPSS. Finally, you will be guided through several sample analyses of the information. This project will give you a more complete understanding of the research process. It also will enable you to compare the people in your sample with the respondents to the 1990 General Social Survey.

1

INTRODUCTION: WHAT HAVE YOU GOTTEN YOURSELF INTO?

Many people hate working with computers or statistics, and you are now in the position of having to do both. Hatred of a task is often grounded in an unspoken fear that "I won't be able to do it right." To become an *expert* at programming or statistics can be a long, difficult learning process, but you need not be an expert to do useful statistical analysis with computers.

The best way to learn to use SPSS is by example. As a learning example, we will analyze how various types of people differ in their likelihood of being happy. Are men happier than women? Are college graduates happier than people who end their education with high school? Are the affluent or the poor happier than the middle class? Are single people happier than married people? Are people with children happier than people without children? In the coming chapters, you will learn how SPSS can help you answer these and a wide range of other questions.

This book's primary goal is to teach you to use SPSS. Although we review many statistical concepts when they first appear in the text, we presume that you have some knowledge of statistics. Take the Background Test at the end of this chapter to check whether your statistical knowledge is at the expected level. If your grasp of statistics concepts is shaky, you may wish to have handy an introductory statistics text for reference. An easy introduction is *Statistics without Tears* by Derek Roundtree (New York: Charles Scribner's Sons, 1981). A more advanced introduction is Hubert Blalock's *Social Statistics: Revised*

Second Edition (New York: McGraw-Hill, 1979). A statistics text that also discusses SPSS commands is *Through the Maze: Statistics with Computer Applications* by Margaret Jendrek (Belmont, Calif.: Wadsworth, 1985).

1.1 About SPSS: Friend or Foe?

We now provide some basic background about SPSS, computer programs, and data. These beginning terms are like your car tires. They are not the most exciting part of the vehicle, but you cannot go anywhere without them.

What Is SPSS?

SPSS is a set of computer programs that enable researchers to do many types of statistical analyses. Sometimes researchers analyze data they have collected; other times they analyze data sets acquired from other researchers. With SPSS you can

- count the number of cases in each category of a variable
- compute score means for variables
- do crosstabulations to examine associations between variables
- compute correlations between variables
- do multiple regressions, analyses of variance, discriminant function analyses, log-linear analyses, factor analyses, and other sophisticated multivariate analyses
- display data in a variety of report and graphic formats

Although other statistics programs are available, SPSS is easier to learn than most programs and is available at more installations than any other program package.

What Are Data and What Data Will We Use?

Broadly defined, **data** are any kind of information; however, the term often is used to refer particularly to information that is organized for computer processing. The word *data* is the plural form of *datum,* so we use *data* with the plural form of verbs, which may sound peculiar at first.

SPSS is a tool that can analyze all sorts of data about a countless variety of topics. What you use it for depends on your interests. SPSS has been used in studies of such diverse subjects as

- business payrolls
- school registrations
- earthquakes
- income distributions
- death rates
- population growth
- unemployment trends
- attitudes about nuclear weapons
- which kinds of people are most likely to be very happy or very unhappy

The subject of happiness is one we will use for examples throughout this book. For these examples, we employ data gathered by the National Opinion Research Center (NORC), a nonprofit research branch of the University of Chicago. Founded in 1941, NORC is one of the oldest national survey research facilities in the country and does work for a wide range of clients. Academic researchers, marketing managers, city planners, and political campaigners are some of the variety of people involved in survey research who have utilized the services or data of NORC.

Among its many research projects, NORC has conducted a General Social Survey almost every year since 1964. (The exceptions were in 1979 and 1981, when government funding for the project was insufficient.) This survey measures people's social, psychological, and political attitudes. The NORC General Social Survey also gathers information about age, sex, income level, level of education, ethnicity, race, marital status, and other social characteristics.

Our examples use data from the 1990 survey (see Appendix B). We also give assignments involving this data file as you progress chapter by chapter. Appendix B lists the questions used by NORC in their data collection. (Assignment Question 1.1 at the end of this chapter will begin preparing you to use this file.)

For comparisons with another year we have also made available data from NORC's 1984 General Social Survey (see Appendix B). Techniques for using data from both years are discussed in Chapter 8.

You can also collect data of your own using the Happiness Questionnaire in Appendix C. These data can be compared with the data from the NORC survey. Look at Appendix C now to get an idea of what the course research project entails. (The Research Project Work at the end of this chapter begins the research project.)

Perhaps you have already collected your own data on a question of interest to you. If so, this book will take you step-by-step through what you need to know to analyze them.

What Is a Program?

A **program** is a set of instructions to a computer to make it perform tasks that the user wants done.

A common mistake of beginning students is to think that a computer program already has the data and that they need only ask their questions. This is not true. For example, if you want to know the mean length of employment at Wadsworth, Inc., a statistics program can calculate the mean only if you supply employment data about the individuals working for Wadsworth. Unless someone has already stored the necessary data set in the system's memory and your program makes reference to its location, you must provide the data along with your commands.

The following is an example of an SPSS "job" that includes the data (the lines of numbers between BEGIN DATA and END DATA). A **job** or **run** is the submission of a program to a computer for execution.

```
DATA LIST  /    ID  1—2
                EDUC  3—4
                SEX  5
                HAPPY  6
BEGIN DATA
010912
021223
031521
041222
050611
061612
071522
081612
091821
101412
111321
121611
130922
141212
151221
161821
170821
```

```
181222
191613
20142
```
END DATA
FREQUENCIES   **EDUC**
                  SEX
                  HAPPY

There is nothing magical about this (or any) program. Preceding the commands in the example there would have to be operating system commands. These commands, which differ slightly for each computer installation, indicate the user's name, what account is to be billed, and where the output is to be sent. If the user were going to use data on a memory device within the system, other operating system commands and subcommands might be needed. You will need to learn from local people the operating system commands used at your installation. When the user gives a command like DATA LIST, certain procedures are carried out according to the instructions in the SPSS program. (The work done by the DATA LIST command is explained in Chapter 2.) The commands are merely a shorthand to activate the more complete instructions contained in the SPSS program, which is stored in the computer's memory. The lines in bold print in the example are the SPSS commands.

Each space in a line represents a column. All SPSS commands begin in column 1. If the command will not fit on one line, it is continued on the following line, but after column 1. If by mistake you begin the continuation of a command in column 1, SPSS will try to read the line as a new command and an error will probably result. You must not split any words or variable names when you continue on a new line. At most installations, the SPSS commands normally cannot extend beyond column 72. (If you enter the command UN-NUMBERED as the first SPSS command, however, your SPSS commands can extend through column 80.)

Most SPSS commands have two parts: (1) a command keyword beginning in column 1 and (2) a specification field, which provides details of the command. In our example, FREQUENCIES is a command keyword calling for a frequencies analysis. (FREQUENCIES is explained in Chapter 3.) Following the command keyword is the specification field EDUC SEX HAPPY, which names the specific variables for which the frequencies are to be produced. Most SPSS commands begin with a command keyword, followed by specifications. However, some commands use a command phrase containing two keywords—for example, DATA LIST—and a few command keywords do not require specifications—for example, BEGIN DATA. (DATA LIST and BEGIN DATA are discussed in Chapter 2.)

How Do You Learn to Use SPSS?

You learn SPSS step by step, just as you learned to read. Our book takes you through the process of learning to use SPSS to analyze social science data. For further reference see the *SPSS Reference Guide,* (Chicago: SPSS, Inc., 1990). All our references to the *SPSS Reference Guide* are to the second edition. This large, intimidating volume is an encyclopedic reference tool for the SPSS user. A section at the end of each chapter, entitled "Where to Look in the *SPSS Reference Guide,*" will cite where in the *Guide* to find more discussion of the material covered in the chapter. A copy of the *SPSS Reference Guide* should be available at your installation for reference, and it is sold in most college bookstores.

1.2 About Using Computers

If you have no experience with a computer, learning to use a computer may be the hardest part of learning to use SPSS. Just remember that you cannot break a computer by using it, even if you make mistakes. A deliberate attack, perhaps with an axe or a sledgehammer, can damage a computer. (Sometimes you will feel like destroying it. Don't!) Dropping a computer down a flight of stairs or pouring coffee into it can damage it, but making errors while using a computer will not damage it. So don't be nervous about hurting it.

What Is a Computer?

What is usually called a **computer** is actually a system of machines that can receive, process, store, and send out information. Remember that you are dealing with a mindless system of machines that does only what it is instructed to do and holds in memory only what it is told to store. (Human and mechanical malfunctions can mess up the ideal state of operation.) We use computers because, once programmed correctly, they perform tasks very quickly and accurately. What we hate about computers are the difficulties encountered in programming them correctly. User-friendly (easy to use) programs like SPSS reduce the difficulties.

What Are the Basic Parts of a Computer System?

The basic parts of a computer system are the input devices, the central processing unit, the storage devices, and the output devices (see Figure 1.1).

At most computer installations, the input device you will use is a **terminal** that consists of a **keyboard** (similar to that of a typewriter) and a **video display**

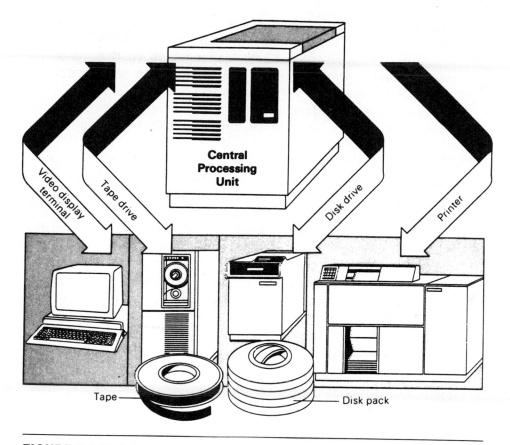

FIGURE 1.1 Typical components of a mainframe computer system

screen (similar in appearance to a television screen). Different types of terminals have small differences in how they are used. Computer installations will also differ in the program that operates the terminal. To give you a rough idea of what happens, we describe in Section 1.3 how information is entered at a TELEX terminal at UTEP (University of Texas at El Paso).

We presume in this text that you will not use an optical scanner, which can extract the information for the computer directly from questionnaires or answer sheets. We also presume that you will not conduct computer-assisted interviews in which the questions are displayed on a screen and the responses entered directly into the computer's memory. Both these techniques can expedite the work of entering data.

Another input device is a **card reader** into which cards with punched holes are fed. The punched holes are a code for letters, numbers, and other characters. The holes are made by a **keypunch machine,** which can make entries in 80 numbered columns on the card. The card devices have been almost completely superseded by more efficient electronic devices.

The **central processing unit** (CPU) of the computer coordinates the parts of the system, processes data, and has a memory core for storing data and instructions.

Programs and data must be stored in such a way that the computer can access them when so instructed. The most common **storage devices** are magnetic tapes and disks and also the memory core of the CPU. To store or retrieve information on a tape requires a machine called a tape drive that is linked with the computer's CPU. Disks usually come in packs; some are permanently mounted on a disk drive whereas others are removable.

Often the output from the computer will be on the same video display screen that indicates your input. For example, if you make a typing error when entering a command, you may receive an error message on the screen. Or, if your output is stored in a file in the computer's memory, you may be able to have the file displayed on your video screen.

Another option is to have your output printed on paper as a **hard copy.** This requires a **printer** and instructions, in the system language, telling the computer to print the output at a particular printer. A common practice is to send the output to a file, examine it on a video screen to ensure that it is correct, and then, if it is correct, have it printed. The commands to perform this operation vary from one computer installation to another.

You may never see all the parts of the computer system with which you are working. Often the user sits at a terminal that can exchange information with the system's CPU. The CPU may be in another room, in another building, or even thousands of miles away. The communication is like talking over a telephone. In fact, with the help of devices called **modems,** phone lines usually can be used to communicate between the terminal and the CPU. All that matters is that the electronic signals you are entering at the keyboard are being sent to the CPU and its responses are being sent back to you.

SPSS is normally run with a mainframe computer. **Mainframe** is a term used to describe a powerful CPU that works quickly and has a large memory core. A mainframe computer is capable of running more than one job at a time and capable of communicating with more than one input or output device simultaneously. Usually a mainframe computer is linked to tape drives and disks.

SPSS/PC+ is an interactive version of SPSS for **personal computers** like the IBM PC (see Chapter 14). A personal computer has a small CPU with less speed and memory than a mainframe. A PC fits on a desk, usually contained in a rectangular case under the display screen.

As the speed and memory core of computers continue to increase, PCs become more powerful and capable of performing more of the traditionally mainframe functions such as operating a network of terminals. At the same time, smart terminals and interactive programs are making mainframes more like PCs in how they are used. **Smart terminals** have data processing and storage capacities independent of the mainframe to which they are linked. **Interactive programs** are those in which the computer responds with output to individual commands as they are entered. (The output may be merely an acknowledgment that a legitimate command has been entered.) This method contrasts with the **batch entry** method, in which a complete set of commands is submitted at one time, and then, after processing all the commands, the computer gives one set of output.

Taking the Computer Plunge: What Do You Do First?

A good first step is to visit your computer installation and learn how it works. What are the input and output devices? Who is available to provide help when you need it? What are the hours of operation? What operating system commands are needed at the beginning of a job? Where will your hard copy output be sent? (If you submit a program and receive no output, your system language commands probably contain an error.)

1.3 Example of a Session at a Terminal

The description that follows is to give you some preparation for using a terminal. Remember, however, that systems will differ. Even within a system, procedures may vary depending on what type of terminal is being used. They also change over time. Life is full of little trials, one of them being to learn the idiosyncrasies (individual characteristics) of your particular computer system. Although tricky at first, operating your system will become old hat, and you'll wonder how it ever could have been a problem.

At each terminal at the University of Texas at El Paso (UTEP), the screen usually displays a UTEP logo or a message that the last user has signed off. (If a screen is totally blank and dark, make sure the machine is switched on and the brightness is turned up high enough. At many installations, the power is switched off or the brightness turned down when the machine is not in use.) Press the ENTER key, and a message will appear on the screen instructing you to enter your account number. (Information is **entered** by typing it and then pressing the ENTER key.) After entering your account number, you are asked to enter your password. After you have entered your password, the system indicates that you are signed on by printing some preliminary messages and the word *GO. At this point you can call up many programs, including one named **EDIT**, which is used to create, change, or store a file. This type of program is called an **editor**.

To use EDIT at UTEP, you type the word EDIT followed by the name of the file you are creating. For example, to begin a file named PROJECT, you would enter the line EDIT PROJECT. The computer would respond with a screen that is mostly blank. At the top is the name of the file (PROJECT). A line at the bottom of the screen indicates the cursor position and what mode the editor is in. (These details will be explained shortly.) Above the bottom line is a command line for entering commands to the editor.

Commands entered at the command line will be executed immediately. Above the command line is an area for entering or editing information in a file. Your entries in this area will be stored but not executed at the time of entry.

The information-entry area of the screen is a grid like graph paper in which each position can be identified by two numbers: a line number and a column number. Think of each position as being a seat in a concert hall. The line number indicates the location of a row of seats (or positions). The column number indicates the location of a particular seat (or position) in that row. A light marker called a **cursor** shows where you are. The cursor is usually a rectangular patch of light about the size of one position. As mentioned, the final line displayed on the screen indicates the line number and column number of the cursor's position. You can move the cursor by using keys with arrows on them. Press the Up arrow and the cursor moves up. Press the Down arrow and the cursor moves down. Similarly, the Left arrow moves the cursor to the left, and the Right arrow moves the cursor to the right.

When the editor is in the Insert mode, what you type appears in the space by the cursor without deleting any of the surrounding characters. When the editor is in the Replace mode, what you type replaces the character in the cursor position. You can switch the editor back and forth between the Insert mode and the Replace mode by pressing the INSERT key.

When you press a key on the keyboard, that key's character will appear on the video display screen. You can make changes when in the Insert mode by using the DELETE key to erase what is incorrect and then inserting what is desired. You can make changes when in the Replace mode by simply typing over the error with the correct character. The arrow keys allow you to position the cursor for deletion of unwanted characters and insertion of new characters.

When you finish and want to store the file, you move the cursor to the command line and type the command FILE PROJECT. The file named PROJECT will be stored, and the message *GO will appear on the screen, indicating that the system is ready for you to call up another program.

If your file named PROJECT is an SPSS program that you are now ready to run, you enter the command SEND PROJECT. The system will respond with a message indicating that the program PROJECT has been sent to be executed. Then the *GO message will appear on the screen.

If you have finished working with the computer, after receiving the *GO message, you enter the word OFF. The OFF command causes your account to be logged off (signed off) the machine, and a message appears confirming the log off. If you press the ENTER key again, the UTEP logo will appear on the screen and you will be back where you started when you sat down at the terminal.

1.4 Summary

In this chapter you've learned that

- *SPSS* is a program that enables researchers to organize data sets, transform variables, and do many types of statistical analysis.
- *Programs* are sets of instructions that the user gives to a computer to command desired operations.
- *Data* are pieces of information to be stored or processed.
- A *job* or *run* is the submission of a program to a computer for execution.
- *Computers* receive, store, process, and transmit information.
- *Terminals* transmit information to and receive information from computers.
- *Printers* produce computer output on paper.
- *Video display screens* produce visual images of computer output.
- *Computer tapes* and *disks* are devices that store information in a magnetic code.
- *Keypunch machines* are devices used to punch holes in computer cards.

RESEARCH PROJECT WORK FOR CHAPTER 1

Administer the Happiness Questionnaire in Appendix C to a sample of 20 people.

REVIEW QUESTIONS FOR CHAPTER 1

(Answers to Review Questions are given at the back of the book.)

1.1   In which column do SPSS commands begin?

1.2   In which column do continuations of SPSS commands begin?

1.3   Which is the highest numbered column that can be used by an SPSS command if the UNNUMBERED command is not used?

1.4   Which is the highest numbered column that can be used by an SPSS command if the UNNUMBERED command is used?

1.5   Which is the highest numbered column that can be used for operating system commands at most computer installations?

1.6   Can the operating system commands from another computer installation be used at your computer installation?

1.7   Can the SPSS commands used in this chapter's example be used at your computer installation?

1.8   What are the various storage devices used by computer systems?

1.9   When you use SPSS, is the machine at which you enter data a self-contained computer?

1.10   What is the difference between program commands and data?

ASSIGNMENT QUESTION FOR CHAPTER 1

(Solutions to the Assignment Questions are given in the *Instructor's Manual*.)

Look through the questions in Appendix B and make a list of the variable names that relate to

1.   family background
2.   satisfaction with aspects of one's life
3.   attitudes toward freedom of speech

BACKGROUND TEST

This book assumes that you are familiar with basic statistical terms and concepts. To check your knowledge and refresh your memory, fill in the blanks in the statements below using the terms provided. (The answers are provided after the final question.)

(a)   case
(b)   central tendency
(c)   Pearson correlation coefficient
(d)   interval measure
(e)   *N*

(f)   nominal measure
(g)   mean
(h)   median
(i)   mode
(j)   ordinal measure
(k)   population
(l)   range
(m) sample
(n)   score
(o)   standard deviation
(p)   statistical significance
(q)   *t*-test
(r)   unit of analysis
(s)   variable
(t)   *Z* score

1. One specific example of what is being studied is called a ___a___.

2. The number of cases in your study is called the ___e___.

3. The type of entity being studied is termed the ___r___.

4. The total set of what you are studying is called the ___k___.

5. A smaller number of the total set of what you are studying is termed a ___m___.

6. A set of mutually exclusive attributes that can be used to classify cases according to a characteristic (for example, income) is a ___s___.

7. The measure of a particular case on a variable is its ___n___ for that variable.

8. The point in a distribution around which other scores tend to cluster is the ___p___.

9. The ___h___ is a measure of central tendency that is the point in a distribution above which and below which half the scores fall.

10. A measure of central tendency that is the average—that is, the sum of scores divided by the number of cases—is called the ___g___.

11. The score that occurs most frequently is called the ___i___.

12. A measure that has categories that can be ranked but are not of equal size is termed ___j___.

13. A measure that has categories of equal size that can be ranked is called
    _____ *d* _____.

14. A measure that has distinct categories that cannot be ranked is called
    _____ *f* _____.

15. The difference between the highest score and the lowest score is called
    the _____ *l* _____.

16. The _____ *o* _____ is a measure of the typical distance from the mean score
    in a distribution. It is the square root of the sum of the deviations from the
    mean squared divided by the number of cases. $\sqrt{\dfrac{\Sigma\,(X - \bar{X})^2}{N}}$

17. A score minus the mean divided by the standard deviation $(X - \bar{X})/s$ is a
    _____ *of z-score* _____.

18. The probability that a given result could be caused by sampling error is
    called the _____ *p* _____.

19. One test of the statistical significance of the distance between the means
    of two sets of scores is the _____ *q* _____.

20. A measure of the strength of association between two interval variables
    is the _____ *RC* _____.

Answers to Background Test

1. a	8. b	15. l
2. e	9. h	16. o
3. r	10. g	17. t
4. k	11. i	18. p
5. m	12. j	19. q
6. s	13. d	20. c
7. n	14. f	

2

GETTING STARTED

New SPSS Commands:

DATA LIST
BEGIN DATA
END DATA
MISSING VALUES
SAVE
GET

After the NORC researchers interviewed 1372 people for the 1990 General Social Survey and recorded their answers, they needed to feed the data into the computer in a form it could use. If you have collected responses to the Happiness Questionnaire in Appendix C, you are facing the same task. What you need to know now is how to code data and how to tell that code to the computer.

2.1 Coding Your Data to Be Computer Readable

In this section we discuss how to prepare information so that it can be analyzed with a computer. Suppose you did the Research Project Work in Chapter 1, which involved administering the Happiness Questionnaire to 20 people. Now you have data from 20 people marked on questionnaires. What is the next step?

Because computers store information in columns, we usually convert verbal responses to numbers that will require fewer columns. For example, in our Happiness Questionnaire, one question is: "Would you say that you are very happy, pretty happy, or not too happy?" The person is asked to choose from three answers:

1	2	3
Very happy	Pretty happy	Not too happy

To store the verbal responses in columns, we would need to reserve as many columns as there are letters and spaces in the longest response—that would be 13 columns for "not too happy." Instead of this approach, we can have each response correspond to the number above it. Fantastic! Now we need only one column reserved for the number that corresponds to the response for that case.

At first, converting the responses to numbers may seem odd; however, this convention saves a tremendous amount of column space. An equally important reason to use numbers is that we often are dealing with variables for which we want to calculate the mean (average of all scores) and other statistics. In the above example, we might like to know the mean of the responses. If it were 1.6, we would know that in our sample the average of the responses was between "pretty happy" and "very happy."

There may be times when you want to work with words instead of numbers. For example, you may be conducting a study for which you want to be able to make a directory of respondents with names and addresses. To work with words you need to use string variables, which are discussed in Appendix A.

Once we have coded the data, we must store them in a way that enables the computer to find them. Think of your data for each case as being stored on a line. These lines are called **records.** Every column in a line of data is numbered sequentially starting with 1. Each **column** can hold one character—a number, letter, or other symbol. If columns 1 and 2 hold the case identification numbers for case 1, columns 1 and 2 will hold the case identification numbers for all other cases as well. This setup, known as a **fixed format,** is the formatting we will use in this book. Other types of formats are available, but the fixed format is most commonly used for statistical data. (See Appendix A for a discussion of free format.)

TABLE 2.1 Example Data Set

Name	Years of Education	Sex	Happiness Level
Acuna	09	male	pretty happy
Adams	12	female	not too happy
Bates	15	female	very happy
Beall	12	female	pretty happy
Cunningham	06	male	very happy
Dunham	16	male	pretty happy
Estrada	15	female	pretty happy
Franklin	16	male	pretty happy
Graham	18	female	very happy
Hadi	14	male	pretty happy
Hedgepeth	13	female	very happy
Jordan	16	male	very happy
Kim	09	female	pretty happy
Lawrence	12	male	pretty happy
MacKenzie	12	female	very happy
Morrison	18	female	very happy
Palafox	08	female	very happy
Practor	12	female	pretty happy
Razkowski	16	male	not too happy
Zirl	14	female	no answer

The number of columns in each line is the **record length.** The most common record length is 80 columns. What if you need to enter more data for this case? You go to the next record—the next line—and use two or more records for each case.

The concepts of cases, columns, and records will be more clear if we go through an example of coding data for a set of cases. Table 2.1 shows a small data file before it is coded. The data in this file, except the names, are real cases taken from a NORC General Social Survey, described in Appendix B. This data set will be used throughout Part I to provide examples of SPSS procedures. We will refer to it as our "example data set."

There are many ways to code a data set, so the researcher has to make some decisions. We could code this data file as follows:

- Case number: The first two columns will be for the case number code; each individual will be given a unique code number to identify who the data are for.

- Education: The third and fourth columns will be education, coded in years.
- Sex: The fifth column will indicate the respondent's sex (1 = male, 2 = female).
- Happiness: The sixth column will be happiness level (1 = very happy, 2 = pretty happy, 3 = not too happy).

We also need codes to indicate missing information. The simplest approach is to leave columns blank to indicate missing data. For example, the last case above, Zirl, did not answer the question about happiness, so the column for that variable will be left blank on the line for Zirl. If you want to distinguish between different types of missing data, you need to use the MISSING VALUES command discussed in Section 2.4.

The coding system described above would result in the following data file:

```
010912
021223
031521
041222
050611
061612
071522
081612
091821
101412
111321
121611
130922
141212
151221
161821
170821
181222
191613
20142
```

Each line above is one record and represents the variable codings for one person. Thus the first line of numbers, 010912, represents the responses of Acuna, the first case in our data file. The first two digits, 01, are the case number that identifies Acuna. The second two digits, 09, indicate that Acuna has 9 years of formal education. The 1 following the 9 shows that Acuna is male. The 2 following the 1 shows that Acuna responded that he was pretty happy.

The second line, 021223, is the coded information for Adams, our second case. The digits 02 beginning the line are Adams' identification number. The 12 following the 02 indicates that Adams has 12 years of education. The 2 following the 12 indicates that Adams is female. The 3 following the 2 indicates that Adams is not too happy.

Likewise, each following line is for a subsequent case. Note that the sixth column for Zirl, the last case, is blank because the information was missing for that variable, and we are using blanks to indicate missing data. Having carefully coded and entered your data, you need to explain these codes and data locations to the SPSS program. This communication with the SPSS program is done via the DATA LIST statement, which is discussed in the next section.

2.2 Telling the Computer How Your Data Are Organized: DATA LIST

The **DATA LIST** command tells the SPSS program the name of each variable that you intend to use and the location of the columns being used for each of these variables. (You do not need to use all of your variables on every run.) Variable names must not be over eight characters long and must begin with a letter. Using variable names that are too long or that do not begin with a letter is a common error made by beginners. Blanks, commas, and periods are not permitted in a variable name, but numbers and other symbols are okay. There are several words that SPSS reserves in its programming that the user cannot employ as a variable name. The **reserved words** are: ALL, AND, BY, EQ, GE, GT, LE, LT, NE, NOT, OR, THRU, TO, and WITH. A good practice is to give your variables names that will remind you of the nature of the variable. For instance, we gave the name HAPPY to the variable containing the responses to the question about happiness.

Normally the DATA LIST command is positioned immediately after the operating system commands (discussed in Chapter 1). However, the UNNUMBERED command, if used, goes between the operating system commands and the DATA LIST command. By itself, the DATA LIST command does not produce any output. It simply provides the SPSS program with information needed to perform other commands. (If your data are in an SPSS system file, you will not use DATA LIST. See Section 2.5.)

Let's consider an example of a DATA LIST command:

```
DATA LIST  /   ID 1—2
```

The words DATA LIST alert the SPSS program that the rest of the command will describe the names and locations of the variables for this run. The words DATA LIST must begin in column 1 of the command and there must be one space and only one space between DATA and LIST. A slash (/) after LIST indicates the beginning of variable names and locations.

The expression ID 1—2 indicates that the first variable name is ID and that the ID information is located in columns 1 and 2.

There must be at least one space between the variable name and the column numbers—in this example, between ID and 1—2. If the data span two or more columns, enter the number of the first column, a hyphen, and then the number of the second column—in this example, 1—2.

Usually you will be concerned with more than one variable. The following DATA LIST command contains information for the four variables described in the coding example at the beginning of this chapter:

```
DATA LIST  /   ID 1—2
               EDUC  3—4
               SEX  5
               HAPPY  6
```

In this longer DATA LIST command, the EDUC 3—4 indicates the name of the second variable and the location of the education responses in columns 3 and 4.

In the command, the variable names are on separate lines. Each variable name must be separated from the column numbers of the preceding variable by one or more commas or spaces. The same convention for separating a list of variable names is followed in other SPSS commands. In this text, we will sometimes use two spaces where one would suffice or use a comma instead of a space. We do so for the sake of clarity. Writing commands that can be read easily, quickly, and correctly is as important as writing commands as compactly as possible.

The third variable is SEX; its data are located in column 5. The fourth variable is named HAPPY; its data are located in column 6.

The DATA LIST command is one of two places where you can indicate whether your data contain decimal points. Indicate the number of digits that are to the right of the decimal point in parentheses following the column location information. For example, if you had a variable named WAGE (hourly wages) in columns 11–15 and you wanted a decimal point to the left of the last two columns, your code would be:

```
DATA LIST /   WAGES 11-15  (2)
```

You could also simply enter the wage data with a decimal point before the last two digits; the (2) would then be unnecessary. For example, if an hourly wage of $7.50 were entered as 7.50, the decimal would not have to be indicated on the DATA LIST command. However, the practice of including decimal points in the data uses up more columns than indicating the decimal place in the DATA LIST command.

Two more examples of coding are provided by the NORC Codebook in Appendix B and the Happiness Questionnaire in Appendix C. (If you are still unclear about coding, take time to look at these appendices now.) Throughout Part I we will refer to the example data set in this chapter, the NORC Codebook in Appendix B, and the Happiness Questionnaire in Appendix C. They will be used in the Review Questions, the Assignment Questions, and the Research Project Work because they are realistic examples of the types of data sets researchers collect and analyze.

2.3 Indicating Where Your Data Records Begin and End: BEGIN DATA and END DATA

Before doing a statistical procedure in SPSS, you need to instruct the computer to begin reading data. This is done with the BEGIN DATA command:

```
BEGIN DATA
```

This command is followed by the data records—the lines of data. After all the data are entered, instruct the computer to stop reading data with the command

END DATA

The DATA LIST, BEGIN DATA, and END DATA commands, as well as the data themselves, are all omitted from your commands when you use an SPSS system file. (We discuss SPSS system files in Section 2.5 below.)

2.4 Indicating Where Data Are Missing: MISSING VALUES

As we explained earlier in this chapter, the easiest way to handle missing data is to leave the columns for that variable blank when entering data. The blanks signal the SPSS program that the data are missing.

At times, however, the researcher will want to distinguish among different types of missing data. The **MISSING VALUES** command enables us to do this. As an example, information on education might be missing because the interviewer forgot to ask that question or because the respondent refused to answer. We could code the education variable -9 to indicate that the interviewer forgot to ask the question and 99 when the respondent refused to answer. The choice of values -9 and 99 is arbitrary. We could have used 98 and 99 or any numbers that would not be confused with an actual response to the education question. We could not use 09 as a missing value because some respondents might have had nine years of formal education.

Now we can distinguish between a respondent's refusal—which we code as 99—and an interviewer's forgetfulness—which we code as -9. We might want to distinguish between these two types of missing data because the person who refuses to answer is showing some reluctance about the interview. This information may be significant in evaluating other answers of that respondent. The following example shows the SPSS command necessary to give the EDUC variable two missing values: -9 and 99.

MISSING VALUES EDUC $(-9,99)$

This command indicates that, if the code in the EDUC columns is -9 or 99, then the response is missing for that case. In the MISSING VALUES command, the two missing values must be separated by at least one comma or space.

We are limited to specifying individually three missing values per variable; however, two values can be used with the keyword THRU to specify a range such as (90 THRU 99). Also the RECODE command (discussed in Chapter 4) allows us to change the code value given to a response to one of the missing values.

If no numbers appear within parentheses immediately after a variable, the missing values will be the same as those for the first variable following on the MISSING VALUES command that does have missing value information. In the example below, HAPPY is not followed by a number in parentheses, whereas SEX, the variable after HAPPY, is followed by a missing value of 0. Thus, the missing value for HAPPY is also 0.

```
MISSING VALUES   HAPPY
                 SEX (0)
```

Not all the variables in the DATA LIST command need to be listed in the MISSING VALUES command, nor does the order of variable names in the MISSING VALUES command need to be the same as the order in the DATA LIST command.

A nice convention is to give all the variables the same missing values, but sometimes this practice is awkward. For income or years of education, for example, one would not use the number 0 to designate missing data because 0 could be a legitimate response. Often a negative number is used for variables that have 0 as a response category. A negative number takes up two columns, however, and you would not want to use it universally if your data set has many variables that can be fit in one column. The use of blanks to indicate missing values is not only convenient, because it will not require a MISSING VALUES command; it also is efficient because it does not require two columns like a negative number.

Procedures are available in some of the SPSS analyses for giving missing values another value, such as the mean for the variable, so that those cases may be included in the analysis. (See the *SPSS Reference Guide* for a discussion of the OPTIONS available for the technique you want to use.) This reassignment of values is often done when an analysis includes so many variables that the number of cases with missing data on one or more variables is quite high. It is possible, especially in an analysis with many variables, for every case to have missing data on one or more of the variables. Under these circumstances, the analysis is impossible unless new values are assigned to the cases' missing data or unless some of the variables are dropped from the analysis.

Where in the program you place the MISSING VALUES command is important. This command must be placed somewhere after the DATA LIST command and before the first statistical procedure command for which the specified values are to be treated as missing. The missing values will stay in effect for the entire run following the MISSING VALUES command unless the command is superseded by a second MISSING VALUES command. Below we have added a MISSING VALUES command to our example:

```
DATA LIST  /   ID 1-2
               EDUC 3-4
               SEX 5
               HAPPY 6
BEGIN DATA
010912
021223
031521
041222
050611
061612
071522
081612
091821
101412
111321
121611
130922
141212
151221
161821
170821
```

```
181222
191613
20142
END  DATA
MISSING VALUES    EDUC (-9,99)
                  HAPPY
                  SEX (0)
FREQUENCIES    EDUC
               SEX
               HAPPY
```

As you can see from this example, when the data and commands are on one file, the file can soon become very bulky. SPSS system files, which we discuss in the next section, provide a solution to this problem.

2.5 Using SPSS System Files

You can think of an **SPSS system file** as a data file that is saved along with the DATA LIST and MISSING VALUES commands. This type of file is a great convenience because you need not enter all this information every time you want to do an analysis of the file. If you use an SPSS system file, DATA LIST, MISSING VALUES, BEGIN DATA, the data themselves, and END DATA are omitted from your commands.

SPSS system files can be combined easily, which is useful when you have a set of related data files that you use in different combinations. For example, you may have a file for each census tract in a city and want to do a series of analyses using different groupings of tracts.

Creating an SPSS System File

In creating an SPSS system file, you need to place information in the operating system commands about where this file will be stored.

The SPSS command you use to create an SPSS system file is **SAVE**. This command must be accompanied by the specification field **OUTFILE =** followed by the name under which to store the file. To create a system file with the name PROJECT, you would use the command

SAVE   OUTFILE=PROJECT

Normally this command is placed at the end of your program so that any transformations and variables created during the program will be saved as well. The
SPSS commands and data needed to create an SPSS system file from our
learning example data set are:

```
DATA LIST  /   ID  1-2
               EDUC  3-4
               SEX  5
               HAPPY  6
BEGIN DATA
010912
021223
031521
041222
050611
061612
071522
081612
091821
101412
111321
121611
130922
141212
151221
161821
170821
181222
191613
20142
END DATA
MISSING VALUES    EDUC  (-9, 99)
                  HAPPY
                  SEX  (0)
SAVE    OUTFILE=PROJECT
```

Note that you need DATA LIST, BEGIN DATA, END DATA, and the data themselves among your commands when you create an SPSS file. Once the file is created, however, you need not include these commands or the data when you use the file. In the run to create the system file PROJECT, statistical procedure commands such as FREQUENCIES could have followed after END DATA.

Accessing a System File

You would use the **GET** command to access the system file named PROJECT that we saved in the preceding example. A **FILE=** specification field is also necessary, so the entire GET command would be:

```
GET   FILE=PROJECT
```

To produce the frequency distributions (see Section 3.2) for all the variables in the SPSS system file PROJECT, the SPSS commands would be

```
GET   FILE=PROJECT
FREQUENCIES   ALL
```

2.6 Summary

In this chapter we explain how to code information into numbers.

We explain how to use the DATA LIST command to tell the computer what our variables are and what columns contain each variable's information.

We show how to set off data with the BEGIN DATA and END DATA commands.

We explain how to indicate missing data with blanks or with the MISSING VALUES command.

Finally, we explain how to create and access SPSS system files using the SAVE and GET commands.

2.7 Where to Look in the SPSS Reference Guide

- The information on coding that is presented in this chapter is not given in the *SPSS Reference Guide.*
- DATA LIST is discussed on pages 109–121.
- BEGIN DATA and END DATA are discussed on pages 72–73.
- MISSING VALUES is discussed on pages 65–68.
- SPSS system files are discussed on pages 6 and 655.
- SAVE is discussed on pages 652–655.

RESEARCH PROJECT WORK FOR CHAPTER 2

1. Enter into a memory device at your installation the data you gathered doing the Chapter 1 research project work. For all but the final question, you can use the codes provided for each response on the Happiness Questionnaire. The final question is not precoded, however, so you will have to decide how to categorize the answers and what code value to give each category.

2. Write DATA LIST and MISSING VALUES commands for the data file you have stored.

REVIEW QUESTIONS FOR CHAPTER 2

(Answers to Review Questions are given at the back of the book.)

Hint: The variables in these problems can be coded in more than one way.

2.1 Using the variables and the coding system from our example data set, what would be the data record for the following case: Hedderson, whose identification number is 25, whose sex is male, who has 21 years of formal education, and who states that he is very happy.

2.2 How would you code the variable *age?*

2.3 How would you code the variable *political affiliation?*

2.4 How would you code the variable *annual salary?*

REVIEW USING DATA LIST

2.5   Write a DATA LIST command that would allow you to use the education variable from our example data set presented in this chapter.

2.6   Do you need to use a DATA LIST command if the file you are using is an SPSS system file?

2.7   For the file that would be created from the Happiness Questionnaire discussed in Appendix C, write a DATA LIST command that would allow you to use variables named INCOME and SEX.

REVIEW USING MISSING VALUES

2.8   Write a MISSING VALUES command that would assign a missing value of −9 to the variable EDUC.

2.9   Write a MISSING VALUES command that would assign missing values of −9 and −8 to the variable INCOME.

2.10   Write a MISSING VALUES command that would assign a missing value of 0 to the variables SEX, RELIGION, and PARTY.

2.11   What must be done in order for a blank to be treated as a missing value?

ASSIGNMENT QUESTIONS FOR CHAPTER 2

(Solutions to the Assignment Questions are given in the *Instructor's Manual*.)

2.1   Using the variables and the coding system from our example data set, what would be the data record for the following case: Foster, whose identification number is 33, whose sex is female, who has 18 years of formal education, and who states that she is very happy.

2.2   How would you code the variable *number of months* employed by Wadsworth?

2.3   How would you code the variable *number of dependents?*

2.4   How would you code the variable *religious affiliation?*

2.5   Write a DATA LIST command that would allow you to use the happiness variable from our example data set.

2.6   Would a DATA LIST command be needed to use the variables AGE and INCOME on the SPSS system file NORC90, discussed in Appendix B?

2.7   Write a DATA LIST command for the variables in the Happiness Questionnaire given in Appendix C.

2.8   Write a MISSING VALUES command that would assign a missing value of −9 to INCOME.

2.9   Write a MISSING VALUES command that would assign missing values of −8 and −9 to a variable named AGE.

2.10   Write a MISSING VALUES command that would assign a missing value of 0 to the variables MARITAL, STATE, and RELIGION.

3

TAKING A FIRST LOOK
AT YOUR DATA

New SPSS Commands:

```
LIST
FREQUENCIES
SELECT IF
```

When you analyze your data for the first time, one of your obvious concerns will be the general distribution of cases for each variable. For instance, in considering the example data set presented in Chapter 2, you might ask what percentage of the cases were "very happy," "pretty happy," and "not too happy," respectively. The answer would be the frequency distribution of cases for the variable HAPPY. In this chapter we learn how to produce frequency distributions with SPSS.

Less obvious concerns, however, that should take precedence over analyzing the distribution of cases for each variable are to ensure (1) that the data were entered correctly into memory and (2) that your program is reading them correctly.

It is very important to check your data for errors in coding and data entry. If the data set is given to you on cards, tapes, or disks by someone who has already checked it extensively, it may be "clean"—that is, free of errors. However, if you or someone else types in the data from a coding sheet, questionnaires, or your scribbled class notes, errors in data entry are likely to occur.

The LIST command, covered in this chapter, allows you to list by case the values entered for each variable.

The FREQUENCIES command, which we also cover in this chapter, allows you to learn about the frequency distribution of the cases for each variable. Interesting in itself, the frequency distribution is also useful for revealing errors in data entry.

The SELECT IF command, the final command introduced in this chapter, allows us to limit an analysis to whatever types of cases we choose to specify.

Together, the LIST, FREQUENCIES, and SELECT IF commands provide you with tools for tracking down errors in data entry and for taking a first look at the distribution of your cases by variable category.

3.1 Printing Out Data for Cases of Interest: LIST

Perhaps you have received a data set on a tape and want to see if it matches an accompanying codebook that explains the variable codings. Perhaps a data set has just been entered onto a storage device and you want to check each case's data to be sure they were entered correctly. Perhaps a statistical analysis has led you to suspect that the data were entered incorrectly for a particular case and you want to list all the data entries for that case. You can accomplish these types of tasks with the **LIST** command.

A listing is an output that gives the values that have been entered in your data file. You may want to list the scores for some or all of your cases or for some or all of your variables. If you want to see all the data entries for all your cases, the command is simply

```
LIST
```

For example, to list all the data entries for our example data set from Chapter 2, the data and necessary SPSS commands would be as follows. (Once again, you must first use the operating system commands for your installation.)

```
DATA LIST  /   ID  1-2
               EDUC  3-4
               SEX  5
               HAPPY  6
BEGIN DATA
010912
021223
031521
041222
050611
061612
071522
081612
091821
101412
111321
121611
130922
141212
151221
161821
170821
181222
191613
20142
END DATA
LIST
```

The output produced by this set of commands is given in Table 3.1. Note that a period is printed for the final case, which has missing data in the column for HAPPY. Preceding and following the output will be many lines summarizing what operations were done by the computer system during execution of the program. The operating system commands and the SPSS commands that you submitted will also be printed. If the job did not run properly, you may see an error message. An **error message** is a statement produced by the SPSS program when it encounters something amiss in trying to read or execute your commands. The message will be a statement that tries to explain what went wrong. It will normally be printed in the output immediately after the command with the error.

TABLE 3.1 Output from the LIST Command

ID	EDUC	SEX	HAPPY
1	9	1	2
2	12	2	3
3	15	2	1
4	12	2	2
5	6	1	1
6	16	1	2
7	15	2	2
8	16	1	2
9	18	2	1
10	14	1	2
11	13	2	1
12	16	1	1
13	9	2	2
14	12	1	2
15	12	2	1
16	18	2	1
17	8	2	1
18	12	2	2
19	16	1	1
20	14	2	

If your data file has a large number of variables and you do not want to print them all, you can specify which ones to print after the LIST command. Adding ID HAPPY would cause only the values for these two variables to be listed for each case. The command at the end of our example would then be

LIST   ID HAPPY

If your data file is very large and you do not want to list all the cases, you can specify the number of cases you want listed. If we substituted the following command in our example, the program would list the scores for ID and HAPPY for the first 25 cases.

LIST   ID HAPPY/
       CASES=25

(The full output generated by this command appears in Table 3.6 at the end of the chapter.)

CASES= is a subcommand to indicate how many cases you want to list. For example, CASES=25 will list 25 cases. CASES=ALL would list all the cases, and this is also what would happen by default if CASES= was omitted. Slash (/) is used to separate the CASES= subcommand from the last variable name. We recommend placing the CASES= subcommand on its own line starting after column 1. In our example, we aligned CASES= with ID to improve readability. It can be placed on the same line as the last variable name. However, placing it on the same line makes it more difficult for a user to find CASES= in the program.

3.2 Learning the Distribution of Cases: FREQUENCIES

The **FREQUENCIES** command instructs the computer to print out all the code numbers that occur for each variable and the number of cases in each of the code-number categories. For example, the variable SEX in our example data set has the code numbers 1 for males, 2 for females, and a blank if the information is missing. The FREQUENCIES command would print out that there was a category coded 1 and the number of cases in this category; it would also print out that there was a category coded 2 and the number of cases in this category. Similarly, it would print out the number of cases for which the data are missing.

In addition to giving the distribution of cases by variable, the FREQUENCIES command is an excellent way to check the validity (accuracy) of your data file. If a value that is impossible appears to have cases, we can be sure that the data were entered incorrectly for those cases or that the DATA LIST command contains an error. Thus, if for some case the value of SEX is listed as 3, when only code values 1, 2, and blank are being used, you would know an error occurred in data entry for that case.

The FREQUENCIES output will not catch errors that are realistic in appearance. For example, if, for the variable SEX, a 1 were entered instead of a 2, nothing would look wrong. One would assume that the case was a male and not realize that it was a female whose gender data had been entered incorrectly. (The LIST command, covered in the previous section, must be used to detect less obvious errors by checking the printout against the original data.)

To do a FREQUENCIES procedure for the variable HAPPY in our example data set, you would use the following command:

```
FREQUENCIES   HAPPY
```

FREQUENCIES must begin in column 1, as with all SPSS commands. Leave at least one blank space between FREQUENCIES and the variables being specified. Variable names must be separated by at least one comma or space.

Placed in the context of the operating system commands, other SPSS commands, and the data for our example data set described in Chapter 2, the preceding FREQUENCIES command would instruct SPSS to produce the frequencies for the variable HAPPY. In the following display we have provided an example omitting operating system commands. Notice that the FREQUENCIES command follows directly after the END DATA command. As we will illustrate later in this chapter, more than one SPSS command may be placed after END DATA.

```
DATA LIST  /    ID  1-2
                EDUC  3-4
                SEX  5
                HAPPY  6
BEGIN DATA
010912
021223
031521
041222
050611
061612
071522
081612
091821
101412
111321
121611
130922
141212
151221
161821
170821
181222
191613
20142
END DATA
FREQUENCIES   HAPPY
```

TABLE 3.2 Simplified Output from a FREQUENCIES Command

HAPPY

VALUE	FREQUENCY	PERCENT
1	8	42.1
2	9	47.4
3	2	10.5
.	1	MISSING
TOTAL	20	100.0

These commands and data would produce the output in Table 3.2. The column headed VALUE indicates what the code categories are for the variable HAPPY. The numbers under FREQUENCY indicate the number of cases in each category. The numbers under PERCENT indicate the percent of all cases that are in each category.

Recall from the coding we did in Chapter 2 that, in our example data set, the value 1 stands for "very happy," the value 2 stands for "pretty happy," and the value 3 stands for "not too happy." In our sample of 20 people, 42 percent responded that they were very happy, 47 percent responded that they were pretty happy, and 10 percent responded that they were not too happy.

To produce a table that presents the number of cases in each category for all variables, you would substitute the following FREQUENCIES command in the preceding example:

FREQUENCIES   ALL

The **ALL** in this example is a specification keyword that has the same meaning in SPSS and in everyday usage. (Specification **keywords** are words used in commands and subcommands to facilitate the expression of what must be done. Their meaning is generally apparent, and we will cover them as we introduce the SPSS commands and subcommands.) In this example, ALL calls for FREQUENCIES to be done for all the variables in the DATA LIST command. ALL can be used with many SPSS commands.

Before doing a FREQUENCIES run, review your variables to be certain that none of them contains more categories than you want printed out. Otherwise your printout may be far bulkier than you want. For example, family income to the nearest dollar might have as many categories as the number of cases, and for a large data set the frequencies for family income would be an enormous table. The best way to solve this problem is to combine many values into fewer large categories. This combining of values is done with the RECODE command, discussed in Chapter 4.

3.3 Doing FREQUENCIES with an SPSS System File

The use of FREQUENCIES with an SPSS system file differs from the example in the previous section. The GET command replaces the DATA LIST, MISSING VALUES, BEGIN DATA, and END DATA commands, and you do not enter the data with your commands. (The program will go to the memory device where you stored the file referred to in your GET command. SPSS will know the location from the directions in the operating system commands.) To do a FRE-QUENCIES run of all the variables in the SPSS system file NORC90, you would use the following commands. (Again the operating system commands for your installation must precede the SPSS commands.)

GET FILE=NORC90
FREQUENCIES   ALL

Part of the output produced by the preceding commands is replicated in Table 3.3. In this table for the 1372-case NORC90 file, we can see a few differences in format from Table 3.2. First, there are value labels for the values, because NORC90 was saved with the VALUE LABELS command. (Creation of value labels is discussed in Chapter 4.) Second, there are some cases with data missing. A check of the NORC90 Codebook in Appendix B will show that DK stands for "don't know" and NA stands for "no answer."

There are also very noticeable differences in the distribution of HAPPY for this sample. The frequency of "very happy" is 33 percent instead of 42 percent (we will round off to the nearest percent in the text), the frequency of "pretty happy" is 58 percent instead of 47 percent, and the frequency of "not too happy" is 9 percent instead of 10 percent. The NORC90 sample is much larger than our 20-case example, so we presume that it more accurately reflects what the percentages would be if we surveyed the entire population of the United States.

TABLE 3.3 Partial Output of FREQUENCIES Using the NORC90 SPSS System File

HAPPY

VALUE LABEL	VALUE	FREQUENCY	PERCENT
VERY HAPPY	1	455	33.4
PRETTY HAPPY	2	784	57.6
NOT TOO HAPPY	3	122	9.0
DK	8	0	MISSING
NA	9	11	MISSING
	TOTAL	1372	100.0

From Table 3.3 we learn that a little more than half the respondents in the NORC90 sample reported being pretty happy, another third reported being very happy, and the remaining 9 percent were not too happy. (In Chapter 4 we will begin to investigate how various types of people differ in their likelihood of being in each of these categories.)

3.4 Producing More with FREQUENCIES: Subcommand STATISTICS

Using the subcommand **STATISTICS** in a FREQUENCIES command will produce the high score, low score, mean, and standard deviation for each variable named. (Other statistics can be produced as well. See Section 18.18 of the *SPSS Reference Guide.*) The format to obtain frequencies and statistics on the variable HAPPY from the NORC90 system file would be

FREQUENCIES   HAPPY/
               STATISTICS

Note that the subcommand STATISTICS is separated from the variable name HAPPY by a slash. For greater visual separation, we have placed the STATISTICS subcommand on a separate line. A good practice is to make it as

TABLE 3.4 Actual Output from the Command
FREQUENCIES   HAPPY/
                  STATISTICS

HAPPY   GENERAL HAPPINESS

VALUE LABEL	VALUE	FREQUENCY	PERCENT	VALID PERCENT	CUM PERCENT
VERY HAPPY	1	455	33.2	33.4	33.4
PRETTY HAPPY	2	784	57.1	57.6	91.0
NOT TOO HAPPY	3	122	8.9	9.0	100.0
DK	8	0	0.0	MISSING	
NA	9	11	.8	MISSING	
	TOTAL	1372	100.0	100.0	

MEAN   1.782   STD DEV   .655   MINIMUM   1.000
MAXIMUM   3.000

VALID CASES   1361   MISSING CASES   11

---

easy as possible to pick out the various parts of your SPSS commands. Any continuation of an SPSS command on a subsequent line must be indented at least one column; therefore, we have indented STATISTICS, a continuation of the FREQUENCIES command. (We indented more than one space for clarity.) Note, however, that following some commands, STATISTICS is used as a command itself, beginning in column 1 (see Section 5.4).

The output from the preceding commands for the variable HAPPY in the NORC90 SPSS system file is given in Table 3.4. This table replicates all the output produced by FREQUENCIES for HAPPY. Note that it includes a variable label, GENERAL HAPPINESS, and valid percent and cum percent (cumulative percent) columns.

For a simple description of the characteristics of a set of cases, the information provided by FREQUENCIES will often be sufficient. But what if you want to focus on a subset of your cases? For example, your employer's personnel department may have assigned you the task of describing the salaries, positions, and length of employment of all female personnel. Or you may want to select those cases with invalid data and print the ID variable. This output would give you the identification number of all cases that need corrections in their data. The SELECT IF command, presented in the next section, will allow you to focus on such subsets of your set of cases.

3.5 Focusing on Cases of Interest: SELECT IF

Often in an analysis you will not want to include all the cases in your data file. Perhaps you want to obtain a description of only the women in your sample. The **SELECT IF** command allows you to select certain cases. Study the following command (remembering that female is coded 2 for the SEX variable):

```
SELECT IF   SEX EQ 2
```

There must be one space and only one space separating SELECT and IF; otherwise the spacing on this command is flexible. The reserved word **EQ** symbolizes "equal," hence this command selects only the women in the data file.

The SELECT IF command must be placed after the DATA LIST command and before any commands for which you want it to apply. The following example illustrates the normal placement of the SELECT IF command:

```
DATA LIST  /   ID 1-2
               EDUC 3-4
               SEX 5
               HAPPY 6
BEGIN DATA
010912
021223
031521
041222
050611
061612
071522
081612
091821
101412
```

```
111321
121611
130922
141212
151221
161821
170821
181222
191613
20142
END DATA
SELECT IF    SEX EQ 2
FREQUENCIES   EDUC SEX HAPPY/
          STATISTICS
```

To do the same procedures for our SPSS system file NORC90, the SPSS commands would be:

```
GET   FILE=NORC90
SELECT IF    SEX EQ 2
FREQUENCIES   ALL/
          STATISTICS
```

If we did two jobs, one selecting for females and the other selecting for males, we would obtain on separate outputs one frequency distribution for females and one for males. Pooling the information from these outputs, we could put together Table 3.5. (In Chapter 4 we will learn how the TEMPORARY command enables us to select for females and then later select for males in the same job.) In the table, the numbers in the first row under the word PERCENT indicate that 34 percent (rounding to the nearest percent) of the males are very happy. (Recall that the response "very happy" has the value 1.) The second part of the table concerns females, and the first row of that part indicates that 33 percent of the females report being very happy.

We can see then that males are slightly more likely than females to report being very happy. We will look at this relationship more closely in later chapters, as we examine how other variables are associated with the likelihood of being happy.

TABLE 3.5 Table Constructed for HAPPY from FREQUENCIES Outputs

MALES

VALUE LABEL	FREQUENCY	PERCENT
VERY HAPPY	205	34.1
PRETTY HAPPY	344	57.2
NOT TOO HAPPY	52	8.7
TOTAL	601	100.0

FEMALES

VALUE LABEL	FREQUENCY	PERCENT
VERY HAPPY	250	32.9
PRETTY HAPPY	440	57.9
NOT TOO HAPPY	70	9.2
TOTAL	760	100.0

Perhaps you want to do an analysis using only the people with over 15 years of education among your cases. The following command would select that subset:

SELECT IF   EDUC GT 15

The reserved word **GT** symbolizes "greater than," so GT 15 indicates that only those cases with an EDUC value greater than 15 will be used in this analysis. If **LT** were used in place of GT, only those whose EDUC value was less than 15 would be used. If EQ were used in place of GT, only those whose EDUC value equaled 15 would be used. The following abbreviated expressions (called *relational operators*) may be used with SELECT IF:

EQ   equal

NE   not equal

LT   less than

GT   greater than

LE   less than or equal to

GE   greater than or equal to

What if you want to select cases in a certain range of values? For example, you want to study only adults with 13 to 16 years of education. No problem. Note the following example (with double spaces for clarity between the parts of the command):

SELECT IF   EDUC GT 12   AND   EDUC LT 17

The EDUC GT 12   AND   EDUC LT 17 part of this command means that only cases with an EDUC value that is both above 12 and below 17 will be selected.

You can also select people from two or more of the categories on one variable. For example, the following command would select both those who had 13 years of education and those who had 14 years of education:

SELECT IF   EDUC EQ 13   OR   EDUC EQ 14

If you want to use two or more variables in your selection process, you can combine them as follows:

SELECT IF   EDUC GT 12   AND   SEX EQ 2

This command would select only those respondents whose EDUC value was greater than 12 and whose SEX value was 2; in our data set, these would be women with more than 12 years of education.

You may want to select people who are in a particular category in either of two variables. That, too, is no problem. For example, to select people who have less than 16 years of education *or* are not too happy, one would use the following command:

SELECT IF   EDUC LT 16   OR   HAPPY EQ 3

SELECT IF commands can become quite convoluted. Often you will want to place your conditions in several commands, rather than have one complex command. Be careful! A series of SELECT IF commands will be interpreted as if they are linked by AND. In other words, only those cases that meet all the specifications of all the commands will be selected for the analysis. For example, the two commands

SELECT IF   EDUC GT 16
SELECT IF   SEX EQ 1

together would dictate that only those with both a value over 16 on EDUC *and a* value of 1 on SEX will be included in the analysis.

SELECT IF can also be used to examine cases for which the data seem incorrect. This cleaning operation is done using SELECT IF together with the LIST command. For example, you might want to list the ID numbers of cases that obviously have false data entered. Suppose you have a variable named SEX coded 1 for males, 2 for females, and blank for missing. Any other value entered in the SEX data column of the data file would be an error that you would want to discover and correct. The following command would list the ID numbers of cases for which SEX had not been coded as either blank, 1, or 2:

```
SELECT IF   SEX NE 1   OR   SEX NE 2
LIST
```

The first line of these commands selects cases that have not been coded as missing, 1 (male), or 2 (female). The second command instructs SPSS to print all the variable codings for these cases. This list will include the ID number of each case so you can go back to the file or questionnaire to see what error occurred when the datum for SEX was entered. Having the values of the other variables may also help you detect the error. Perhaps a variable was omitted so that the positions of all the other variables after it were offset by the number of columns in the missed variable.

To select missing value cases, such as those coded blank, the specification MISSING is used followed by the variable name in parentheses. For example,

```
SELECT IF   MISSING(SEX)
```

This command would select the cases coded blank for missing on the variable SEX.

3.6 Summary

In this chapter we explain the LIST command, which produces the data entered by case. LIST can be used for all the variables or for a subset of them; it can be used for all the cases or for a subset of the cases.

The FREQUENCIES command produces the distribution of cases by categories of a variable. It can be used for all the variables or for a subset of the variable set. STATISTICS is a subcommand that causes particular statistics to be added to or deleted from the output. Most SPSS procedure commands allow tailoring of output by STATISTICS.

The SELECT IF command causes SPSS to focus its analyses on subsets of the cases in the data file. The cases kept in the analyses following SELECT IF are those that meet the conditions specified in the SELECT IF command. If more than one SELECT IF command is used, a case must meet the conditions specified by all the commands to be kept in the analysis.

3.7 Where to Look in the SPSS Reference Guide

- FREQUENCIES is discussed on pages 501–510.
- SELECT IF is discussed on pages 183–185.

RESEARCH PROJECT WORK FOR CHAPTER 3

1. Produce a listing and the frequencies for all the variables in the data set you created from the Happiness Questionnaire.

2. Clean the data set of any errors that were made in entering the data.

REVIEW QUESTIONS FOR CHAPTER 3

(Answers to Review Questions are given at the back of the book.)

LIST

3.1 Write a set of commands that will output the data entries for all variables for all cases of our example data set.

3.2 Write a set of commands that will output the data entries for all variables for the first 20 cases of the SPSS system file NORC90, presented in Appendix B.

3.3 Write a set of commands that will list all the data entries for the variable INCOME from the SPSS system file NORC90.

FREQUENCIES

3.4   Write all the commands necessary to produce the frequencies for all the variables in our example data set.

3.5   Write all the commands necessary to produce the frequencies for the variables AGE, SEX, and MARITAL from the SPSS system file NORC90 (Appendix B).

3.6   What would you need to do before using a FREQUENCIES command for a variable named INCOME, which is the annual income of the respondent to the nearest dollar?

3.7   What would be the meaning of the following output?

NEIGHBOR

VALUE	FREQUENCY	PERCENT
1	3	30.0
2	5	50.0
3	2	20.0

MISSING CASES 1

SPSS System File

3.8   Write the commands necessary to produce a FREQUENCIES procedure for all the variables in the NORC90 file.

3.9   Write the command necessary to print out the frequencies for variables in the NORC90 file that concern attitudes toward abortion.

3.10   Write the commands necessary to produce frequencies for the variables concerning the respondent's education, health, and happiness in the NORC90 file.

SELECT IF

3.11   Write a SELECT IF command that will select only those cases that are coded 1 on the variable SEX.

3.12   Write a SELECT IF command that will choose only those cases that have a value of 65 or greater on the variable AGE.

3.13   Write a SELECT IF command that will choose only those cases that are over 16 on the EDUC value or over 30000 on the INCOME value.

3.14   Write a SELECT IF command that will choose only those cases that have a value greater than 15 and less than 66 on the variable AGE.

3.15   Write a SELECT IF command that will choose only those cases that are coded 2 on the variable SEX and also coded between 14 and 45 on the variable AGE.

3.16   Write a set of commands that will list the data entries for all the variables for the first 25 cases that are coded above 15 on EDUC and coded 2 on SEX from the SPSS system file NORC90, presented in Appendix B.

ASSIGNMENT QUESTIONS FOR CHAPTER 3

(Solutions to the Assignment Questions are given in the *Instructor's Manual.*)

3.1   Write all the commands necessary to produce all the frequencies for the variable named EDUC in our example data set (given in Chapter 2).

3.2   Write all the commands necessary to produce the frequencies for the variables AGE, INCOME, and TVHOURS from the SPSS system file NORC90, described in Appendix B.

3.3   What would you need to do before using a FREQUENCIES command for a variable named SQFEET, which is the area of housing units to the nearest square foot?

3.4   What would be the meaning of the following output?

```
POLPARTY
        VALUE           FREQUENCY           PERCENT
          1                 7                 35.0
          2                 9                 45.0
          3                 4                 20.0


        MISSING CASES 1
```

(You need to be familiar with the SPSS system file NORC90, explained in Appendix B, to work the following problems.)

3.5 Write the SPSS commands necessary to produce a FREQUENCIES procedure for all the variables in the NORC90 file. We know you did this task before as a Review Question, but you will want to perform this task frequently and we want to be sure you remember. Besides, this is one of the easy questions.

3.6 Write the SPSS commands necessary to print out the frequencies for variables in the NORC90 file that concern anomie.

3.7 For the NORC90 file, write the commands necessary to produce frequencies for the variables concerning whether the respondent has been unemployed any time in the past 10 years and concerning his or her current employment.

3.8 Write a SELECT IF command that will select only those cases coded 1 on the variable named RACE.

3.9 Write a SELECT IF command that will choose only those cases that have a value of 40 or less on the variable AGE.

3.10 Write a SELECT IF command that will choose only those cases coded below 12 on EDUC or under 10000 on INCOME.

3.11 Write a SELECT IF command that will choose only those cases that have a value less than 16 or greater than 65 on the variable AGE.

3.12 Write a SELECT IF command that will choose only those cases that are coded 2 on the variable RACE and also are coded between 21 and 65, inclusive, on the variable AGE.

3.13 Write a LIST command that will output the data entries for all the variables for the first 20 cases.

3.14 Write a LIST command that will output the data entries for the variable ID for all the cases in the file.

3.15 Write a set of commands that will list the data entries for the variable ID for all the cases coded above 3 on the variable RACE.

3.16 Write a set of commands that will list the data entries for all the variables for the first 20 cases that are coded above 15 on EDUC and coded 2 on SEX.

TABLE 3.6 Actual Output from Command:
LIST   VARIABLES=ID HAPPY/CASES=25

ID HAPPY

ID	HAPPY
1	3
2	1
3	3
4	2
5	2
6	2
7	1
8	3
9	3
10	1
11	9
12	1
13	2
14	2
15	3
16	1
17	1
18	1
19	1
20	2
21	1
22	2
23	2
24	2
25	2

NUMBER OF CASES READ = 25   NUMBER OF CASES LISTED = 25

4

TRANSFORMING VARIABLES AND LABELING OUTPUT

New SPSS Commands:

RECODE
COMPUTE
IF
TEMPORARY
VARIABLE LABELS
VALUE LABELS

In Chapter 3 we used the FREQUENCIES and SELECT IF commands to find that, in the NORC90 data file, 33 percent of the respondents reported they were very happy and that men were slightly more likely than women to report being very happy. In this chapter we will learn whether the likelihood of being very happy is affected by the variable AGE. Before we begin, we need to cover some of the data transformation commands available in SPSS. A problem frequently encountered is that the existing coding of your data is different from the coding you need for a particular analysis. This annoyance can be remedied using the RECODE, COMPUTE, and IF commands described in this chapter. The TEMPORARY command, also covered in this chapter, allows you to confine the effects of the data transformation commands to the statistical procedure immediately following TEMPORARY instead of being in effect for all following procedures.

Finally, we explain how to use the VARIABLE LABELS and VALUE LABELS commands to make the output easier to read.

4.1 Changing Variable Categories Where Necessary: RECODE

Suppose you coded information on education that ranged from 0 to 22 years of formal education, and now you need to do an analysis using only three education categories: respondents who did not complete high school, those who completed high school but not college, and those who completed college. The data you enter for a variable can be reclassified using the **RECODE** command. Carefully study the following example:

```
RECODE   EDUC   (0 THRU 11=1) (12 THRU 15=2) (16 THRU 30=3)
```

The RECODE command indicates that some changes follow in one or more variable codings. EDUC indicates that the first data to be recoded will be for the variable named EDUC. THRU is a reserved keyword in SPSS that can be used to indicate a range of values in many commands. (0 THRU 11=1) indicates that the numbers 0, 1, 2, 3, 4, 5, 6, 7, 8, 9, 10, and 11 will now all be treated as though they have the value 1. (12 THRU 15=2) indicates that the numbers 12, 13, 14, and 15 will all be treated as though they have the value 2. (16 THRU 30=3) indicates that the numbers 16 through 30 will all be treated as though they have the value 3. A statistical procedure done after the RECODE command changes the values of EDUC will use the new values. Thus, a new FREQUENCIES of the EDUC variable would now reveal that the case scores have a range of from 1 to 3 instead of from 0 to 22.

For a variable that is being recoded, if some of the numbers fall outside the range of the RECODE command, these numbers will keep their original values. For example, if someone had 31 years of education, that value in the data columns for education would remain unchanged, because the command recoded only values up to 30. Although someone could have more than 30 years of education, you should verify the data for that case before adjusting the RECODE command.

RECODE allows the use of two terms—**HI** and **LO**—to encompass extreme scores. Using these terms, our previous example would read:

```
RECODE   EDUC   (LO THRU 11=1) (12 THRU 15=2) (16 THRU HI=3)
```

A hazard of using the LO and HI terms, however, is that you might accidentally encompass your MISSING VALUES. In the above example, if 99 were the missing value for refusing to answer for EDUC, all the cases with missing values would be recoded from 99 to 3 and no longer treated as cases with missing data. Likewise, if −9 were the missing value for EDUC, it would be recoded to 1.

The RECODE command must follow the DATA LIST command and appear somewhere before any command for which you want to use the recoded information. However, the RECODE command need not *immediately* precede commands for which you want to use the recoded information. The data will stay recoded throughout the run unless a TEMPORARY command is placed before the RECODE command. The TEMPORARY command, which we discuss in Section 4.4, would keep the recoding in effect for only the first statistical procedure following the RECODE command.

The following set of commands illustrates the file placement of the RECODE command using our example data set:

```
DATA LIST  /   ID 1-2
               EDUC 3-4
               SEX 5
               HAPPY 6
BEGIN DATA
010912
021223
031521
041222
050611
061612
071522
081612
091821
101412
111321
121611
130922
141212
151221
161821
170821
```

```
181222
191613
20142
END DATA
MISSING VALUES   EDUC (-9,99)
RECODE   EDUC   (0 THRU 11=1)(12 THRU 15=2)(16 THRU 30=3)
FREQUENCIES   ID
              EDUC
              SEX
              HAPPY
```

4.2 Making New Variables from Old Variables: COMPUTE

At times you will want to create new variables from variables already in your data file. For example, you may have a variable for family income named IN-COME and a variable for family size named FAMSIZE. In addition to these two variables, you might want to have a variable for family income per capita—that is, the family income divided by the number of persons in the family.

We can create a new variable for income per capita, INCOMPER, with the COMPUTE command as follows. (Note how a slash is used to indicate division.)

```
COMPUTE   INCOMPER=INCOME/FAMSIZE
```

Anywhere in your program following this COMPUTE command, you can refer to the INCOMPER variable just as you refer to any variable contained in your DATA LIST command.

The SPSS equivalents of the basic arithmetic operators are as follows:

+   addition

−   subtraction

/   division

∗   multiplication

∗∗   exponentiation (raising to a power)

SQRT   taking the square root

These operations can be done with actual numeric values, with variables, or with a mixture of both. First we will give examples of doing the arithmetic operations with numbers. Then we will give examples of doing the arithmetic operations with variables.

COMPUTE Commands with Numbers

Addition—Example 1:

COMPUTE   ANSWER1=450+200

In this example, after the COMPUTE command ANSWER1 would equal 650.

Subtraction—Example 2:

COMPUTE   ANSWER2=450-200

In this example, after the COMPUTE command ANSWER2 would equal 250.

Multiplication—Example 3:

COMPUTE   ANSWER3=450*2

In this example, after the COMPUTE command ANSWER3 would equal 900.

Division—Example 4:

COMPUTE   ANSWER4=450/50

In this example, after the COMPUTE command ANSWER4 would equal 9.

Exponentiation—Example 5:

COMPUTE   ANSWER5=5**3

In this example, after the COMPUTE command ANSWER5 would equal 125— that is, 5^3.

Square Root—Example 6:

COMPUTE   ANSWER6=SQRT(81)

In this example, after the COMPUTE command ANSWER6 would equal 9.

COMPUTE Commands with Variables

The previous operations were done with numbers. The following examples illustrate each of these operations with variables.

Addition—Example 7: To compute a new variable, total income (TINC), equal to Wife's Income (WINC) plus husband's income (HINC):

```
COMPUTE   TINC=WINC+HINC
```

Subtraction—Example 8: To compute a new variable, years until retirement (RETIRE), equal to 65 minus age (AGE):

```
COMPUTE   RETIRE=65-AGE
```

Multiplication—Example 9: To compute a new variable, total pay (TPAY), equal to daily salary (DSALARY) multiplied by number of days worked (DAYS):

```
COMPUTE   TPAY=DSALARY*DAYS
```

Division—Example 10: To compute a new variable, average salary (AVESAL), equal to payroll (PAYROLL) divided by number of employees (NEMPLOYS):

```
COMPUTE   AVESAL=PAYROLL/NEMPLOYS
```

Exponentiation—Example 11: To compute a new variable, the deviation from the mean squared (DEVSQ), equal to income minus the mean of income (INC-MINC) squared:

```
COMPUTE   DEVSQ=(INC-MINC)**2
```

Square Root—Example 12: To compute a new variable, absolute deviation (ABDEV), equal to the square root of the deviation from the mean squared (DEVSQ):

```
COMPUTE   ABDEV=SQRT(DEVSQ)
```

Many other functions can be used with the COMPUTE command—nearly 50 in all. (See the *SPSS Reference Guide,* pages 85–91, for a more complete description of these functions.)

COMPUTE Commands and Missing Values

What happens if a variable you use in a COMPUTE command has missing values? For example, you may want to COMPUTE the household's income per person, but for some of the households the income variable is missing. SPSS will assign the **system missing value** (usually blanks) for the variable being computed to any case that has a missing value for any variable used in the computation. The system missing value will be displayed as a period in the output. For example, if you do a FREQUENCIES procedure for a variable and the value for one of the categories appears as a period, then the category of cases has missing data on that variable.

The system missing value will also be assigned to cases for which the computation is mathematically impossible. For example, you cannot divide by zero or take the square root of a negative number. If you gave the command COMPUTE INCOMPER=INCOME/CHILDS, the system missing value would be assigned to all cases for which the value of CHILDS was 0.

4.3 The IF Statement

At times you will want to compute new variables for some cases but not for others. The **IF** command allows this type of operation. You can think of it as a combination of a SELECT IF command and a COMPUTE command. The first part of the command selects the cases for which the procedure is to be done; the second part computes the new variable. For example, you may want to use an individual's income for a person not living with his or her parents but use the parents' income if the person lives with them. To do so, the following SPSS commands could be used. Assume we have a variable named LPARENT, for "living with parent(s)," coded 1 for yes. Assume also that we have a variable named PARENT$, income of parent(s). The following command would make INCOME equal to PARENT$ when the individual lives with his or her parent(s) (two spaces are inserted between the parts of the command to improve readability):

```
IF   LPARENT EQ 1   INCOME=PARENT$
```

Notice the similarity in syntax between each of the two parts of this command and the SELECT IF and COMPUTE commands, respectively:

(like SELECT IF)   (like COMPUTE)

```
IF   LPARENT EQ 1   INCOME=PARENT$
```

All the relational operators used in the SELECT IF command can be used in the IF command. They are

EQ   equal

NE   not equal

LT   less than

GT   greater than

LE   less than or equal to

GE   greater than or equal to

All the functions used in the COMPUTE command can be used in the second part of the IF command. (These functions are explained in Section 4.2)

Parentheses can be used where necessary to clarify the command. For example, we can rewrite the preceding example as

```
IF   (LPARENT EQ 1)   INCOME=PARENT$
```

Another example using IF would be to create a new variable AGEGROUP, which groups age into 10-year categories, from AGE, which records an individual's actual age. (Note that the IF command must be used instead of the RECODE command in this case, if you want to retain the original values for AGE.)

Grouping AGE into new categories for the variable AGEGROUP could be accomplished with the following commands:

```
IF   AGE LE 9   AGEGROUP=1
IF   AGE GT 9 AND AGE LE 19   AGEGROUP=2
IF   AGE GT 19 AND AGE LE 29   AGEGROUP=3
```

```
IF   AGE GT 29 AND AGE LE 39   AGEGROUP=4
IF   AGE GT 39 AND AGE LE 49   AGEGROUP=5
IF   AGE GT 49 AND AGE LE 59   AGEGROUP=6
IF   AGE GT 59 AND AGE LE 69   AGEGROUP=7
IF   AGE GT 69 AND AGE LE 79   AGEGROUP=8
IF   AGE GT 79   AGEGROUP=9
```

The treatment of missing data and impossible computations for the IF command is the same as for the COMPUTE command (discussed in Section X4.2). For example, if a case was coded 99 for AGE, which has 99 as one of its missing values, then AGEGROUP would be assigned the system missing value.

In Appendix A we discuss the DO IF-END IF structure. For further discussion of complex IF commands and DO IF-END IF, see the *SPSS Reference Guide*, pages 285–288 and 145–152.

4.4 Making a Transformation for Only One Procedure: TEMPORARY

The TEMPORARY command signals SPSS to do the data transformations that follow it only for the next statistical procedure. For example, this useful command allows you to do separate FREQUENCIES for different subsets on the same run. To do two FREQUENCIES—one for males and one for females—on the same run, the following procedure could be used. After the TEMPORARY command, use SELECT IF for males (code 1) and then do a FREQUENCIES procedure. Following this FREQUENCIES, add another TEMPORARY command, use SELECT IF for females (code 2), and do another FREQUENCIES. The result will be two FREQUENCIES outputs, one for males and one for females:

```
DATA LIST /   ID 1-2
              EDUC 3-4
              SEX 5
              HAPPY 6
BEGIN DATA
010912
021223
031521
041222
```

```
050611
061612
071522
081612
091821
101412
111321
121611
130922
141212
151221
161821
170821
181222
191613
20142
END DATA
TEMPORARY
SELECT IF   SEX EQ 1
FREQUENCIES   ALL/
             STATISTICS
TEMPORARY
SELECT IF   SEX EQ 2
FREQUENCIES   ALL/
             STATISTICS
```

The first SELECT IF would select only males for the first FREQUENCIES. Because this selection is for only the first statistical procedure after the TEMPORARY command, following the FREQUENCIES procedure we have our entire sample back. The second SELECT IF would select the female cases, and they would be used for the second FREQUENCIES. Combining the output from these two FREQUENCIES commands, we can compare men and women in our sample data. The second TEMPORARY command is not necessary because only one command follows it. We included it as if these commands were part of a longer program.

   For the same procedures with our SPSS system file NORC90, the SPSS commands would be

```
GET   FILE=NORC90
TEMPORARY
SELECT IF   SEX EQ 1
FREQUENCIES   ALL/
              STATISTICS
TEMPORARY
SELECT IF   SEX EQ 2
FREQUENCIES   ALL/
              STATISTICS
```

Pooling the information from the two frequency distributions these commands produce, we could construct tables for all the variables like Table 3.5 for the variable HAPPY. However, by using TEMPORARY only one job is needed instead of two.

As another example, we could select first the respondents in the SPSS system file NORC90 who are under age 40 (respondents had to be at least 18) and then the respondents age 40 and over. (In NORC90, ages 98 and older were coded 97, because 98 and 99 were used as missing values and the variable AGE had only 2 columns for data.) Then we will do a separate FREQUENCIES for each group and find whether being in either group increases the likelihood of being happy. The SPSS commands required would be

```
GET FILE=NORC90
RECODE   AGE  (18 THRU 39=1) (40 THRU 97=2)
TEMPORARY
SELECT IF   AGE EQ 1
FREQUENCIES   HAPPY
TEMPORARY
SELECT IF   AGE EQ 2
FREQUENCIES   HAPPY
```

The output from the preceding commands would include the information in Table 4.1.

The first set of percentages is for the under-40 respondents. Rounding to the nearest percentage point we can see that 35 percent of them report being very happy. The second set of percentages is for respondents 40 and over. We can see that 32 percent of these respondents report being very happy. Hence

TABLE 4.1 Happiness by Age for the NORC84 File

PERSONS AGE 18-39

VALUE LABEL	FREQUENCY	PERCENT
VERY HAPPY	212	34.8
PRETTY HAPPY	352	57.7
NOT TOO HAPPY	46	7.5
NA	4	MISSING
TOTAL	614	100.0

PERSONS AGE 40 AND OVER

VALUE LABEL	FREQUENCY	PERCENT
VERY HAPPY	243	32.4
PRETTY HAPPY	432	57.5
NOT TOO HAPPY	76	10.1
NA	7	MISSING
TOTAL	758	100.0

the likelihood of being very happy appears to be greater for the younger respondents.

So far we have seen that one's likelihood of being very happy is improved slightly by being male and by being under 40. You might complain that you have no control over these variables. Fair enough. In the next chapter and beyond, we will consider the effects of some variables that you can control: education, income, marital status, and number of children.

4.5 Identifying Variables: VARIABLE LABELS

In SPSS variable names are limited to eight or fewer characters. At times you will want to give a variable a longer label in order to express more clearly what it is. The **VARIABLE LABELS** command enables the user to attach a label of 40 characters or less to a variable. (Starting with Release 2.1, up to 120 characters can be used. However, most procedures will truncate long labels in the output.) The label may contain more than one word; it may also contain punctuation.

The label is placed after the variable name and must be enclosed in quotation marks. Either single or double quotation marks may be used. If you use double quotation marks, do not place double quotation marks within the label. If you use single quotation marks, do not place single quotation marks within the label.

The following command would give the label YEARS OF EDUCATION to the variable named EDUC:

```
VARIABLE LABELS  EDUC 'YEARS OF EDUCATION'
```

The VARIABLE LABELS command must begin in column 1 and there must be one space and only one space between the word VARIABLE and the word LABELS.

Two or more variables can be given labels with the same VARIABLE LABELS command. The variables' specifications are separated by one or more spaces or commas. The following example gives labels to EDUC, HEALTH, and INCOME:

```
VARIABLE LABELS  EDUC 'YEARS OF EDUCATION'
                 HEALTH 'SELF-ASSESSMENT OF HEALTH'
                 INCOME 'TOTAL FAMILY INCOME'
```

Although more than one variable label can be put on a line, the program is easier to read if each label is on a separate line. This setup also keeps the user from splitting a label across two lines, which cannot be done without additional special punctuation. (For a discussion of how to split a label across two lines, see the *SPSS Reference Guide,* page 712.)

4.6 Identifying Codings: VALUE LABELS

With the **VALUE LABELS** command, you can label the categories of a variable in the output with more than the number code in the data file. The format for this command is as follows, where labels are being given to categories of the variable SEX:

```
VALUE LABELS   SEX 1 'MALE' 2 'FEMALE'
```

   The VALUE LABELS command is similar to the VARIABLE LABELS command with one important exception: if the VALUE LABELS command contains more than one variable, the variables' specifications must be separated by a slash (/). For example, the following command would create value labels for the categories of EDUC, HEALTH, and INCOME:

```
VALUE LABELS
   EDUC    1 '0 TO 11 YEARS'
           2 '12 TO 15 YEARS'
           3 '16 YEARS AND OVER'/
   HEALTH  1 'EXCELLENT'
           2 'GOOD'
           3 'FAIR'
           4 'POOR'/
   INCOME  1 'UNDER $5,000'
           2 '$5,000 TO $9,999'
           3 '$10,000 TO $14,999'
           4 '$15,000 TO $19,999'
           5 '$20,000 TO $24,999'
           6 '$25,000 TO $34,999'
           7 '$35,000 TO $49,999'
           8 'OVER $50,000'
```

VALUE LABELS cannot exceed 20 characters in releases preceding Release 2.1, after which they can have up to 60 characters. As with long variable labels, long value labels will be truncated in the output of many statistical procedures.
   If you create an SPSS system file, the labels you define before saving the file will be saved with it. (Saving SPSS system files is described in Chapter 2.)
   The next two chapters describe the CROSSTABS and MEANS statistical procedures. These procedures have great utility in themselves, and they also are the preliminary steps for doing more advanced statistical analyses.

4.7 Summary

The RECODE, COMPUTE, IF, and TEMPORARY commands covered in this chapter enable us to transform data.

The RECODE command allows us to regroup categories of a variable and change their coded values.

COMPUTE enables us to calculate new variables from our old variables.

IF allows us to restrict the recoding or computation of variables to cases that meet specified conditions.

TEMPORARY enables us to make transformations for one statistical procedure without changing the data set for the balance of the job.

The VARIABLE LABELS and VALUE LABELS commands enable us to make our output easier to interpret.

4.8 Where to Look in the SPSS Reference Guide

- RECODE is discussed on pages 573–576.
- COMPUTE is discussed on pages 85–92.
- IF is discussed on pages 285–288.
- TEMPORARY is discussed on pages 698–699.
- The VARIABLE LABELS and VALUE LABELS commands are discussed on pages 710–712.

RESEARCH PROJECT WORK FOR CHAPTER 4

1. Write a VARIABLE LABELS command for your research project data file.

2. Write a VALUE LABELS command for your research project data file.

REVIEW QUESTIONS FOR CHAPTER 4

(Answers to Review Questions are given at the back of the book.)

RECODE

Hint: Before you can do a RECODE command for a variable, you need to know its missing values.

4.1 For a variable named MARITAL, married people were coded 1, never-married people were coded 2, divorced people were coded 3, and widowed people were coded 4. Recode MARITAL so that all three types of unmarried people are coded 2. The missing value for MARITAL is blanks.

4.2   A variable named HEIGHT has each respondent's height coded in inches. Recode HEIGHT so that people under 60 inches are coded 1, people 60 to 70 inches are coded 2, and people over 70 inches are coded 3. The missing value for HEIGHT is blanks.

4.3   A variable named CARS was coded 0 if the family had no car, 1 if the family had one car, 2 if the family had two cars, 3 if the family had three cars, and so on. Recode CARS so that any families with two or more cars will be coded 2. The missing value for CARS is −1.

4.4   A variable named AGE has been coded in one-year intervals; that is, someone who is 20 years old was given a value of 20, someone who is 66 years old was given a value of 66. The missing value for this variable is −9. Recode AGE into three categories: those under 16, those 16 to 65, and those over 65.

COMPUTE and IF

4.5   Write a command that will compute a variable named FAMILY$, which is to be WIFE$ (wife's income) plus HUSBAND$ (husband's income).

4.6   Write a command that will divide a variable named SALARY (monthly salary) by 160 to make an estimate of HOURLY$ (average hourly salary of the subjects).

4.7   Create a new variable named NEWEXEC (new executives) that will be coded 1 when an executive's TENURE with the company, measured in months, is less than 12.

4.8   Write a command that will place a family in category 1 of a variable named INCOME if the value on a variable named FAMINCOM is greater than the value of a variable named AVEINCOM.

TEMPORARY

4.9   Using the TEMPORARY, SELECT IF, and FREQUENCIES commands, write the commands necessary to compare the FREQUENCIES output for women on the variable INCOME with the FREQUENCIES output for men on the same variable for the file NORC90, discussed in Appendix B.

4.10   Using the TEMPORARY, SELECT IF, and FREQUENCIES commands, write the SPSS commands necessary to compare the education of persons age 50 and over with the education of persons age 25 to 49 in the file NORC90, discussed in Appendix B.

VARIABLE LABELS and VALUE LABELS

4.11 Write a command that would assign to a variable named CHILDS the variable label NUMBER OF CHILDREN.

4.12 Write a command that would assign to a variable named INCOME the variable label GROSS INCOME and to a variable named NET the variable label NET INCOME.

4.13 Write a command for the variable POLVIEWS that would give the category coded 1 the value label LIBERAL, give the category coded 2 the label MIDDLE OF THE ROAD, and give the category coded 3 the label CONSERVATIVE.

4.14 Write a command for the variable named OVERDUE that will create the value label LESS THAN 60 DAYS for the category coded 1 and MORE THAN 60 DAYS for the category coded 2. As part of the same command, for a variable named MILITARY, create the label MILITARY PERSONNEL for category 1 and the label CIVILIAN PERSONNEL for category 2.

ASSIGNMENT QUESTIONS FOR CHAPTER 4

(Solutions to Assignment Questions are given in the *Instructor's Manual*.)

4.1 RECODE the variable CHILDS in the SPSS system file NORC90 so that any families with more than two children will be coded 3.

4.2 RECODE the variable AGE in the SPSS system file NORC90 into three categories: those under 16, those 16 to 65, and those over 65.

4.3 Write a command that will compute a variable named RELATIVE, which is CHILDS (number of children) plus SIBS (number of siblings).

4.4 Write a command that will divide a variable named INCOME (annual income) by PERSONS (number of persons in the family) to make a new variable named INCOMPER.

4.5 Create a new variable named GRAD that will be coded 1 when EDUC is greater than 15 and 0 otherwise.

4.6 Using the variable INCOME in the SPSS system file NORC90, create a variable named UPPER that will be coded 1 for a family with an income of $25,000 or more and 0 for a family with an income below $25,000.

4.7   For a variable named AGED, assign the variable label NUMBER OF PER-
        SONS AGE 65 AND OLDER.

4.8   Using the TEMPORARY, SELECT IF, and FREQUENCIES commands,
        write the commands necessary to compare the FREQUENCIES output
        for blacks on the variable EDUC with the FREQUENCIES output for
        whites on the same variable for the SPSS system file NORC90, dis-
        cussed in Appendix B.

4.9   Using the TEMPORARY, SELECT IF, and FREQUENCIES commands,
        write the commands necessary to compare the income of persons age
        40 and over with the income of persons between ages 18 and 39, in-
        clusive, in the system file NORC90, discussed in Appendix B.

4.10   For a variable named GRASS, write the variable label FAVOR LEGALIZ-
        ING MARIJUANA, and in the same command give a variable named CUT
        SPEND the label FAVOR LESS SPENDING ON EDUCATION.

4.11   For the variable named RELIG, label category 1 PROTESTANT, category
        2 CATHOLIC, category 3 JEWISH, category 4 NONE, category 5
        OTHER, and category 9 NO ANSWER.

4.12   For the variable named UNEMPLOY, label category 1 YES, category 2
        NO, category 8 DO NOT REMEMBER, and category 9 NO ANSWER. In
        the same command, for the variable named CLASS, label the categories
        as follows: 1 LOWER, 2 WORKING, 3 MIDDLE, 4 UPPER, and 9 NO
        ANSWER.

5

CROSSTABULATIONS OF TWO OR MORE VARIABLES

New SPSS Command:

CROSSTABS

We often begin an analysis suspecting that one variable affects another. For example, students invest time, energy, and money for each additional year of education. One might ask whether this effort pays off in happiness. Are people with more education happier than their less-educated peers? This question is "bivariate," which means that it concerns the association between two variables. (The prefix is the Latin word *bi,* meaning *two.*)

One way to investigate a bivariate question is by doing a crosstabulation. If we "crosstabulate" a happiness variable with an education variable, the output will reveal the percentage of people in each education category who are in each happiness category. We can then look for differences in happiness levels among the educational categories. Such differences would indicate an association between education and happiness. For example, if the percentage of highly educated people in the high-happiness category is greater than the percentage of less-educated people in the same category, increasing one's education would seem to increase the likelihood of being happy.

Described verbally, crosstabulations sound confusing. The example we present next will clarify what we mean.

5.1 An Introduction to Crosstabulations

Consider the crosstabulation presented in Table 5.1. It is an analysis of the association between happiness and education using our example data set from Chapter 2.

The three columns in Table 5.1 represent the coding categories for the education variable. (Recall that we have recoded the values as 1 to mean 0–11 years of education, 2 to mean 12–15 years of education, and 3 to mean 16 or more years of education.) Column 1 represents the people coded 1 on education. Column 2 represents the people coded 2 on education. Column 3 represents the people coded 3 on education. The column total for column 1 is 4, which means that 4 respondents were coded 1 on education.

The row numbers under HAPPY correspond to the categories of that variable. Row 1 represents the people who responded "very happy," coded 1. Row 2 represents those who responded "pretty happy," coded 2. Row 3 represents those who responded "not too happy," coded 3.

The upper left-hand cell of the table (row 1, column 1) is the conjunction of people who were coded 1 on both EDUC and HAPPY. The 50.0 in that cell indicates that 50.0 percent of the people with 0–11 years of education stated they felt very happy. The middle cell of column 1 (that is, in row 2) is the conjunction of people who were coded 1 on EDUC and 2 on HAPPY. The 50.0 in that cell

TABLE 5.1 Crosstabulation of Happiness by Education

		EDUC		
		1	2	3
HAPPY	1	50.0	33.3	50.0
	2	50.0	55.6	33.3
	3		9.1	16.6
COLUMN TOTAL		4	9	6

indicates that 50.0 percent of the people with 0–11 years of education stated they felt pretty happy. The bottom cell of column 1 is blank, which means that none of the people with 0–11 years of education responded that they were not too happy.

It is easy to become confused when reading a crosstabulation table, especially one that shows more than two variables. You must think carefully about (1) what the percentages represent, and (2) what comparisons are meaningful. In our example, each percentage has as a base the number of people in that column, and each column is an education category. (Note that for each column the sum of the percentage equals 100.)

We can compare up and down the columns. In our example, the percentage of people in the top cells is greater than the percentage of people in the bottom cells, which means that the percentage of people who are very happy is greater than the percentage of people who are not too happy.

We can also compare across rows. In our example, if we compare across the top row, we find that 50.0 percent of those with less than 12 years of education (column 1) or more than 16 years of education (column 3) are very happy, whereas 33 percent of those with 12 to 15 years of education (column 2) are very happy. Thus we have no clear pattern here. Among both those with the least education and those with the most education, 50.0 percent stated they were very happy; however, the sample size of our example is small. The association between variables will be clear when we replicate this crosstabulation in Section 5.3 using the larger sample in the NORC90 SPSS system file.

5.2 The CROSSTABS Command

In SPSS, crosstabulations are produced by the CROSSTABS command. The following CROSSTABS command, using two of its OPTIONS, produced the output in Table 5.1:

```
CROSSTABS   HAPPY BY EDUC/
            CELLS=COLUMN
```

The CROSSTABS command must begin in column 1. We recommend placing the variable you think is being affected (the dependent variable) before the BY and the variable you think is causing an effect (the independent variable) after the BY. This way the dependent variable will always appear as row categories along the side of your table.

The number of cases in each cell can be obtained by multiplying the cell percentage by the number of cases in that column. For example, in Table 5.1 the upper left cell (row 1, column 1) is the conjunction of people who have 0–11 years of education and are very happy. The percentage in this cell, 50.0 percent, multiplied by the column total, 4, gives the number of cases in that cell: $0.5 \times 4 = 2$. Thus two cases are represented in the upper-left cell. Following these procedures, the total cases for each cell can be calculated. Another option for obtaining the count for each cell is to add COUNT to the CELLS= subcommand.

Placed with the other SPSS commands necessary to produce a run with our example data set, the commands needed to generate the CROSSTABS output in Table 5.1 would be

```
DATA LIST  /   ID 1-2
               EDUC 3-4
               SEX 5
               HAPPY 6
RECODE   EDUC  (0 THRU 11=1)  (12 THRU 15=2)  (16 THRU 30=3)
BEGIN DATA
010912
021223
031521
041222
050611
061612
071522
081612
091821
101412
111321
121611
130922
141212
151221
161821
170821
```

```
181222
191613
20142
END DATA
MISSING VALUES   EDUC (-9,99)
                 HAPPY
                 SEX (0)
CROSSTABS   HAPPY BY EDUC/
            CELLS=COLUMN
```

A problem arises when we do CROSSTABS with a small number of cases. Some of the cells are empty and, more important, the results are not likely to be generalizable. For example, when we have only 4 individuals with less than 12 years of education, we are not confident that they are likely to be typical of all people with less than 12 years of education.

5.3 Using CROSSTABS with an SPSS System File

To illustrate the problem of representativeness and to give you a more accurate impression of the relationship between education and happiness, we now do an identical CROSSTABS for the entire SPSS system file NORC90, described in Appendix B. The commands needed to do a crosstabulation of the variables HAPPY and EDUC in the NORC90 file are as follows:

```
GET   FILE=NORC90
RECODE   EDUC (0 THRU 11=1) (12 THRU 15=2) (16 THRU 30=3)
CROSSTABS   HAPPY BY EDUC/
            CELLS=COLUMN COUNT
```

Table 5.2 is constructed from the output produced by these commands. The entire sample size is 1372 cases. Consequently we now have no empty cells and the percentages, based on a much larger sample, are more likely to portray accurately the relationship between education and happiness in the United States. Adding the COUNT option to the CELLS subcommand causes the number of cases in each cell to be printed above the column percentage.

TABLE 5.2 Crosstabulation of Happiness by Education Using the
NORC90 System File

	EDUC		
	1	2	3
HAPPY			
VERY HAPPY	92	242	121
	30.8	31.5	41.4
PRETTY HAPPY	167	462	153
	55.9	60.2	52.4
NOT TOO HAPPY	40	64	18
	13.4	8.3	6.2
COLUMN TOTAL	299	768	292

NUMBER OF MISSING OBSERVATIONS = 13

Along the top of Table 5.2 are the education categories; each column under an education value corresponds to the people in that category. Along the left side of the table are the happiness categories; each row corresponds to the people in that category.

Look at the percentage of less-educated people in the very happy category—the upper-left cell (row 1, column 1). The 31 percent (rounded) demonstrates that about one-third of the people with less than 12 years of education are very happy. Compare this figure with the percentage of highly educated people who report being very happy—41 percent. We see that more education appears to increase the likelihood of being very happy.

Interpretation of what causes what, however, is tricky. Perhaps people who are happy tend to stay in school longer. If this statement is true, then happiness increases the likelihood of high educational attainment rather than educational attainment's increasing the likelihood of being happy. Perhaps both effects are at work: higher education increases the likelihood of being happy and being happy increases the likelihood of high educational attainment. We should also remember that associations in society are usually far from absolute. Fifty-nine percent of the highly educated people are *not* very happy (100 percent minus 41 percent), so we would conclude that obtaining more education is far from a good guarantee that one will be very happy.

5.4 Multivariate Analysis with CROSSTABS

We have seen that the probability of respondents' reporting that they are very happy is linked to their sex and educational achievement. Another question we might ask is whether the association of happiness with education is the same for women and men. When two or more independent variables are present, the analysis is called *multivariate*.

To add a third variable to a CROSSTABS analysis, we simply add the word BY and the name of the third variable. For our example with the NORC90 system file, the CROSSTABS and accompanying SPSS commands would be

```
GET   FILE=NORC90
RECODE   EDUC (0 THRU 11=1) (12 THRU 15=2) (16 THRU 30=3)
CROSSTABS   HAPPY BY EDUC BY SEX/
            CELLS=COLUMN/
            STATISTICS=CHISQ PHI
```

In this analysis SEX is called the *control variable* because we will see the effects of education when we control for SEX. Note that the control variable is the last in the command sequence. If the positions of EDUC and SEX were reversed in the command, we would see the effects of SEX when we control for EDUC.

Note also that we have added the subcommand STATISTICS=CHISQ PHI. This subcommand, when following CROSSTABS, will produce three statistics: chi-square, phi, and Cramer's *V*. Cramer's *V* is easy to interpret. It ranges from 0.0, when there is absolutely no association between two variables, to 1.0, when there is a perfect association. Phi will not be used in this text.

χ^2 (chi-square, pronounced "kai square") is another useful statistic because it has a known sampling distribution and its significance level is included in the output. In calculating chi-square, the value expected for each cell (if the variables were not associated) is compared to the actually observed values through a somewhat complex formula. The resulting chi-square statistic does not have a simple range such as 0.0 to 1.0; hence, to assess its importance immediately is not easy. Cramer's *V* is a transformation of χ^2 that standardizes for the number of cells in the crosstabulation table so that the range becomes 0.0 to 1.0 and easier to interpret. Consequently, the significance level of Cramer's *V* is the same as the significance level of χ^2.

TABLE 5.3 Output from Multivariate Crosstabulation

CROSSTABULATION OF HAPPY BY EDUC CONTROLLING FOR SEX
SEX   VALUE=1

	COL PCT	EDUC 1	2	3	
HAPPY					
VERY HAPPY	1	35.4	31.9	37.8	
PRETTY HAPPY	2	53.8	58.5	57.4	
NOT TOO HAPPY	3	10.8	9.6	4.7	
	COLUMN TOTAL	130	323	148	601

CHI-SQUARE	SIGNIFICANCE
5.1	0.275

STATISTIC	VALUE
CRAMER'S *V*	0.07

CROSSTABULATION OF HAPPY BY EDUC CONTROLLING FOR SEX
SEX   VALUE=2

	COL PCT	EDUC 1	2	3	
HAPPY					
VERY HAPPY	1	27.2	31.2	44.5	
PRETTY HAPPY	2	57.4	61.3	47.9	
NOT TOO HAPPY	3	15.4	7.4	7.5	
	COLUMN TOTAL	169	445	146	760

CHI-SQUARE	SIGNIFICANCE
20.4	0.000

STATISTIC	VALUE
CRAMER'S *V*	0.12

NUMBER OF MISSING OBSERVATIONS = 11

The output will be on different pages for each category of the control variable. In our example the output will be spread over two pages. The first page will contain the HAPPY BY EDUC table for men (SEX value=1) and the second will contain the HAPPY BY EDUC table for women (SEX value=2).

Table 5.3 is the simplified output produced by the preceding commands. Notice how the addition of the STATISTICS subcommand has produced the chi-square and Cramer's *V* statistics at the bottom of each portion of the table. Actual output is like Table 5.4 at the end of this chapter.

Looking at the percentages in the two portions of the table, we can see that for females the difference in percentage between the least educated and the most educated who are very happy is greater than for males. For females the difference in the top row (the very happy respondents) between the respondents with 16 or more years of education (44.5) and the respondents with less than 12 years of education (27.2) is 17.3 percent. The corresponding difference for males is 2.4 percent. This result suggests that a higher level of education improves the likelihood of being very happy more for females than for males.

5.5 Summary

In this chapter we explain how CROSSTABS can be used to produce the crosstabulations of two or more variables. These crosstabulations are useful for examining the associations between variables. We show how chi-square is used to assess the statistical significance of associations in a crosstabulation. We describe Cramer's *V*, which is a transformation of chi-square that ranges on a scale from 0.0 to 1.0. Crosstabulations can be very simple and easy to interpret; they can likewise be very complex and arduous to interpret. Some of the techniques we cover in Part 2 are methods of searching through complex crosstabulations for the most important associations.

We now know that we can increase our likelihood of being happy by being more educated. This variable is the first we have examined over which individuals have any control. By now we hope your curiosity is aroused as to why certain variables are associated with happiness. Are more educated people generally happier because they generally have more money? Are older people generally happier because they are less likely to be parents? We will be better able to tackle these multivariate questions using the techniques presented in Part 2 of this text. The researcher's never-ending task is to try to push our understanding a bit further, knowing full well that answering one question leads immediately to asking more questions.

5.6 Where to Look in the SPSS Reference Guide

- CROSSTABS is discussed on pages 99–108.

RESEARCH PROJECT WORK FOR CHAPTER 5

1.   a. For the data set you gathered, replicate the crosstabulations of HAPPY BY EDUC and HAPPY BY EDUC BY SEX done in this chapter.

       b. Describe any differences between the results in your sample and the results for the NORC90 file given in Tables 5.2 and 5.3.

       c. If there are differences, what do you think caused them?

2.   a. Produce a crosstabulation of HAPPY by another variable in the data set that you think might affect happiness.

       b. Discuss whether the results are as you expected.

REVIEW QUESTIONS FOR CHAPTER 5

(Answers to Review Questions are given at the back of the book.)

5.1   Write the CROSSTABS command and CELLS subcommand that would crosstabulate a variable named INCOME with a variable named SEX. Your hypothesis is that the SEX variable is causing differences in IN- COME. Remember that whether the variables are independent or causal affects the order of the variables on the command.

5.2   Write the CROSSTABS command including CELLS and STATISTICS sub- commands that would crosstabulate a variable named DAY with a vari- able named SALES. Your hypothesis is that the DAY variable is affecting the SALES variable.

5.3   Write all the commands necessary to crosstabulate EDUC with SEX in our example data set. Assume that SEX is the causal variable and recode EDUC into the categories specified in Section 5.1. Include CELLS and STATISTICS subcommands.

5.4   Write the commands that are needed to demonstrate through a crosstabulation the effects of the variable RELIGION on the variable POLVIEWS for the SPSS system file NORC90, described in Appendix B.

5.5   Write the CROSSTABS commands and subcommands that would produce three crosstabulations demonstrating the association of the in- dependent variable named EDUC with the variables HAPPY, HEALTH, and INCOME for the SPSS system file NORC90, described in Appendix B. Include CELLS and STATISTICS subcommands.

5.6 Write the CROSSTABS commands and subcommands that would produce a crosstabulation demonstrating the association of the dependent variable HAPPY with the variable MARITAL, controlling for the variable SEX.

5.7 What subcommand must be added to the CROSSTABS command to produce the chi-square and Cramer's *V* statistics?

5.8 Explain the difference between chi-square and Cramer's *V*.

ASSIGNMENT QUESTIONS FOR CHAPTER 5

(Solutions to the Assignment Questions are given in the *Instructor's Manual*.)

5.1 Write the CROSSTABS command that would crosstabulate a variable named AGE with a variable named SEX. Your hypothesis is that there are differences between the sexes in death rates and, therefore, in age distribution.

5.2 Write the CROSSTABS command that would crosstabulate a variable named HEALTH with a variable named EDUC. Your hypothesis is that the education level of respondents affects the likelihood of good health.

5.3 Write all the commands necessary to crosstabulate HAPPY by SEX in our example data set. Assume that SEX is the causal variable.

5.4 Write the commands that are needed to demonstrate through a crosstabulation the effects of the variable named INCOME on the variable named ATTEND for the SPSS system file NORC90, described in Appendix B. Include the subcommand specification needed to print the number of cases in each cell.

5.5 Write the commands needed to produce three crosstabulations demonstrating the effects of the variable named INCOME on the variables SATFAM, SATFRND, and SATJOB for the SPSS system file NORC90, described in Appendix B.

5.6 Write all the commands necessary to crosstabulate INCOME by EDUC controlling for SEX using the NORC90 SPSS system file, described in Appendix B. Include the command necessary to produce the chi-square and Cramer's *V* statistics.

TABLE 5.4 One Page of Actual Output from CROSSTABS HAPPY BY EDUC BY SEX/
CELLS=COLUMN

	CROSSTABULATION OF	
HAPPY GENERAL HAPPINESS	BY EDUC	HIGHEST YEAR OF SCHOOL COMPLETED

CONTROLLING FOR . . .
  SEX   RESPONDENT'S SEX   VALUE =   1. MALE

COL PCT	EDUC			ROW TOTAL
	1	2	3	
HAPPY				
VERY HAPPY 1	33.5	27.1	38.8	185 31.7
PRETTY HAPPY 2	45.9	58.9	53.7	315 53.9
NOT TOO HAPPY 3	20.6	13.9	7.5	84 14.4
COLUMN TOTAL	170 29.1	280 47.9	134 22.9	584 100.0

CHI-SQUARE	D.F.	SIGNIFICANCE	MIN E.F.	CELLS WITH E.F. <5
16.54304	4	0.0024	19.274	NONE

STATISTIC	VALUE	SIGNIFICANCE
CRAMER'S V	0.11901	

6

COMPARING MEANS

New SPSS Command:

MEANS

We know from previous chapters that men, people with more education, and persons age 40 and younger are more likely to report being very happy. You should be curious about these associations. Many questions are unanswered. For example, are the more educated happier because they have higher incomes? Are men at all income levels happier than women?

Crosstabulations are difficult to interpret for variables like income that have many categories. The MEANS command provides output that is simpler to read and is a useful tool when the dependent variable is an ordinal or interval level measure. To clarify this point, we need to explain levels of measurement.

6.1 Levels of Measurement

Nominal level of measurement variables have categories that cannot be ranked from lesser to greater. One's religious affiliation is a nominal variable. Another example of a nominal variable is place of birth. It does not make sense to calculate a mean (average) or median (midpoint of a distribution) for such variables. (Nominal variables are also called *categorical* variables.)

Ordinal level of measurement variables have categories that can be ranked. **Interval** level of measurement variables have categories that can be ranked *and* are of equal size. In our example data set presented in Chapter 2, the HAPPY variable is ordinal and the EDUC variable is interval. HAPPY is an ordinal variable because we can rank the categories "very happy," "somewhat happy," and "not too happy" in an order on the dimension of happiness. The EDUC variable is interval because the categories can be ranked and each interval is of an equal size—that is, the distance between 9 years of education and 11 years of education is the same as the distance between 13 years of education and 15 years of education. Some statistical techniques are designed to be used only with interval variables.

Two-category nominal variables like SEX are called *dichotomous* or *binomial*. They are a special case of nominal variables because, after being coded with numerical values, they can be used in interval level statistical analyses like Pearson correlations (see Chapter 7). [For a discussion of this point, see Roderick P. McDonald's *Factor Analysis and Related Methods* (Hillsdale, N.J.: Lawrence Erlbaum Associates, 1985), pages 9–11, 198–202.] As an example, look at our treatment of the SEX variable in Chapter 7.

Further distinctions can be made between levels of measurement, and the classification of a variable's level of measurement is not always clear-cut (see Blalock, 1979, pages 15–26). At times there are disputes over whether variables are "interval enough" to justify the use of statistics designed for interval measures. Researchers like to use interval measure statistics because they are better than ordinal measure statistics for handling multiple variable analyses and for detecting weak associations between variables. Consequently, there is a tendency to use interval level statistics with ordinal variables. The risk of this practice is that the results may be biased. However, William L. Hays' *Statistics for the Social Sciences,* Second Edition (New York: Holt, Rinehart and Winston, 1973, pages 87–90), observes that at issue here is not really mathematics and statistics but the good judgment of the researcher in selecting a method for the problem at hand and interpreting the meaning of the results. There is no simple, hard-and-fast rule about which statistical technique to use for a particular set of variables.

6.2 Comparing Means between Groups: MEANS

The command MEANS produces an analysis that compares group means on a dependent or criterion variable. This technique, however, can be employed only when the mean is a useful measure for the dependent variable. (Recall that a dependent variable is the one we think is being affected by another variable in the analysis. The independent variable is the one having an effect.)

We can consider, for example, whether there are differences between males and females in happiness. Because we are considering whether the respondent's sex affects the probability of his or her being happy, sex is the independent variable and happiness is the dependent variable. Happiness is an ordinal variable, so we can use MEANS.

To determine the effect of a person's sex on the probability of happiness, the MEANS command would be

```
MEANS   HAPPY BY SEX
```

The word MEANS must begin in column 1. Again, as with the CROSSTABS commands, we place the dependent variable, HAPPY, before the BY and the independent variable, SEX, after the BY.

For our example data file, described in Chapter 2, the necessary set of SPSS commands for a MEANS is:

```
DATA LIST  /   ID 1-2
               EDUC 3-4
               SEX 5
               HAPPY 6
BEGIN DATA
010912
021223
031521
041222
050611
061612
071522
081612
091821
101412
111321
121611
130922
141212
151221
161821
170821
```

```
181222
191613
20142
END DATA
```
MEANS   HAPPY BY SEX

Table 6.1 is part of the output that would be produced by this BREAK-DOWN. The first line of the sample output presented in the table reads "CRITE-RION VARIABLE HAPPY." The **criterion variable** is the one whose mean scores will be given by the MEANS output—in our example, it is HAPPY. The second line of output indicates that the criterion variable HAPPY is "broken down by SEX." Thus we see the mean score for HAPPY in each SEX category.

The line reading "VARIABLE CODE MEAN N" provides the column headings. On the following line, the word SEX indicates the independent variable. The 1 under the word CODE indicates that this line is for cases coded 1 on SEX—that is, the male cases. The 1.8 is the mean for these cases on the criterion variable. The 8 indicates the number of cases in this category. The final line provides information for the cases coded 2 on the variable SEX—the females. The mean for the females on the criterion variable HAPPY is 1.5.

Recall that the HAPPY variable is coded 1 for "very happy" and 3 for "not too happy." Therefore, the fact that the mean value for women is lower than for men indicates that, on the average, the women were happier than the men. These findings are based on a sample of only 20 respondents; when the analysis is repeated with the entire SPSS system file NORC90 with 1372 respondents, men are happier but the difference is not as great.

TABLE 6.1 Partial Output Produced by MEANS   HAPPY BY SEX

```
CRITERION VARIABLE      HAPPY
    BROKEN DOWN BY      SEX

 VARIABLE    CODE  MEAN    N

    SEX       1    1.8     8
    SEX       2    1.5    11
```

6.3 Using MEANS with an SPSS System File

The SPSS commands necessary to do the MEANS of HAPPY by SEX with the NORC90 file (described in Appendix B) are

```
GET  FILE=NORC90
MEANS  HAPPY BY SEX
```

In this analysis the direction of causality is certain—we know that one's level of happiness does not affect the likelihood of being male or female. Exactly why men are more likely to respond that they are very happy is one of those thought-provoking questions that lead researchers to call for further study of a subject. Are the health and lifestyle of men more likely than those of women to yield happiness? Are men more reluctant to say they are not happy? Is the objective situation of men better than that of women? Our analysis does not answer these questions. It shows only that, in general, men are more likely than women to tell pollsters they are happy.

In our next MEANS example, we will consider the question "Does money buy happiness?" Both money and happiness are variables for which a mean score is useful. Our hypothesis, however, is that money affects happiness, so we will break down the mean level of happiness for each income category. In other words, happiness will be our dependent variable. Using our SPSS system file NORC90, the necessary commands are as follows:

```
GET  FILE=NORC90
MEANS  HAPPY BY INCOME
```

As before, the happiness variable has three categories: the lower the mean score on the variable HAPPY, the happier are the respondents. Table 6.2 contains the overall mean and the mean score for each income group. We can see that the higher income categories have lower mean scores on the happiness variable. Since lower scores indicate greater happiness, our findings show that people in higher-income families tend to be happier.

In this analysis we have some uncertainty in deciding the direction of causality. Perhaps happy people are more successful at making money because people like to do business with them; that is, maybe happiness earns money rather than money buying happiness.

TABLE 6.2 Partial Output Produced by MEANS   HAPPY   BY   INCOME

```
CRITERION VARIABLE      HAPPY
     BROKEN DOWN BY      INCOME

VARIABLE                        MEAN        N

FOR ENTIRE POPULATION           1.8       1,223

INCOME    LESS THAN $10000      1.9         200
INCOME    $10000-19999          1.8         258
INCOME    $20000-29999          1.8         211
INCOME    $30000-39999          1.7         193
INCOME    $40000-49999          1.6         109
INCOME    $50000-59999          1.7          82
INCOME    $60000+               1.5         170

TOTAL CASES=1,372

MISSING CASES=149 OR 10.9 PERCENT
```

6.4 Multivariate Analysis with MEANS

We can do multivariate analyses using the MEANS command, as with CROSS-TABS. For example, we can examine the association between income and happiness to find out whether the relationship is the same for women as for men. The command to produce this analysis would be

MEANS   HAPPY BY SEX BY INCOME

This command would produce the output presented in Table 6.3 for the NORC90 file. The output is usually easier to read if the control variable is listed before the independent variable. Thus, in our example, SEX is placed in the MEANS command before INCOME.

Table 6.3 shows that the mean happiness level tends to be lower (indicating greater happiness) as income goes up for both males and females.

Assignment Question 6.9 asks you to answer the first question we posed at the beginning of the chapter about whether the more educated are happier because they have higher income. You can answer this question by doing a

TABLE 6.3 Output Produced by BREAKDOWN   HAPPY BY SEX BY INCOME

CRITERION VARIABLE   HAPPY
   BROKEN DOWN BY   SEX
                     INCOME

VARIABLE			MEAN	N
FOR ENTIRE POPULATION			1.7	1,223
SEX	MALE		1.7	543
	INCOME	LESS THAN $10000	1.9	65
	INCOME	$10000-19999	1.8	101
	INCOME	$20000-29999	1.8	106
	INCOME	$30000-39999	1.7	101
	INCOME	$40000-49999	1.6	57
	INCOME	$50000-59999	1.7	34
	INCOME	$60000+	1.6	79
SEX	FEMALE		1.8	680
	INCOME	LESS THAN $10000	1.9	135
	INCOME	$10000-19999	1.8	157
	INCOME	$20000-29999	1.8	105
	INCOME	$30000-39999	1.6	92
	INCOME	$40000-49999	1.6	52
	INCOME	$50000-59999	1.8	48
	INCOME	$60000+	1.5	91

TOTAL CASES=1,372

MISSING CASES=149 OR 10.9 PERCENT

breakdown of happiness by education controlling for income. (Remember that EDUC needs to be recoded and that the proper sequence of the command would be MEANS HAPPY BY INCOME BY EDUC.)

6.5 The STATISTICS Subcommand with MEANS

If we wanted to test for the statistical significance of the mean differences in happiness by income, we would add the subcommand STATISTICS ALL. The statistical significance is the probability that the differences are because of sampling error.

The output produced by the STATISTICS subcommand for MEANS gives the F ratio from which the statistical significance level for the differences in happiness between income categories is calculated. (For a discussion of the logic and calculations of F, see Blalock, 1979, pages 336–346.) Furthermore, the association is broken down into its linear and nonlinear components. The linear component assumes that the effects of a particular difference in INCOME are the same throughout its range—for example, that the effects of the difference between \$5,000 and \$10,000 are the same as the difference between \$20,000 and \$25,000.

Note that the statistical significance test is only for the first MEANS variable. Therefore, the control variable would have to be dropped from the MEANS command on runs using STATISTICS ALL. Otherwise the statistics would be for the control variable. For example, if we added the STATISTICS ALL subcommand to the command

MEANS   HAPPY BY SEX BY INCOME

without deleting the control variable SEX, the statistical significance test would be only for the association between HAPPY and SEX. The correct commands to examine the statistical significance of the association between HAPPY and INCOME would be

MEANS   HAPPY BY INCOME /
        STATISTICS ALL

The output produced by the STATISTICS ALL command would include the statistics presented in Table 6.4. The abbreviation SIG. stands for statistical significance, which is the probability that between-groups mean differences of this magnitude would be due to sampling error. A statistical significance of .000 indicates that the probability is less than .001. Table 6.5 at the end of this chapter provides an example of the complete output from the MEANS command.

If we want to focus on the mean differences between just two groups—an analysis similar to the traditional t-test—all we need to do is use a SELECT IF statement to limit the MEANS to those two groups. Once the analysis is complete, taking the square root of the F ratio will give the t value. The statistical significance level is the same as for the F ratio. Doing multiple t-tests, however, is to be avoided because the significance levels for t-tests are based on individual trials. Looking at a set of t scores increases the probability that one will discover a score that is "significant." (See Blalock, 1979, pages 347–348, for further discussion of this point.)

TABLE 6.4 Partial Output of Statistics for BREAKDOWN

ANALYSIS OF VARIANCE

SOURCE	D.F.	F	SIG.
BETWEEN GROUPS	6	7.9	.000
LINEARITY	1	39.7	.000
DEVIATION FROM LINEARITY	5	1.6	.171

6.6 Summary

In this chapter we explain how to use MEANS to analyze the differences between groups in their means on a variable. The variable for which means are calculated is called the criterion variable; usually it is thought of as the dependent variable in the analysis.

Using the STATISTICS command with MEANS produces a table that indicates the statistical significance of the differences between group means. Also produced in the table are two advanced statistics explained further in Part 2: the significance of the linear regression using the group variable as a predictor and the significance of deviations from the linear model.

The analysis in this chapter showed that reported happiness increases with income. This association remains when we control for sex.

6.7 Where to Look in the *SPSS Reference Guide*

- MEANS is discussed on pages 457–462.

RESEARCH PROJECT WORK FOR CHAPTER 6

For the following work you might want to pool your data file with that of other students in your class so that the group means are based on five or more cases. An alternative would be to recode variables that have too few cases in some categories.

1. Using your research project data file, compute means for SATFAM, SATFRND, and SATJOB by INCOME controlling for SEX.

2.   Describe the associations you find in the means from Problem 1.

3.   Discuss what might be causing the associations you find in the means from Problem 1.

REVIEW QUESTIONS FOR CHAPTER 6

(Answers to Review Questions are given at the back of the book.)

6.1   Write a command that would produce the mean scores on the variable INCOME for each category of the variable SEX.

6.2   Write a command that would produce the mean scores on the variable HEALTH for each category of the variable EDUC and for each category of the variable INCOME.

6.3   Write all the commands necessary to produce the mean scores on the variable HAPPY for each category of the variable EDUC for our example data set given in Chapter 2.

6.4   Write all the commands needed to produce the mean scores on the variable HAPPY for each category of the variable HEALTH for the SPSS system file NORC90, described in Appendix B.

6.5   What is the criterion variable in a MEANS output?

6.6   In a MEANS analysis, does the dependent variable appear before or after the word BY in the MEANS command?

6.7   What command would be used to produce the mean scores on INCOME for each category of EDUC controlling for SEX?

6.8   What commands would produce the statistics that would enable the user to judge whether the differences in income by education were statistically significant?

6.9   What commands would be needed to determine whether the mean income for those with 15 years of education is statistically different from those with 12 years of education?

ASSIGNMENT QUESTIONS FOR CHAPTER 6

(Solutions to the Assignment Questions are given in the *Instructor's Manual.*)

6.1 Write all the commands necessary to produce the mean years of education completed for each of the categories of the variable HAPPY in our example data set from Chapter 2.

6.2 For the SPSS system file NORC90, write all the commands necessary to produce the mean score on the variable POLVIEWS for each category of the variable SEX.

6.3 For the SPSS system file NORC90, write all the commands necessary to produce the mean score on the variable HAPPY for each category of the variable POLVIEWS.

6.4 For the SPSS system file NORC90, write all the commands necessary to produce the mean score on the variable HAPPY for each category of the variable CHILDS.

6.5 For the Happiness Questionnaire in Appendix C, write the MEANS command necessary to produce the mean score on SATJOB for each category of the variable SEX.

6.6 For the Happiness Questionnaire in Appendix C, write the MEANS command necessary to produce the mean score on the variable HAPPY for each category of the variable TVHOURS.

6.7 What MEANS command would you need to produce the mean score on the variable HAPPY for each category of the variable TVHOURS controlling for the variable SEX?

6.8 What commands would be needed to produce statistics indicating the statistical significance of the association between HAPPY and TVHOURS?

6.9 Use the SPSS system file NORC90 to do a breakdown of happiness by education controlling for income.

TABLE 6.5 Complete Output from Commands: MEANS HAPPY BY INCOME /
STATISTICS ALL

SUMMARIES OF   HAPPY   IS RESPONDENT HAPPY
BY LEVELS OF   INCOME   TOTAL FAMILY INCOME

VARIABLE	VALUE	LABEL	MEAN	STD DEV	CASES
FOR ENTIRE POPULATION			1.7490	.6068	1223
INCOME	1.00	LESS THAN $10000	1.9100	.5862	200
INCOME	2.00	$10000-$19999	1.8256	.6211	258
INCOME	3.00	$20000-$29999	1.8104	.6265	211
INCOME	4.00	$30000-$39999	1.6632	.5912	193
INCOME	5.00	$40000-$49999	1.5963	.5793	109
INCOME	6.00	$50000-$59999	1.7317	.5676	82
INCOME	7.00	$60000 OR MORE	1.5706	.5634	170

TOTAL CASES   = 1372
MISSING CASES = 149 OR 10.9 PCT.

****

*   A N A L Y S I S   O F   V A R I A N C E   *

****

SOURCE	SUM OF SQUARES	D.F.	MEAN SQUARE	F	SIG.
BETWEEN GROUPS	16.8902	6	2.8150	7.9046	.0000
LINEARITY	14.1294	1	14.1294	39.6756	.0000
DEV. FROM LINEARITY	2.7608	5	.5522	1.5504	.1713

R = -.1772   R SQUARED = .0314

| WITHIN GROUPS | 433.0461 | 1216 | .3561 | | |

ETA = .1937   ETA SQUARED = .0375

****

7

CORRELATIONS AND SCATTERGRAMS

New SPSS Commands:

CORR
SAMPLE
PLOT

We have done frequencies, crosstabulations, and breakdowns to determine that the variable HAPPY is associated with SEX, AGE, EDUC, and INCOME. To do these analyses, however, we recoded AGE and EDUC. INCOME also would have been recoded if the data were not already grouped into large intervals on the SPSS system file NORC90. Whenever we recode data into large intervals, detail is lost and we cannot study the association as precisely as we could before recoding the data. CORR and PLOT provide two analytical methods that do not require the regrouping of data into a small number of intervals. However, these methods were designed only for interval level variables.

In this chapter we will use CORR to re-examine the associations of SEX, AGE, EDUC, and INCOME with HAPPY and with one another. We will use PLOT to present the association between INCOME and EDUCATION. We will add to our analysis the variable HEALTH from the SPSS system file NORC90. HEALTH is the response to the question: "Would you say your own health, in general, is excellent, good, fair, or poor?" The answers were coded excellent

(1), good (2), fair (3), and poor (4). Strictly speaking HEALTH is an ordinal level of measurement variable because the categories can be ranked but the intervals are not clearly of equal size. A common practice, however, is to assume that the categories on a variable like HEALTH represent roughly equal steps on the measurement and to use the variable as an interval variable. This is done by assigning sequential numbers to the categories as we have done in our coding of the HEALTH variable. Dichotomous (two-category) nominal variables like SEX can also have their categories assigned numerical values and be used with statistical techniques like Pearson's correlation coefficient that are designed for interval level variables.

7.1 When and How to Use CORR

The output of the CORR command summarizes the strength of an association through the Pearson correlation coefficient, which is in the range from -1.0 to $+1.0$. One advantage of the Pearson correlation coefficient is that it indicates whether the association is positive or negative. A negative coefficient means that, when one variable is higher in value, the other variable tends to be lower in value. A positive coefficient means that, when one variable is higher, the other variable also tends to be higher. For example, we might expect the correlation between education and income to be positive.

The best indicator of the strength of the association between a pair of variables is the Pearson correlation coefficient squared. A correlation of .20 is four times as strong as a correlation of .10, because $(.20)^2 = .04$ and $(.10)^2 = .01$. However, once the coefficient is squared, it no longer indicates whether the association is positive or negative. Thus tables usually present the unsquared coefficient.

CORR requires the assumptions that the variables are interval level and linearly associated. For example, if income is low for young adults, peaks in late middle age, and drops off after age 60, the association is not linear and would be underestimated by Pearson's correlation coefficient. Other types of non-linear associations would not be appropriate material for CORR analysis. Two hypothetical examples are given in scattergrams in Figure 7.1.

To run CORR, we simply list after the command the variables whose associations we want printed. For example, to look at the association between each of the variables we have considered so far, use the following commands:

```
CORR   HAPPY  SEX  AGE  EDUC  INCOME  HEALTH
```

FIGURE 7.1 Nonlinear Associations That Would Be Inappropriate for CORR Analysis: (a) Exponential Increase—For Example, Number of Big Macs Sold Each Year, 1960–1985; (b) Logistic Curve—For Example, Resident Population Size of a Housing Development by Months Since Opening

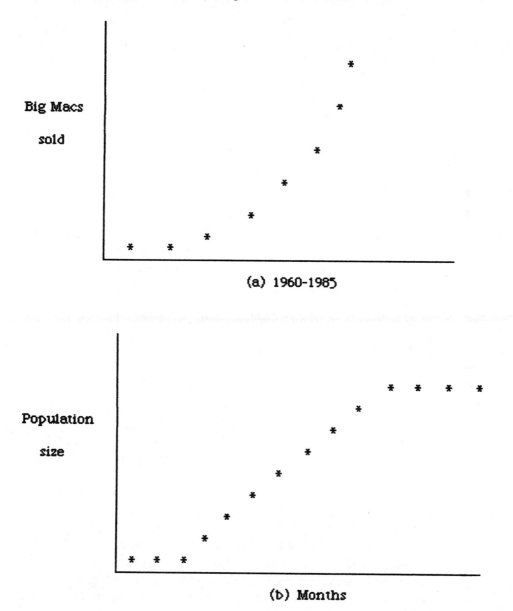

TABLE 7.1 Partial Output Produced by
CORR   HAPPY SEX AGE EDUC INCOME HEALTH /
      FORMAT SERIAL

PEARSON CORRELATION COEFFICIENTS

VARIABLE
PAIR   .037   -.047

HAPPY .015   HAPPY .030   HAPPY -.097
WITH N(1361)   WITH N(1357)   WITH N(1359)
SEX SIG .290   . AGE SIG .134 EDUC SIG .002

HAPPY -.177   HAPPY .251
WITH N(1223)   WITH N(911)
INCOME SIG .000 HEALTH SIG .000

For users unfamiliar with correlation matrices, the output will be easier to read
if the subcommand FORMAT SERIAL is also used. Without FORMAT SERIAL
the variable labels are in the margins instead of next to each correlation. Together the commands would be

CORR   HAPPY SEX AGE EDUC INCOME HEALTH /
      FORMAT SERIAL

Part of the Pearson correlation output from these commands is given in
Table 7.1. (An example of complete output is in Table 7.2 at the end of this chapter.) In this output the Pearson correlation coefficient is the number to the right
of the top variable (HAPPY) of each pair. In the upper-left part of the table, we
see that for HAPPY with SEX the correlation coefficient is .015. The N(1361)
under HAPPY indicates the number of cases used in calculating the correlation.
This number is different for each pair because the number of missing cases is
not the same for all variables. The SIG .290 shows that a correlation this size
would occur because of sampling error only 290 times out of 1000.
The correlation for HAPPY with HEALTH is .251, the highest for any of the
pairs. Only the correlation of HAPPY with INCOME is nearly as great. Although
the correlation with EDUC is less strong, it is still greater than a random association that might be expected from sampling error. So, the old folklore that to
be healthy, wealthy, and wise brings happiness has some empirical support in
our NORC90 survey.

FIGURE 7.2 Simplified Output of PLOT / PLOT-INCOME WITH AGE (hypothetical data)

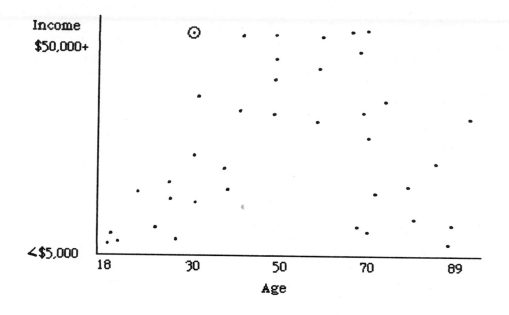

7.2 When and How to Use PLOT

The PLOT command produces a "scattergram" of the association between two variables by plotting a point for each case. These points lie on a plane in which each axis corresponds to the intervals of one of the variables. To understand PLOT, one picture is truly worth a thousand words. Look at Figure 7.2. The circled dot represents the case of someone age 30 earning over $50,000 per year. (We should all do so well!) The dot's distance from the vertical axis corresponds to the age interval 30, and its distance from the horizontal axis corresponds to an income of $50,000+. You can see that the scatter of cases tends to be higher on the vertical income axis for the older cases, which are more to the right on the age axis. At the oldest ages, however, income once more is at lower levels.

PLOT output is difficult to interpret when either variable has fewer than five intervals. For this reason we did not use the variable HAPPY in a scattergram example. PLOT output is also difficult to interpret when there are hundreds more cases than there are intervals in the two variables. We can solve the problem of too many cases by taking a sample of our cases before doing the PLOT. We do so with the command **SAMPLE** followed by the proportion of the cases we want in the sample. For Table 7.3, which is at the end of this chapter and gives complete output, we sampled .1, or 10 percent, of the males over age 34 to use in a scattergram of income with education.

To run PLOT you need to use the command followed first by / PLOT-then by the name of the variable you want on the vertical axis, then the word WITH, and finally the name of the variable you want on the horizontal axis. Normally, dependent variables are placed on the vertical axis and independent variables on the horizontal axis.

The commands to obtain a scattergram of INCOME with AGE like that in Figure 7.2 are

```
SAMPLE    .1
 / PLOT-PLOT   INCOME WITH AGE
```

In the next chapter we will discuss the analytical technique known as multiple regression. This technique will enable you to look at the combined effects of several independent variables. At the same time, you can control for the effects of the independent variables on one another's association with the dependent variable. Sounds like fun, huh? Please, no groans.

7.3 Summary

In this chapter we explain how to produce scattergrams and Pearson correlation coefficients by using the SPSS commands PLOT and CORR. Both procedures use interval level data or ordinal data that approximate interval data. Dichotomous (two-category) nominal level variables can be used in Pearson correlation analyses. Both procedures are well suited for handling variables with a large number of values.

An advantage of PLOT is that it depicts nonlinear relationships accurately, but its disadvantage is its inability to handle variables that have only a few values. CORR does not indicate accurately the association between two variables if the association is nonlinear.

We also introduced the command SAMPLE, which enables you to use a randomly selected portion of your cases when you want to reduce the sample size.

7.4 Where to Look in the SPSS Reference Guide

- CORR is discussed on pages 92–96.
- PLOT is discussed on pages 523–528.
- SAMPLE is discussed on pages 650–651.

RESEARCH PROJECT WORK FOR CHAPTER 7

1.   For your research project data set, do a PLOT of the association between TVHOURS and INCOME.

2.   For your data set, produce the Pearson correlation coefficients of all the variables with one another.

REVIEW QUESTIONS FOR CHAPTER 7

(Answers to Review Questions are given at the back of the book.)

7.1   Write a command to produce a scattergram with INCOME on the vertical axis and EDUC on the horizontal axis.

7.2   Write a command to produce two scattergrams, one with INCOME on the vertical axis and AGE on the horizontal axis and one with EDUC on the vertical axis and AGE on the horizontal axis.

7.3   Write a command to produce the Pearson correlation coefficient of HAPPY with HEALTH.

7.4   Write the commands to produce the Pearson correlation coefficients of INCOME, AGE, FAMSIZE, and CARSIZE in the output format discussed in this chapter.

7.5   Would a scattergram with number of cars per family on the vertical axis and family income on the horizontal axis be very revealing?

7.6   What problem would arise if you produced a scattergram of income (coded into 10 categories) with education using a data file with 10,000 cases? How could you solve the problem?

7.7   What types of variables can be used in a CORR analysis?

7.8   Infant deaths drop off exponentially as infant weight increases. Why would it be poor methodology to use CORR to analyze the association between infant death rates and infant weight without transforming one of the variables? Which variable would you transform and how?

7.9   What is the difference between a Pearson correlation coefficient of −.50 and a Pearson correlation coefficient of +.50?

7.10 If the Pearson correlation coefficient between HEALTH and EDUC were .20 and the Pearson correlation coefficient between HEALTH and IN-COME were .30, how would you describe the relative strength of the two associations?

ASSIGNMENT QUESTIONS FOR CHAPTER 7

(Solutions to the Assignment Questions are given in the *Instructor's Manual*.)

7.1   Write the commands necessary to produce a scattergram with INCOME on the vertical axis and AGE on the horizontal axis.

7.2   Write the commands necessary to produce three scattergrams (including Pearson correlation coefficients) with EDUC on the vertical axes and MAEDUC, PAEDUC, and SPEDUC on the horizontal axes.

7.3   Write a command to produce the Pearson correlation coefficient for the association between HEALTH and EDUC.

7.4   Write the commands necessary to produce the Pearson correlation coefficients for all the variables in a data file with one another. Include the command that will produce the format used in this chapter.

7.5   Why would a scattergram of the NORC90 variables HAPPY and HEALTH be inappropriate?

7.6   Would it be correct to use CORR to examine the association between the NORC90 variables HAPPY and MARITAL? Why?

7.7   What is the difference in meaning between positive and negative Pearson correlation coefficients?

7.8   If the Pearson correlation coefficient between AGE and HAPPY were .20 and the Pearson correlation coefficient between HEALTH and HAPPY were .40, what would we know about their relative strength?

TABLE 7.2 Complete Output from Command CORR HAPPY SEX AGE EDUC INCOME HEALTH / FORMAT SERIAL

P E A R S O N   C O R R E L A T I O N   C O E F F I C I E N T S

VARIABLE PAIR	VARIABLE PAIR	VARIABLE PAIR	VARIABLE PAIR	VARIABLE PAIR	VARIABLE PAIR
HAPPY WITH AGE .0146 N(1361) SIG .295	HAPPY WITH EDUC .0300 N(1357) SIG .134	HAPPY WITH INCOME -.0773 N(1359) SIG .002	HAPPY WITH HEALTH -.1772 N(1223) SIG .000	SEX WITH AGE .2507 N(911) SIG .000	SEX WITH EDUC .0610 N(1368) SIG .012
SEX WITH INCOME .0164 N(1370) SIG .272	SEX WITH HEALTH -.0807 N(1229) SIG .002	AGE WITH EDUC .0536 N(914) SIG .053	AGE WITH INCOME -.1843 N(1366) SIG .000	AGE WITH HEALTH -.1181 N(1226) SIG .000	AGE WITH HEALTH .2962 N(910) SIG .000
EDUC WITH HEALTH .3699 N(1228) SIG .000	INCOME WITH HEALTH -.2849 N(914) SIG .000	INCOME WITH HEALTH -.2542 N(1223) SIG .000			

SIG IS 1-TAILED, ' . ' IS PRINTED IF A COEFFICIENT CANNOT BE COMPUTED.

7.9   What distortion would probably occur if the association between IN-
       COME and AGE were measured with the Pearson correlation
       coefficient?

7.10   What could be done to make the Pearson correlation coefficient a better
       measure of the associaton between INCOME and AGE?

TABLE 7.3 Complete Output Using NORC90 File from Commands
        SELECT IF   SEX EQ 1   AND   AGE GT 34
        SAMPLE   .1
        PLOT/PLOT=INCOME WITH EDUC

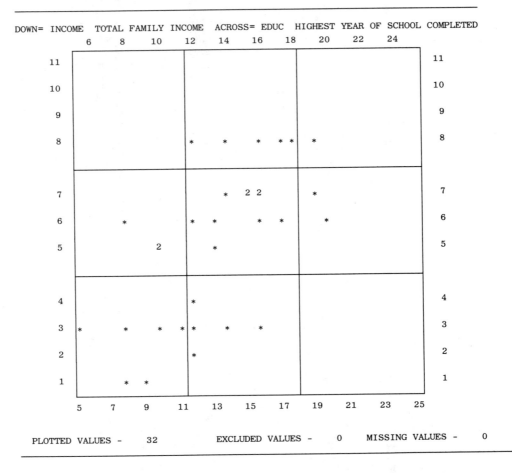

DOWN= INCOME TOTAL FAMILY INCOME   ACROSS= EDUC HIGHEST YEAR OF SCHOOL COMPLETED

PLOTTED VALUES -   32   EXCLUDED VALUES -   0   MISSING VALUES -   0

8

COMPARING DATA FROM DIFFERENT FILES

New SPSS commands:

ADD

There will be occasions when you want to compare data from two or more files. Perhaps you were sent data already in SPSS files from different test sites. Or you may want to add the latest month's balances from an SPSS file to an existing SPSS file containing past information on customers.

Another common task is having to join files from two time periods for comparison. In this chapter we will demonstrate how to combine SPSS files using the ADD command. The example that we will use is adding together the NORC84 and NORC90 General Social Survey files described in Appendix B of this book. After showing how to join the files we will discuss some of the issues in comparing from time periods, locations, or other such sets of data files.

8.1 Using the ADD Command to Join Files

The basic SPSS command for bringing together two files is simply

```
ADD FILES / FILE=NORC84/
             FILE=NORC90
```

where NORC84 and NORC90 are the files being joined. Up to 50 files can be joined on one ADD command. SPSS files must be made from non-SPSS files before they can be used on the ADD command. (See Chapter 2.) The ADD command may use the active file that the program has created up to that point by using * in place of a file name on a FILE=subcommand.

An important preliminary step is to ensure that there is a variable, such as YEAR, that distinguishes your files. If this is not so, you can create such a variable with a COMPUTE command. For example, we can retrieve the NORC84 file with the command GET NORC84. Then we can use the command COMPUTE YEAR=1984 to create the variable YEAR, which will have the value 1984 for all cases in that file. This file, including the new variable YEAR, can be saved with the command SAVE OUTFILE=NORC84. Altogether the commands would be

```
GET FILE NORC84
COMPUTE YEAR=1984
SAVE OUTFILE=NORC84
```

As you can see in Appendix B for NORC84 and NORC90, the variable YEAR, which distinguishes between them, has already been created.

8.2 Looking for Changes in Central Tendency

We could make variable-by-variable comparisons between the two years to see whether there have been any changes. Remember, however, that these are samples used to estimate much larger populations. Looking at 100 comparisons would probably produce at least one difference that could occur only one time out of 100 because of sampling variability. It would be better, therefore, to have a focused research agenda in mind. The research theme running throughout this book is what is associated with happiness, so a logical begin-

TABLE 8.1 Partial Output from CROSSTABS HAPPY BY YEAR.

	1984	1990
	COL PCT	
VERY HAPPY	34.7	33.4
PRETTY HAPPY	52.3	57.6
NOT TOO HAPPY	12.9	9.0
Column Total	1445	1361

CHI-SQUARE	SIGNIFICANCE
14.0	.001

ning point is to see whether responses to the happiness question changed between 1984 and 1990. A convenient way to address this inquiry is to produce a crosstabs of HAPPY by YEAR. The required commands would be

```
ADD FILES  /  FILE=NORC84  /
              FILE=NORC90
CROSSTABS     HAPPY BY YEAR  /
              CELLS=COLUMN  /
              STATISTICS=CHISQ PHI
```

The results are presented in Table 8.1. We can see that the largest change was in the "pretty happy" category, which increased from 52 percent to 58 percent. The percentages in both the "very happy" and the "not too happy" categories declined slightly. These changes are not very great, but the chi-square indicates that it is unlikely that the changes are simply due to sampling error.

8.3 Looking for Changes in Associations

Measures of central tendency, such as means, medians, and modes, are not the only statistics to examine for differences or changes. There can also be changes in the spread of scores on a variable or the degree to which it is skewed to one side or the other of the central tendency. At one time or another, almost all the statistics that can be calculated are worthy of examination for changes over time or differences among data sources. In particular, we are often interested in changes in the strength of associations.

Table 8.2 Output from CROSSTABS HAPPY BY SEX BY YEAR.

	CROSSTABULATION OF		
HAPPY	GENERAL HAPPINESS	BY SEX	RESPONDENT'S SEX

CONTROLLING FOR . . .
     YEAR=1984

HAPPY	MALE	FEMALE	ROW TOTAL
VERY HAPPY	186	316	502
	31.7	36.8	
PRETTY HAPPY	315	441	756
	53.8	51.3	
NOT TOO HAPPY	85	102	187
	14.5	11.9	
Column Total	586	859	1445
	100.0	100.0	

CHI-SQUARE	D.F.	SIGNIFICANCE	MIN E.F.	CELLS WITH E.F. <5
4.80514	2	.0905	75.835	None

STATISTIC	VALUE
CRAMER'S V	.05767

Given the lively discussion about changes, or lack thereof, in sex roles, let's consider as an example whether there has been a change between 1984 and 1990 in the association between gender and happiness. We can address this question by crosstabulating HAPPY and SEX controlling for YEAR. The necessary SPSS command would be

```
CROSSTABS HAPPY BY SEX BY YEAR/
         CELLS=COUNT COLUMN/
         STATISTICS=CHISQ PHI
```

TABLE 8.2 Output from CROSSTABS HAPPY BY SEX BY YEAR. (continued)

	CROSSTABULATION OF		
HAPPY	GENERAL HAPPINESS	BY SEX	RESPONDENT'S SEX

CONTROLLING FOR . . .
      YEAR=1990

	MALE	FEMALE	ROW TOTAL
HAPPY			
VERY HAPPY	205 34.1	250 32.9	455
PRETTY HAPPY	344 57.2	440 57.9	784
NOT TOO HAPPY	52 8.7	70 9.2	122
COLUMN TOTAL	601 100.0	760 100.0	1361

CHI-SQUARE	D.F.	SIGNIFICANCE	MIN E.F.	CELLS WITH E.F. <5
1.55280	2	.670905 835	75.835	None

STATISTIC	VALUE
CRAMER'S V	.01480

NUMBER OF MISSING OBSERVATIONS=39

The output from these commands is printed in Table 8.2. We can see that the association between gender and happiness is not very strong in either year, but it has undergone an interesting change. The percentage of women who reported being "very happy" declined from 37 to 33, while the percentage of men who reported being very happy increased from 32 to 34. Among those who reported being "not too happy," the percentage decreased for both men and women; however, it decreased more for men (14 to 9) than for women (12 to 9). Whether this represents a trend toward men's being happier than women or a convergence toward similar happiness levels cannot be determined without seeing what happened after 1990.

The statistics produced indicate the strength of the association for each year, but do not indicate the significance of changes in the association between years. To address this more subtle question, you would have to look at what are termed "interaction effects" using one of the more sophisticated statistical techniques discussed in Part 2 of our text. We're sure that makes you eager to plunge ahead.

8.4 Summary

In this chapter we explain how the ADD command can be used to join a set of two or more SPSS files. We point out that for comparisons among the files there must be a variable in all the files that distinguishes among them. If not, one can be created and saved with each file before the joining process is begun.

There is often great interest in seeing whether data from different sources differ in the central tendencies and other characteristics of their variables. Similarly, researchers often investigate whether associations found in one data set are also found in others. Statistical techniques covered in previous chapters are powerful tools for these comparisons; however, some tests will require the more advanced methods presented in Part 2.

8.5 Where to Look in the *SPSS Reference Guide*

• ADD is discussed on pages 33–38.

RESEARCH PROJECT WORK FOR CHAPTER 8

1. Collect a second sample of data or exchange the SPSS file you created from your research project with another student's research project SPSS file. Join the two files using the ADD command. Be sure there is a variable that identifies the file each case is from.

2. Test to see whether there are noteworthy differences in central tendency between the two files for happiness, age, income, health, and education.

3. Test to see whether there are noteworthy differences in the associations between happiness, age, income, health, and education.

REVIEW QUESTIONS FOR CHAPTER 8

8.1   Write commands that would create the variable REGION for the file NORTH so that all the cases would have the value 1 for the REGION variable.

8.2   Write a command to join four files named NORTH, SOUTH, EAST, and WEST.

8.3   Write the command necessary to join the file BRITAIN to the active file created by the program up to that point.

8.4   Write a CROSSTABS command to compare responses to the happiness question for joined files distinguished by the variable REGION.

8.5   Write a MEANS command to compare income by education for the joined files distinguished by the variable REGION.

ASSIGNMENT QUESTIONS FOR CHAPTER 8

8.1   Write commands that would create the variable QUARTER for the file BIRTHS3 so that all the cases would have the value 3 for the QUARTER variable.

8.2   Write a command to join four files named BIRTHS1, BIRTHS2, BIRTHS3, and BIRTHS4.

8.3   If all four joined files had a variable BIRTHS, and a variable HOSPITAL, what command would indicate the number of births for each hospital for the combined data file?

8.4   Write a MEANS command to compare on the variable BIRTHWT the files distinguished by the variable QUARTER.

8.5   Write a CROSSTABS command to compare the association between EDUC and BIRTHWT for differences among the files distinguished by the variable QUARTER.

PART 2

ADVANCED TECHNIQUES

Very useful analyses can be produced using the statistical procedures discussed in Part 1, and you have to use these procedures to clean your data and become familiar with the distributions of your variables and their bivariate associations. There will come a time, however, when you want to move on to more powerful techniques for analyzing multivariate associations. The procedures we present in Part 2 (multiple regression, analysis of variance, discriminant function analysis, log-linear analysis, and factor analysis) enable you to uncover associations that are difficult or impossible to detect using the techniques discussed in Part 1.

We present the material in Part 2 with the assumption that you now have a basic knowledge of statistics and of SPSS. The examples will present only the statistical procedure commands and will assume that you have already used the GET command to access an SPSS system file.

We present a short discussion of the statistical basis of each procedure, but our primary intent is to introduce the SPSS commands rather than to teach statistics. For a complete explanation of these statistical techniques, you will need to refer to an advanced statistics book. The Russell Sage Foundation publishes a good series of papers on these methods written for the nonmathematician reader: *Quantitative Applications in the Social Sciences*. At the beginning of each chapter we will refer you to the appropriate paper from this series.

The statistical procedures discussed in Part 2 require data sets with at least 100 cases for most analyses. Therefore, to use the research project data that was gathered and used in Part 1, you will need to merge together the data files of several students.

9

EXAMINING COMBINED EFFECTS OF MANY INDEPENDENT VARIABLES: MULTIPLE REGRESSION

New SPSS Command:

REGRESSION

We have seen that health, age, education, income, and sex are all associated with the probability of people's reporting they are happy. However, what if we want to examine the effects of each of those variables controlling for the effects of all the other variables in our analysis? A crosstabulation or breakdown would be very difficult to interpret. Multiple regression is a technique that will do what we want and still be easy to interpret.* Multiple regression will show us the effects of each variable when the effects of other variables are controlled.

9.1 When to Use REGRESSION

The advantage of multiple regression is that it shows both the combined effects of a set of independent variables and the separate effects of each inde-

---

*For a more complete discussion of the statistics of regression analysis, see Michael S. Lewis-Beck's *Applied Regression: An Introduction* (Beverly Hills, CA: Sage Publications, 1980).

pendent variable when the others are controlled. A drawback of multiple regression is that it requires several assumptions about the distribution of each variable and the associations among the variables. Multiple regression applies best to an analysis in which both the dependent variable and the independent variable are normally distributed interval variables (for a discussion of the normal distribution see Blalock, 1979). However, ordinal variables are commonly used as well, and moderate deviations from normality do not bias the results greatly.

Multiple regression also assumes that the effects of the independent variables are linear—that is, that the effect of a unit difference in an independent variable is the same at all points in the range of the variable. (There is further explanation of the nature of this assumption in the Chapter 7 discussion of the Pearson correlation coefficient.)

Another assumption of multiple regression is that the independent variables are not correlated with one another (see Section 9.4).

Multiple regression can be used with categorical variables through a technique known as dummy coding (see Section 9.5).

If the relationship between the independent variable and the dependent variable is nonlinear, the independent variable can be transformed (see Section 9.6).

9.2 How to Use REGRESSION

The command that produces multiple regression analyses in SPSS is **REGRESSION**. REGRESSION has three required subcommands. The first subcommand, **VARIABLES =**, is followed by a list of all the variables that will be used. The second required subcommand, **DEPENDENT =**, is followed by each variable that you want to use as a dependent variable. For both subcommands variable names are separated by one or more spaces or commas. A different multiple regression analysis will be produced for each dependent variable. The third subcommand is **METHOD = ENTER**. (Besides ENTER there are five other methods that are a bit more complex.)

To run REGRESSION with HAPPY as the dependent variable and SEX, AGE, EDUC, INCOME, HEALTH, and MARITAL as independent variables, the following commands are needed. MARITAL was recoded into a dichotomous variable (married = 1, unmarried = 0).

```
REGRESSION   VARIABLES=HAPPY SEX AGE EDUC INCOME
                     HEALTH MARITAL/
             DEPENDENT=HAPPY/
             METHOD=ENTER/
```

TABLE 9.1 Partial Output from REGRESSION Command

MULTIPLE R	.362	F=20.71
R SQUARE	.131	SIGNIF F=.0000
ADJUSTED R SQUARE	.125	

——————————— VARIABLES IN THE EQUATION ———————————

VARIABLE	B	SE B	BETA	T	SIG T
MARITAL	-.301	.046	-.243	-6.61	.000
SEX	-.048	.041	-.038	-1.15	.249
EDUC	-.011	.007	-.056	-1.54	.123
HEALTH	.172	.026	.231	6.52	.006
AGE	-.001	.001	-.038	-1.11	.266
INCOME	-.012	.012	-.004	-.10	.922
(CONSTANT)	1.88	.143		13.19	.000

Note that each subcommand is followed by a slash. Part of the output from these commands is presented in Table 9.1. An example of complete output is given in Table 9.2 at the end of this chapter.

9.3 Interpreting REGRESSION Output

In Table 9.1 the multiple R is the correlation between the dependent variable and the entire set of independent variables. The multiple R squared (R^2) is the proportion of variance in the dependent variable associated with variance in the independent variables. This proportion is a good indicator of the explanatory power of the regression model.

The adjusted R^2 is corrected for the number of cases. A small number of cases relative to the number of variables in the multiple regression can bias upward the estimate of R^2. When your sample size is less than ten cases per variable, you will notice that the adjusted R^2 decreases substantially relative to the unadjusted R^2 if the sample size is reduced.

The beta column indicates the values of the standardized regression coefficient. Beta represents the effect that a standard deviation difference in the independent variable would have on the dependent variable in standard deviation (the standardized scores of the dependent variable). The beta for HEALTH is .231, which means a difference of one standard deviation in HEALTH is predicted to cause a difference of .231 standard deviation in HAPPY. Because the coefficient is positive, a person with a lower score on HEALTH is predicted to

have a lower score on HAPPY. Recall that the happiest category and the healthi-
est category are coded 1, the least healthy category is coded 4, and the least
happy category is coded 3. So the beta for HEALTH indicates that people who
report feeling healthy are more likely to report feeling happy. Based on the
betas, differences in health and differences in marital status have the greatest
impact on happiness.

Because the beta coefficient for MARITAL is negative with married
people coded 1 and unmarried coded 0, we can conclude that married people
tend to be happier than unmarried people.

Another method of evaluating the importance of an independent variable
is to observe the change in the R^2 when it is added to or dropped from the
analysis. This can be done by using more than one METHOD=ENTER subcommand with independent variables specified after ENTER. The variables specified on each METHOD=ENTER subcommand will be added to the ones already
in the analysis. To produce two regressions, one with MARITAL and one without, the commands would be

```
REGRESSION   VARIABLES=HAPPY SEX AGE EDUC INCOME
                      HEALTH MARITAL/
             DEPENDENT=HAPPY/
             METHOD=ENTER   SEX AGE EDUC INCOME HEALTH/
             METHOD=ENTER   MARITAL/
```

The T statistic is a measure of the distance of beta from zero in a probability distribution. The SIG T (significance of *t*) is the probability that such a
deviation from zero would be due to sampling error. For MARITAL, the first predictor variable, the SIG T is .0000, which indicates that a beta this large would
occur from sampling error less than one time out of 1000.

Residuals are the errors in prediction. They are obtained by subtracting
the actual score from the predicted score for each case. If the actual score for a
case were 3 and the predicted score were 2.5, the residual would be 0.5.

Doing a scattergram of the standardized residuals by the standardized predicted scores is a convenient test of whether the model violates assumptions
about linearity. If the model is good, the residuals will be randomly distributed
for each value of the predicted values. At the same time, there should be more
predicted values near zero (the mean of a standardized variable) because the
dependent variable is assumed to be normally distributed. To obtain this scattergram, use the subcommand

```
SCATTERPLOT   (*RES, *PRE) /
```

Like the subcommands given in Section 9.2, SCATTERPLOT must begin after column 1 and is usually aligned with the other subcommands for clarity.

To see a histogram of the residuals, use the subcommand RESIDUAL= HISTOGRAM. (Recall that a histogram is the graphic representation of a frequency distribution by a series of bars.) The histogram of the residuals should reveal that they have a normal distribution.

9.4 Multicollinearity

Before doing a regression analysis, you should do a FREQUENCIES analysis to determine whether the variables are normally distributed. Theoretically, the variables should be normally distributed. In practice, multiple regression is recognized as a robust technique that can include non–normally distributed variables, if their deviations from normality are not extreme.

You also need to know the intercorrelations among the variables, which can be obtained using the CORR command. Theoretically, the independent variables should be correlated with the dependent variable, but not with one another. In practice, one often sees intercorrelations as high as .60 among independent variables in a regression analysis. Use only one of a group of highly correlated variables or construct an index.

9.5 Dummy Variables

Nominal variables may be used in REGRESSION by employing a coding technique known as **dummy variables.** The simplest dummy variable would be for a two-category variable like SEX. Simply code one category 0—let this be the males—and code the other category 1—for the females. This variable can be entered in the REGRESSION as an independent variable. A dummy variable should not be used as a dependent variable in regression if one of the categories contains less than 20 percent of the cases because the assumption of a normally distributed dependent variable would be violated too greatly. Such a violation would tend to produce unreliable estimates of the regression coefficients.

For a nominal variable with more than two categories, a set of dummy variables is used. The number of dummy variables will be one less than the number of categories. For example, the variable RELIG (religious preference) in the NORC90 file has five categories: Protestant, coded 1; Catholic, coded 2; Jewish, coded 3; None, coded 4; and Other, coded 5. To create a set of dummy variables, the following commands could be used:

```
IF    RELIG EQ 1    D1=1
IF    RELIG NE 1    D1=0
IF    RELIG EQ 2    D2=1
IF    RELIG NE 2    D2=0
IF    RELIG EQ 3    D3=1
IF    RELIG NE 3    D3=0
IF    RELIG EQ 4    D4=1
IF    RELIG NE 4    D4=0
```

For each case, except those in the "other" category, one dummy variable would equal 1 and the rest would equal 0. For those in the "other" category, all the dummy variables would equal zero. A Protestant, for example, would have a score of 1 on D1 and a score of 0 on D2, D3, and D4.

D1 through D4 would then be entered as independent variables in the RE-GRESSION. To evaluate the total effects of the RELIG variable on the dependent variable, the dummy variables' collective effects would be used by looking at the R^2 with the set of dummy variables included in the REGRESSION and then the R^2 with the dummy variables dropped from the REGRESSION. The difference in R^2 would be one measure of the impact of the RELIG variable.

Another indicator of the importance of RELIG would be if any of the dummy variables had a statistically significant beta coefficient. The beta coefficient for each dummy variable represents how much greater (or lesser if the sign is negative) cases coded 1 on that variable are predicted to score on the dependent variable (in standardized scores) compared to cases in the category for which all the dummy variables are coded 0. The output in Table 9.2 at the end of this chapter includes RELIG as a dummy variable.

9.6 Nonlinear Effects Corrected through Variable Transformations

When the residual plot reveals nonlinear effects, the researcher can make adjustments by transforming the dependent variable. For example, if the residuals increase in value as the predicted value increases, you can compute the log of the dependent variable and try using that transformed score as the dependent variable to reduce the errors in your predictions.

There are many ways of transforming the predictor variables or the dependent variables to compensate for nonlinear relationships. The SPSS COMPUTE functions make it easy to transform variables, thereby facilitating adjustments for nonlinearity. However, the choice of what transformations to make and how to interpret the coefficients is a complex topic beyond the scope of this book.

9.7 Interaction Effects

An interaction effect exists when the effects of one variable are influenced by scores on another variable. For example, if the effects of income on happiness were greater for high-education respondents than for low-education respondents, there would be an interaction between income and education. Look for interaction effects when knowledge of your research subject suggests that they exist or when you find irregularities in your residuals.

One way to adjust for interaction effects is to include in the analysis a variable that is a composite of the two variables. For our example of income interacting with education, we could adjust by computing a new variable (income multiplied by education) and including this interaction term in the regression as an independent variable along with its two components. If the beta coefficient for the interaction term is statistically significant, it indicates that its variables have a combined effect as well as their separate effects.

9.8 Summary

In this chapter we discuss multiple regression. This technique is used to evaluate the effects of a set of independent variables on one dependent variable.

The output from REGRESSION indicates the combined effects of a set of independent variables and also each independent variable's separate effects when the other independent variables are controlled. The variables are assumed to be interval or ordinal measures; however, nominal variables can be used with a technique known as dummy variable coding.

Multiple regression assumes that the independent variables are normally distributed and not highly correlated with one another.

9.9 Where to Look in the SPSS Reference Guide

- REGRESSION is discussed on pages 585–603.

RESEARCH PROJECT WORK FOR CHAPTER 9

1. For your research project data set, do a REGRESSION using HAPPY as the dependent variable and INCOME, SEX, EDUC, MARITAL, AGE, HEALTH, and TVHOURS as the independent variables. (If your file has

fewer than 100 cases, combine it with those of other students to obtain a minimum of 100 cases.)

2.   Interpret the results from Problem 1.

REVIEW QUESTIONS FOR CHAPTER 9

9.1   What types of variables theoretically can be used in a multiple regression analysis?

9.2   Write the commands necessary to do a multiple regression analysis with HEALTH as the dependent variable and INCOME, EDUC, HAPPY, AGE, and SEX as the independent variables.

9.3   Write the commands necessary to do a multiple regression analysis with HAPPY as the dependent variable and INCOME, HEALTH, and RELIG as the independent variables. (Remember to recode religion into dummy variables.)

9.4   What is the meaning of the multiple R at the top of the table in the RE-GRESSION output (Table 9.1)? How is it related to the predictive strength of the REGRESSION model?

9.5   What does it mean to have multicollinearity problems? How are multi-collinearity problems resolved?

9.6   What would it mean if the SCATTERPLOT of standardized residuals by standardized predicted values was not random?

9.7   Add to the commands required for Review Question 9.2 the subcom-mand necessary to produce the scatterplot of standardized residuals by standardized predicted values.

ASSIGNMENT QUESTIONS FOR CHAPTER 9

9.1   Write the commands necessary to do a multiple regression analysis with INCOME as the dependent variable and EDUC, AGE, and SEX as the in-dependent variables.

9.2   Write the commands necessary to do a multiple regression with the NORC90 file using HAPPY as a dependent variable and INCOME and MARITAL as independent variables. Remember to recode MARITAL into either a dichotomous variable or a set of dummy variables.

9.3 What is the difference between the R^2 and the adjusted R^2 at the top of the table in the REGRESSION output (Table 9.1)?

9.4 Which more accurately indicates the proportion of variance in the dependent variable explained in a multiple regression analysis, the R or the R^2?

9.5 What would you need to do if two independent variables in a multiple regression were correlated at the .95 level?

9.6 How can a researcher detect whether the assumptions of linear effects on the dependent variables are violated?

9.7 What subcommand must be added to the REGRESSION command to plot the standardized residuals by the standardized predicted values?

TABLE 9.2 Complete Output Produced by:

```
RECODE  MARITAL  (2,3,4,5=0)
IF  RELIG EQ 1  D1=1
IF  RELIG NE 1  D1=0
IF  RELIG EQ 2  D2=1
IF  RELIG NE 2  D2=0
IF  RELIG EQ 3  D3=1
IF  RELIG NE 3  D3=0
IF  RELIG EQ 4  D4=1
IF  RELIG NE 4  D4=0
REGRESSION  VARIABLES=HAPPY SEX AGE EDUC INCOME HEALTH MARITAL
                      D1 D2 D3 D4 /
                      DEPENDENT=HAPPY /
                      METHOD=ENTER /
```

LISTWISE DELETION OF MISSING DATA

EQUATION NUMBER 1   DEPENDENT VARIABLE..   HAPPY

BEGINNING BLOCK NUMBER   1.   METHOD: ENTER

* * * *   M U L T I P L E   R E G R E S S I O N   * * * *

Equation Number 1   Dependent Variable..   HAPPY

VARIABLE(S) ENTERED ON STEP NUMBER

   1..   D4
   2..   HEALTH
   3..   SEX
   4..   D3
   5..   D2
   6..   MARITAL
   7..   EDUC
   8..   AGE
   9..   INCOME
  10..   D1

MULTIPLE R   .37459
R SQUARE   .14032
ADJUSTED R SQUARE .12980
STANDARD ERROR   .57651

ANALYSIS OF VARIANCE

	DF	SUM OF SQUARES	MEAN SQUARE
REGRESSION	10	44.32103	4.43210
RESIDUAL	817	271.53767	.33236

F = 13.33527   SIGNIF F = .0000

VARIABLES IN THE EQUATION

VARIABLE	B	SE B	BETA	T	SIG T
D4	.02836	.13878	.01153	.204	.8381
HEALTH	.16472	.02639	.22100	6.242	.0000
SEX	-.04149	.04121	-.03330	-1.007	.3143
D3	.19616	.18394	.04504	1.066	.2865
D2	-.11568	.12348	-.07890	-.937	.3491
MARITAL	-.28537	.04562	-.23041	-6.255	.0000
EDUC	-.01372	7.43572	-.06714	-1.845	.0654
AGE	-.00153696	1.19300	-.04464	-1.288	.1980
INCOME	-.00392680	.01238	-.01262	-.317	.7511
D1	-.14901	.11894	-.11500	-1.253	.2106
(CONSTANT)	2.04698	.18322		11.172	.0000

END BLOCK NUMBER   1   ALL REQUESTED VARIABLES ENTERED.

MULTIVARIATE COMPARISON OF MEANS: ANALYSIS OF VARIANCE AND MULTIPLE ANALYSIS OF VARIANCE

New SPSS Command:

MANOVA

We have seen that, in general, the probability of being happy is higher for people who are more educated, more affluent, healthy, and married. However, what about interactions among these variables? Are the effects of being affluent, for example, greater for men than for women? Are the effects of education the same for both sexes? Are the effects of marital status affected by income?

The MEANS procedure allows multivariate comparisons of means. However, MEANS does not calculate the statistical significance or the strength of the association for more than one predictor variable at a time. In other words, we cannot learn the statistical significance of one variable controlling for the effects of one or more other variables. Nor is it easy to assess the strength of the interactions among the predictor variables.

Several SPSS programs do analysis of variance of one sort or another. Rather than study them all, we will examine MANOVA (multiple analysis of variance), the one most powerful SPSS program for addressing these questions.

10.1 Doing Many Types of Analysis of Variance: MANOVA

The MANOVA program does many types of analysis of variance. Analysis of variance (ANOVA) is especially appropriate when the dependent variable is an interval measure and the predicting variables are nominal.* It is also useful when the predicting variables are interval but nonlinear in their effects.

MANOVA allows us to study the effects of nominal variables and interval variables together. In such an analysis, the interval level variables are termed **covariates** and the technique is called **covariate analysis.**

Finally, MANOVA allows us to look at differences on a set of dependent variables, rather than just one. For example, if we have several measures of happiness, we can do a composite analysis to determine whether groups differ on them. This last application is the actual multiple analysis of variance from which the program received its name—MANOVA.

Analysis of variance assumes that the dependent variable is interval and that the variances are equal for all groups.

10.2 One Dependent Variable with Two or More Independent Variables

We will begin our study of the MANOVA command with the case of one dependent variable and two or more independent variables. (The case of one dependent variable and one independent variable can be handled more easily with the MEANS command. See Chapter 6.)

Consider whether differences in happiness by marital status are the same for both males and females. The only statistical procedure command we need is

MANOVA   HAPPY BY MARITAL(1,5) SEX(1,2)

The (1,5) after MARITAL is required to indicate the low and high categories of MARITAL. The (1,2) after SEX is required to indicate the low and high

---

*For a more complete discussion of the statistics of analysis of variance see Gudmund R. Iversen and Helmut Norpoth's *Analysis of Variance* (Beverly Hills, CA: Sage Publications, 1976).

TABLE 10.1 Partial Output from MANOVA

SOURCE OF VARIATION	MEAN SQUARE	F	SIG. OF F
WITHIN CELLS	.34		
MARITAL	9.55	28.4	.000
SEX	.17	.5	.476
MARITAL BY SEX	.32	1.0	.425

categories of SEX. Missing values should not be included in the range specified on the command. The MANOVA program assumes that there are no empty categories. If MARITAL category 4 were empty, the values would need to be recoded. For example, the cases with a score of 5 could be recoded as 4. (If you are using any value labels, remember to change them as well.)

The output from this command will contain a table entitled "Analysis of Variance," partial contents of which are given in Table 10.1.

The WITHIN CELLS row represents the variance that remains within cells after the cases have been partitioned by the MARITAL and SEX categories. This variance may be thought of as "unexplained." This row does not convey information about an association; hence it has no F ratio.

The MARITAL row represents the association between HAPPY and MARITAL. The F ratio is the mean of the differences on HAPPY between MARITAL categories squared (9.55) divided by the mean within-cells of the differences on HAPPY squared (.32). For MARITAL the F ratio is 28.4, which indicates that, when we control for the effects of SEX, the differences between MARITAL categories are much greater than the differences within the MARITAL categories. The significance level of F is .000, which indicates that a difference this size would occur fewer than 1 time out of 1000 by random sampling error.

The SEX row reveals a mean sum of squares of .17, an F of .5, and a significance level of .476. The last statistic indicates that, controlling for MARITAL, the differences by SEX are so small that the probability is 476 times out of 1000 that such differences could occur because of mere sampling error.

Our purpose in this analysis is to examine the interaction between marital status and sex. In the MARITAL BY SEX row we see that the mean of differences squared by MARITAL and SEX interactions (.32) is about the same as the mean of differences squared within cells (.34). Hence the F is 1, and the significance level of .425 is too high to give us confidence that the MARITAL BY SEX interactions are anything more than sampling error. We would conclude, then, that the effects of marital status are roughly the same for males and females. Similarly, the effects of the variable SEX are the same for all marital statuses.

10.3 One Dependent Variable, Two Group Variables, and One Covariate

At the beginning of this chapter, we raised the question of whether variances in income would affect the MARITAL–HAPPY association. One way to examine this question is to control for income by including it as a covariate; that is, each individual's score will be adjusted for the effects of income. (Depending on the statistical program used and the options specified, the control will be done before, while, or after the group effects are examined. In MANOVA, as we are using it in this chapter, the control for the covariate is done simultaneously with the examination of the group effects. If an association exists between MARITAL and HAPPY only because married couples have more money than unmarried people, then the association between MARITAL and HAPPY will vanish once we control for income by including it as a covariate.

The statistical procedure command necessary to produce this analysis is

```
MANOVA   HAPPY BY MARITAL (1, 5)  SEX  (1, 2)  WITH INCOME
```

Note that the covariate is preceded by the word WITH instead of the word BY. Note also that the name of the covariate is not followed by its low and high values.

Part of the output produced by this MANOVA command using the NORC90 file is given in Table 10.2. Essentially the output at the top of Table 10.2 re-

TABLE 10.2 Partial Output from MANOVA Command

ANALYSIS OF VARIANCE

SOURCE OF VARIATION	MEAN SQUARE	F	SIG. OF F
WITHIN CELLS	.34		
REGRESSION	2.44	7.2	.000
CONSTANT	848.18	2508.8	.000
MARITAL	6.10	18.0	.000
SEX	.18	.5	.443
MARITAL BY SEX	.22	.7	.475

REGRESSION ANALYSIS FOR WITHIN CELLS ERROR TERM

DEPENDENT VARIABLE...HAPPY   GENERAL HAPPINESS

COVARIATE	BETA	T VALUE	SIG. OF T
INCOME	−.077	−2.7	.007

sembles that of the MANOVA without the covariate. Note, however, that the mean sum of squares for MARITAL groups has been reduced from 9.55 to 6.10. This result indicates that roughly one third of the differences by marital status disappear when we control simultaneously for the effects of income. Nonetheless, the remaining mean square has an F of 18.0 with a significance level below .000. Hence the differences by marital status remain significant even after the effects of INCOME are controlled.

The lower portion of the table allows us to evaluate the impact of the covariate INCOME. We are given its standardized regression coefficient, or beta ($-.077$), t value, and significance level, all of which indicate that, for cases with higher incomes, the happiness score is lower. (Recall that lower scores on HAPPY indicate greater happiness.) We can see that the effects of income are significant.

10.4 Multiple Dependent Variables and One or More Group Variables

The distinction between MANOVA and other SPSS programs is that MANOVA can handle multiple dependent variable analysis of variance. For example, instead of using only one dependent variable, you can use a set of dependent variables like SATCITY, SATFAM, SATFRND, and HAPPY. One reason for using multiple variables is that a bias creeps into an analysis that has a large number of tests of group differences. If you do tests of group differences on several dependent variables, you increase the likelihood that a given-sized difference will occur from sampling error—much as you would increase the likelihood of rolling 12 with a pair of dice if you rolled the dice four times instead of once.

The command to test whether there are differences by marital status or sex on this set of dependent variables would be

```
MANOVA    SATCITY  SATFAM  SATFRND  HAPPY BY MARITAL(1,5)  SEX(1,2)
```

When there are multiple dependent variables, the output from MANOVA will present first a set of tables for the interaction effects, then a set for the last variable in the command, then a set for the next-to-last variable, and so forth. Each set of tables covers a page of output. See Table 10.4 at the end of this chapter for an example of complete MANOVA output.

The first statistics on each page are multivariate tests of significance, which are measures of whether groups differ significantly in their scores on the set of dependent variables. The most powerful and robust of these measures is Pillai's trace, which is printed first.

TABLE 10.3 Partial Output from MANOVA Multiple Dependent Variable Command

---

EFFECT .. MARITAL BY SEX

MULTIVARIATE TESTS OF SIGNIFICANCE
TEST NAME	VALUE	APPROX. F	SIG. OF F
PILLAIS	.031	1.7	.036

UNIVARIATE F-TESTS
VARIABLE	HYPOTH. MS	ERROR MS	F	SIG. OF F
SATCITY	1.9	2.0	1.0	.414
SATFAM	5.7	1.6	3.6	.007
SATFRND	.5	1.6	.3	.866
HAPPY	.2	.3	.7	.620

///

EFFECT .. SEX

MULTIVARIATE TESTS OF SIGNIFICANCE
TEST NAME	VALUE	EXACT F	SIG. OF F
PILLAIS	.010	2.2	.069

UNIVARIATE F-TESTS
VARIABLE	HYPOTH. MS	ERROR MS	F	SIG. OF F
SATCITY	4.9	2.0	2.5	.114
SATFAM	12.6	1.6	7.8	.005
SATFRND	6.2	1.6	3.8	.051
HAPPY	.3	.3	.9	.331

///

EFFECT .. MARITAL
MULTIVARIATE TESTS OF SIGNIFICANCE

TEST NAME	VALUE	APPROX. F	SIG. OF F
PILLAIS	.209	12.0	.000

UNIVARIATE F-TESTS
VARIABLE	HYPOTH. MS	ERROR MS	F	SIG. OF F
SATCITY	9.1	2.0	4.6	.001
SATFAM	69.0	1.6	37.3	.000
SATFRND	4.0	1.6	2.5	.043
HAPPY	7.9	.3	24.2	.000

The last statistics on each page are the univariate *F* tests, which indicate whether groups differ on each of the dependent variables considered separately instead of as a set.

Table 10.3 presents the key statistics produced by our example command. For the interaction effects of MARITAL BY SEX, we can see from the significance level of Pillai's trace that the effects of marital status differ between men and women. The univariate *F* tests reveal that the differences in effects of marital status are concentrated in satisfaction with family life.

Pillai's trace is also statistically significant for the effects of SEX. The univariate *F* tests reveal that the differences are concentrated in satisfaction with family and satisfaction with friends.

For the effects of MARITAL, Pillai's trace is again statistically significant. The univariate *F* tests reveal that the differences are statistically significant on all four dependent measures.

10.5 Summary

The MANOVA program does many types of analysis of variance. Analysis of variance is especially appropriate when the dependent variable is an interval measure and the predicting variables are nominal. It is also useful when the predicting variables are interval but nonlinear in their effects.

MANOVA allows us to study the combined effects of nominal variables and interval variables. In such an analysis, the interval-level variables are termed covariates, and the technique is called covariate analysis.

Finally, MANOVA allows us to look at differences on a set of dependent variables instead of just one. For example, if we have several measures of happiness, we can do a composite analysis to determine whether groups differ on them. This last application is the actual multiple analysis of variance for which the MANOVA program is named.

Analysis of variance assumes that the dependent variable is interval and that the variances are equal for all groups.

In multiple analysis of variance, we also assume that (1) the dependent variables are multivariately normally distributed and (2) the covariance matrices are equal for all groups.

10.6 Where to Look in the *SPSS Reference Guide*

- MANOVA is discussed on pages 358–398.

RESEARCH PROJECT WORK FOR CHAPTER 10

1. For your research project data set, replicate the example MANOVA analyses in this chapter, but replace SATCITY with SATJOB for the last example.

2. For your research project data set, reanalyze the effects of INCOME and EDUC on HAPPY. Choose the form of analysis of variance that you think is most appropriate, and explain the reasons for your choice.

REVIEW QUESTIONS FOR CHAPTER 10

(Answers to Review Questions are given at the back of the book.)

10.1   What are the advantages of using MANOVA instead of MEANS?

10.2   What assumptions does MANOVA make about the dependent and independent variables?

10.3   What command is needed to do an analysis of variance of EDUC by MARITAL by SEX using the MANOVA procedure?

10.4   Would there be any difficulty with the command in Review Question 10.3 if no cases were coded 4 for the MARITAL variable?

10.5   What command is needed to do an analysis of variance of EDUC by MARITAL by SEX with INCOME as a covariate?

10.6   What command is needed to do an analysis of variance using CONFINAY to CONARMY in the NORC90 file as a set of dependent variables and RELIG and SEX as predictor variables?

10.7   What does it mean if the significance of F for MARITAL in Review Question 10.3 is .002?

10.8   What would it mean if the significance of F for MARITAL BY SEX in Review Question 10.3 were .000?

10.9   Would marital status be a significant variable in the analysis if the interaction effects of MARITAL BY SEX were significant but the effects of MARITAL were not?

10.10 When there are multiple dependent variables, what statistic indicates whether there are group differences among the predictor groups in their scores on the set of dependent variables?

ASSIGNMENT QUESTIONS FOR CHAPTER 10

(Solutions to the Assignment Questions are given in the *Instructor's Manual.*)

10.1   When is MANOVA preferred over REGRESSION as an analytical technique?

10.2   Would it be appropriate to do an analysis of variance using MANOVA in which MARITAL from the NORC90 file was the dependent variable and the predictor variables were SEX and AGE?

10.3   Write the MANOVA command to do an analysis of variance of INCOME by MARITAL by RELIGION.

10.4   Write the MANOVA command to do an analysis of variance of INCOME by MARITAL by RELIGION using AGE as a covariate.

10.5   Write the MANOVA command to do an analysis of variance using SAT-CITY to SATHEALT from the NORC90 file as a set of dependent variables and REGION by MARITAL as predictor variables.

10.6   What would it mean if the Pillai's trace in the output from the command in Assignment Question 10.4 were significant at the .005 level for the REGION effect?

10.7   What would it mean if, in output for the REGION effect from Assignment Question 10.5, the univariate F test for SATCITY had a significance of .545?

TABLE 10.4
Complete Output Produced by Command: MANOVA SATCITY SATFAM SATFRND HAPPY BY MARITAL(1, 5) SEX(1, 2)

********************** A N A L Y S I S   O F   V A R I A N C E   **********************

885 CASES ACCEPTED.
  0 CASES REJECTED BECAUSE OF OUT-OF-RANGE FACTOR VALUES.
487 CASES REJECTED BECAUSE OF MISSING DATA.
 10 NON-EMPTY CELLS.

  1 DESIGN WILL BE PROCESSED.

EFFECT .. MARITAL BY SEX

MULTIVARIATE TESTS OF SIGNIFICANCE (S = 4, M = -1/2, N = 435)

TEST NAME	VALUE	APPROX. F	HYPOTH. DF	ERROR DF	SIG. OF F
PILLAIS	.031	1.72	16.00	3500.00	.036
HOTELLINGS	.032	1.73	16.00	3482.00	.035
WILKS	.969	1.73	16.00	2664.64	.035
ROYS	.023				

UNIVARIATE F-TESTS WITH (4, 875) D. F.

VARIABLE	HYPOTH. SS	ERROR SS	HYPOTH. MS	ERROR MS	F	SIG. OF F
SATCITY	7.78	1726.9	1.94	1.97	.99	.414
SATFAM	22.92	1407.4	5.73	1.61	3.56	.007
SATFRND	2.04	1412.2	.51	1.61	.32	.866
HAPPY	.86	284.4	.21	.33	.66	.620

EFFECT .. SEX

MULTIVARIATE TESTS OF SIGNIFICANCE (S = 1, M = 1, N = 435)

TEST NAME	VALUE	APPROX. F	HYPOTH. DF	ERROR DF	SIG. OF F
PILLAIS	.010	2.18	4.00	872	.069
HOTELLINGS	.010	2.18	4.00	872	.069
WILKS	.990	2.18	4.00	872	.069
ROYS	.010				

UNIVARIATE F-TESTS WITH (1, 875) D. F.

VARIABLE	HYPOTH. SS	ERROR SS	HYPOTH. MS	ERROR MS	F	SIG. OF F
SATCITY	4.95	1726.9	4.95	1.97	2.51	.114
SATFAM	12.56	1407.4	12.56	1.61	7.81	.005
SATFRND	6.16	1412.2	6.16	1.61	3.81	.051
HAPPY	.31	284.4	.31	.33	.95	.331

EFFECT .. MARITAL

MULTIVARIATE TESTS OF SIGNIFICANCE (S = 4, M = -1/2, N = 435)

TEST NAME	VALUE	APPROX. F	HYPOTH. DF	ERROR DF	SIG. OF F
PILLAIS	.209	12.05	16.00	3500.00	.000
HOTELLINGS	.254	13.81	16.00	3482.00	.000
WILKS	.795	13.01	16.00	2664.64	.000
ROYS	.191				

UNIVARIATE F-TESTS WITH (4, 875) D. F.

VARIABLE	HYPOTH. SS	ERROR SS	HYPOTH. MS	ERROR MS	F	SIG. OF F
SATCITY	36.49	1726.9	9.12	1.97	4.62	.001
SATFAM	239.99	1407.4	60.00	1.61	37.30	.000
SATFRND	16.00	1412.2	4.00	1.61	2.48	.043
HAPPY	31.51	284.4	7.88	.32	24.24	.000

EFFECT .. CONSTANT

MULTIVARIATE TESTS OF SIGNIFICANCE (S = 1, M = 1, N = 435)

TEST NAME	VALUE	APPROX. F	HYPOTH. DF	ERROR DF	SIG. OF F
PILLAIS	.817	970.85	4.00	872.00	.000
HOTELLINGS	4.453	970.85	4.00	872.00	.000
WILKS	.183	970.85	4.00	872.00	.000
ROYS	.817				

UNIVARIATE F-TESTS WITH (1, 875) D. F.

VARIABLE	HYPOTH. SS	ERROR SS	HYPOTH. MS	ERROR MS	F	SIG. OF F
SATCITY	2540.35	1726.8	2540.35	1.97	1287.20	.000
SATFAM	1982.32	1407.4	1982.32	1.61	1232.43	.000
SATFRND	1628.42	1412.2	1628.42	1.61	1008.95	.000
HAPPY	1049.42	284.4	1049.42	.33	3228.56	.000

11

DISCRIMINANT FUNCTION ANALYSIS

New SPSS Command:

DISCRIMINANT

Our regression analysis in Chapter 9 indicated that, when the effects on reported happiness of the variables sex, age, education, income, health, and marital status are considered simultaneously, the most important variable is health, followed by marital status and income. All the variables had statistically significant effects. However, as we discussed, regression requires the assumption that, for each value of the predictor variable, scores on the dependent variable be normally distributed with equal variances. We might be concerned that this assumption is not met adequately by our happiness measure. Or an examination of the residuals might reveal that the assumption is seriously violated. What could we do then?

The discriminant function analysis produced by the command DISCRIMINANT does not require assumptions about the variance of the dependent variable. In fact, it is designed to work with nominal dependent variables.* DISCRIMINANT is a convenient technique for seeing the associations between a

---

*For a more complete discussion of the statistics of discriminant function analysis see William R. Klecka's *Discriminant Analysis* (Beverly Hills, CA: Sage Publications, 1980).

large set of independent variables and a dependent variable. One of its limitations, however, is that it cannot handle well a dependent variable with a large number of values. Interval variables like income or education must be recoded into a small number of categories, a process that involves a loss of detailed information. Hence you would want to use REGRESSION with interval dependent variables, unless they deviate sharply from a normal distribution.

The variable HAPPY can be used with DISCRIMINANT because it has only three categories. In this chapter we will replicate, using DISCRIMINANT, the regression analysis we did of happiness in Chapter 9. We will add to the analysis the variable CHILDS, the number of children the respondent has ever had, which we will refer to as parenthood.

11.1 What Discriminant Function Analysis Is and When to Use It

Discriminant function analysis is a technique for deciding the category of a variable into which a case is most likely to fall. For example, you might want to know whether a job applicant is more likely to succeed in a particular position or is more likely to quit or be fired. Or you might want to know whether a home-mortgage applicant is a good risk or is more likely to default on the loan. Perhaps the least popular user of discriminant analysis is the dreaded Internal Revenue Service (IRS). IRS employs the technique to determine the probability that you cheated in filing your income tax return.

The greatest advantage of discriminant function analysis over regression analysis is that the dependent variable can be a nominal measure. Regression analysis can be used for a dichotomous (two-category) nominal dependent variable if at least 20 percent of the cases are in the smallest category. However, discriminant analysis has the great advantage of being able to classify cases into three or more nominal categories—a task that regression analysis cannot handle. With discriminant analysis, we can judge better whether a person will be a Democrat, Republican, or Independent. We can predict whether one's vacation preference will most likely be Hawaii, Alaska, or Europe.

Discriminant analysis is best served when the independent variables being used to predict the correct classification of cases are interval measures and normally distributed. However, as in regression analyses, nominal independent variables often can be used through dummy variable codings with acceptable results.

11.2 How to Use DISCRIMINANT

Let's consider what occurs in discriminant analysis by replicating our regression analysis of Chapter 9. The dependent variable will still be HAPPY. The discriminant function analysis will predict for each case which of the three happiness scores is most likely. For classification variables we will use sex, age, education, income, marital status, and parenthood.

Our example uses variables from the SPSS system file NORC90. It considers the task of classifying cases into one of the three categories of HAPPY using as predictors the variables SEX, AGE, EDUC, INCOME, and MARITAL. (CHILDS will be added later.)

The SPSS commands would be

```
RECODE   MARITAL (2 THRU 5 = 0)
DISCRIMINANT   GROUPS=HAPPY(1,3) /
               VARIABLES=SEX AGE EDUC INCOME HEALTH
                         MARITAL/
               PRIORS=SIZE/
               STATISTICS TABLE
```

The **GROUPS=** subcommand indicates the dependent variable for which group membership is being predicted. The numbers in parentheses following the variable name indicate the low and high values of the dependent variable.

The **VARIABLES=** subcommand is followed by a list of the predictor variables.

The **PRIORS=SIZE** subcommand is needed when we want the cases to be classified using prior knowledge of the proportion in each category in the sample. For example, if 15 percent of the cases in the sample are in category 1, then the analysis uses this knowledge in making the predicted classifications.

When group sizes are very unequal, small groups can have a low percentage of correct classifications even though the overall correct classification percentage is high. Using PRIORS=SIZE can worsen this problem by causing the classification of a disproportionately large number of cases into the category that has the highest proportion of the cases.

The **STATISTICS TABLE** subcommand produces a table showing the accuracy of the DISCRIMINANT analysis in classifying cases.

11.3 The Accuracy of Discriminant Analysis

We use discriminant analysis to predict group membership; therefore, an obvious measure of our success is the percentage of cases that are classified correctly. Table 11.1 shows a portion of the actual output from our commands of the preceding section, a table entitled CLASSIFICATION RESULTS. The simplest summary statistic to look at is the percentage of cases correctly classified, which is given at the end of the table. In our example, the percentage of cases correctly classified is 59.2 percent. Let's compare this result to how many cases would be correctly classified by random assignment.

   With two groups of equal size, we would expect 50 percent of the classifications to be correct by chance. However, when the groups are not of equal size and when each group is randomly assigned the number of cases equal to its size, the expected percentage of correct classifications is found by squaring the proportion in each group and then summing the squares. In our example, this expected percentage would be $(.33)^2 + (.56)^2 + (.10)^2 \times 100 = 44$ percent. We can evaluate our model by comparing its proportion of errors $(1 - .59 = .41)$ to the proportion of errors that would occur if cases were classified randomly $(1 - .44 = .56)$. Therefore, our model enabled us to reduce the proportion of errors by $[(.56 - .41)/.56] \times 100 = 27$ percent. (This amount is the random-error proportion minus the model-error proportion, and then divided by the random-error proportion so that the reduction in error is expressed as a proportion of the original-error proportion.

   Returning to the classification results given in Table 11.1, note that each horizontal row represents the actual group membership. The first column head-

TABLE 11.1 Partial Output of DISCRIMINANT

ACTUAL GROUP	NO. OF CASES	PREDICTED GROUP MEMBERSHIP 1	2	3
GROUP 1 VERY HAPPY	275	90 32.7%	185 67.3%	0 .0%
GROUP 2 PRETTY HAPPY	469	69 14.7%	400 85.3%	0 .0%
GROUP 3 NOT TOO HAPPY	86	5 5.8%	80 93.0%	1 1.2%

PERCENT OF "GROUPED" CASES CORRECTLY CLASSIFIED: 59.2%

ing is ACTUAL GROUP. Under this heading the 1 identifies the row of group 1's statistics, 2 identifies the row of group 2's statistics, and so on. Proceeding to the NO. OF CASES column, we see that group 1 has 275 cases, group 2 has 469 cases, and group 3 has 86 cases.

The next three columns indicate the predicted group memberships. In this table the correct predictions are given by the diagonal percentages from the upper-left number, 32.7 percent, to the bottom-right number, 1.2 percent. The number above each percentage is the actual number of cases predicted to have that group membership.

11.4 Classifying Unknown Cases

Thus far we have discussed how to derive a predictive discriminant model from a set of cases for which we know the score on the dependent variable. What if, after we have the predictive discriminant model, we want to use it to predict the group membership of cases for which we do not have that information?

The simplest method is to use the SELECT subcommand to choose the cases used for calculating the discriminant function. The STATISTICS TABLE command will produce two sets of classification statistics—one for the SELECT cases and one for the remaining cases. The PLOT CASES command will produce each case's predicted group membership and the probability of its being in that group.

Suppose, for example, we want to predict happiness levels for a sample of people for whom we have data for the predictor variables but not for the dependent variable, HAPPY. We first would create a variable that separated the cases with known HAPPY data from those with unknown HAPPY data. Let's assume that the unknown cases are for the year 1992 and that a variable YR is coded 90 for the known cases and 92 for the unknown cases. If we add the SELECT subcommand to the DISCRIMINANT command, our example will read

```
RECODE   MARITAL (2 THRU 5 = 0)
DISCRIMINANT   GROUPS=HAPPY (1,3)/
               VARIABLES=SEX AGE EDUC INCOME HEALTH
                         MARITAL/
               PRIORS=SIZE/
               SELECT=YR(90)/
               STATISTICS TABLE
               PLOT CASES
```

11.5 Evaluating the Importance of Variables: The Discriminant Function Coefficients

To determine the contribution of a particular variable to the accuracy of the discriminant analysis classifications, you can repeat the analysis but drop or add the variable in question from the VARIABLES= subcommand. The change in the percentage of cases classified correctly when the variable is dropped or added represents the variable's contribution:

Contribution = % correct with variable − % correct without variable

Another method of assessing the importance of a particular variable is to look at its discriminant function coefficient. Discriminant analysis produces discriminant function coefficients for each predicting variable. For each case the score on a variable is multiplied by that variable's discriminant function coefficient. For each case this multiplication is done for all its variable scores and the products are summed. This sum is the case's **discriminant function score.** The discriminant function coefficients are calculated to maximize the differences between the groups in discriminant function scores. In other words, the ratio of between-groups variance to within-groups variance is maximized.

The set of standardized discriminant function coefficients for the predicting variables is produced as part of the DISCRIMINANT output. The standardized coefficients for our example are given in Table 11.2.

The term **standardized** indicates that each variable score is standardized before it is multiplied by the coefficient. In standardizing a variable score, the mean for that variable is subtracted from the score, and then the difference is divided by the standard deviation of the variable. Assume that for AGE the

TABLE 11.2 Partial Output of DISCRIMINANT

STANDARDIZED CANONICAL DISCRIMINANT FUNCTION COEFFICIENTS

	FUNCTION 1	FUNCTION 2
SEX	0.11	0.39
AGE	0.11	−0.01
EDUC	0.17	−0.24
INCOME	0.01	−0.52
HEALTH	−0.66	0.33
MARITAL	0.69	0.78

mean is thirty-four and the standard deviation is eight. Thus, for a case with a score of forty on AGE, the standardized score would be (forty minus thirty-four)/eight equals .75. Algebraically the formula is

$$\frac{X - \bar{X}}{S_x}$$

where X equals a case score on a variable

$\bar{X}$ is the mean for the variable

S_x is the standard deviation for the variable

Standardized variables have a mean of 0 and a standard deviation of 1.

Standardized coefficients are used to remove the effects of differing means and differing standard deviations in the predicting variables. Otherwise, variables with smaller standard deviations would tend to have larger coefficients, making it difficult to assess the relative importance of the predicting variables.

As we show in section 11.6 below, the coefficients for the first function are the most important. As in our regression analysis example in Chapter 9, the variable with the biggest effect on happiness is health, followed by marital status and age. The signs of the coefficients in discriminant analysis have no special meaning. Because the dependent variable is treated as a nominal measure, we cannot think in terms of positive or negative associations.

As in regression analysis, correct assessment of each predictor variable's importance depends on having all the relevant variables in the equation.

The DISCRIMINANT program does not produce an estimate of the statistical significance of each predictor variable. To approximate the contribution of a particular variable to the statistical significance of a discriminant analysis, you will need to drop the variable in question, repeat the analysis, and then compare the statistical significance of the analyses with and without the variable. The variable's contribution is the reduction in the statistical significance, which is the likelihood that the group differences are the result of sampling probability error. (The statistical significance of an analysis is given by the Wilks' lambda, discussed in the next section.)

11.6 Evaluating the Importance of Functions: Eigenvalue, Canonical Correlation, and Wilks' Lambda

Discriminant analysis maximizes the between-groups differences on discriminant scores and minimizes the within-groups differences. Hence, one measure of how well a discriminant analysis worked is to compare the between-groups variance to the within-groups variance. The **eigenvalue,** which in DISCRIMI-

TABLE 11.3 Partial Output of DISCRIMINANT

CANONICAL DISCRIMINANT FUNCTIONS

FUNCTION	EIGENVALUE	CANONICAL CORRELATION
1	0.15	0.36
2	0.00	0.04

AFTER FUNCTION	WILKS' LAMBDA	SIGNIFICANCE
0	0.87	0.000
1	0.99	0.939

NANT output is the between-groups variance divided by the within-groups variance, is one statistic for evaluating the worth of a discriminant analysis. An eigenvalue of 0 means that the discriminant analysis had no discriminating value, whereas an eigenvalue above 0.40 is considered excellent. (The discriminant analysis eigenvalue has no upper limit.) The eigenvalues for our example are given in the second column of Table 11.3.

The canonical correlation squared is the ratio of the between-groups variance in scores on the function to the total variance in scores. It is a good measure of how well the function discriminates between groups on a scale that ranges from 0.0 to 1.0.

Wilks' lambda (also called the *U* statistic) is the within-groups sum of squares divided by the total sum of squares. This ratio can vary from 0.0 to 1.0. The *lower* Wilks' lambda is, the better the discriminating power of the model. The Wilks' lambdas for our example are given in Table 11.3. In the AFTER FUNCTION column, the 0 indicates what the Wilks' lambda in that row is when all the functions are in the analysis. The lambda of 0.87 indicates that differences between groups account for 12 percent of the variance in the predicting variables. The lambda for AFTER FUNCTION 1 indicates what percentage of the variance is accounted for by group differences after the effects of function 1 are removed. The lambda of 0.99 indicates that the proportion of accounted for variance remaining after the effects of function 1 are removed is .00. We can see, therefore, that the effects of function 1 are much greater than the effects of function 2.

Produced with Wilks' lambda is its statistical significance. Table 11.3 shows that, when none of the functions have been dropped from the analysis, the statistical significance is 0.000 and, when the first function is dropped from the analysis, the statistical significance is 0.939.

11.7 Pooled Within-Groups Correlations with Functions

A statistic for examining a variable's association with a discriminant function is the Pearson correlation coefficient between a variable and that function. The DISCRIMINANT output produces this statistic for each of the variables (see Table 11.4).

The first function accounted for 15 percent of the "explained" variance (its canonical correlation squared) in the predictor variables, compared to 10 percent for the second function. Therefore, the correlations with the first function are more important than the correlations with the second function.

Variables that correlate below 0.20 with a function have only a weak association with it, and their effects tend to be unstable. The standardized discriminant function coefficients are better than the correlations for assessing a variable's impact on the discriminant function scores of cases and their predicted classification.

We can also judge the impact of an individual variable by adding or dropping it from the analysis and observing changes in the percentage of cases classified correctly, the eigenvalues, the canonical correlations, and the Wilks' lambda. Table 11.6 at the end of this chapter gives the complete output from DISCRIMINANT when CHILDS is added to the analysis. When CHILDS is included in the analysis, the percentage of correctly classified cases remains the same, while the canonical correlation coefficient increases very slightly. The evidence suggests that parenthood does not have an impact on happiness.

TABLE 11.4 Partial Output for DISCRIMINANT

STRUCTURE MATRIX:
POOLED WITHIN-GROUPS CORRELATIONS BETWEEN DISCRIMINATING VARIABLES
    AND CANONICAL DISCRIMINANT FUNCTIONS
(VARIABLES ORDERED BY SIZE OF CORRELATION WITHIN FUNCTION)

	FUNC 1	FUNC 2
MARITAL	0.71	0.50
HEALTH	-0.70	0.48
INCOME	0.47	-0.39
EDUC	0.32	-0.50
SEX	-0.03	0.34
AGE	0.10	0.24

11.8 Multicollinearity Problems

Two or more of the predictor variables may be highly correlated with each other. This condition is termed **multicollinearity** and results in unstable coefficients. One way to deal with multicollinearity is to combine the highly correlated variables into a composite variable. A second way to eliminate multicollinearity is to drop one of the two highly correlated variables.

Before doing a discriminant analysis, produce a Pearson's correlation coefficient matrix and examine the correlations among the predictor variables. If any of the correlations between two *predictor* variables is above 0.70, consider carefully the possibility of dropping one of the variables from the analysis or combining the variables.

If the group membership variable has only two categories, the higher the correlation between a *predictor* variable and the *dependent* variable the better. Just be sure you do not have a tautological relationship; that is, be sure you are not using one measure of an attribute to predict another measure of the same attribute. For example, it would not be reasonable to use years of education to predict whether a person is a college graduate. If the group membership variable has more than two nominal categories that cannot be ranked, its Pearson correlation coefficients with other variables are useless, even though the program will calculate them (see the discussion in Chapter 6 of levels of measurement).

11.9 Group Centroids

The **group centroid** is the point corresponding to the mean score of the group on each function. In Table 11.6, the mean score for the very happy cases on function 1 is 0.48, and their mean score on function 2 is .03. In classifying cases, the predicted group membership is the one whose centroid is closest to the case's discriminant function scores. For two functions, the group centroids can be plotted on a plane with each function serving as an axis. A case will be classified into the group that has the centroid closest to the case's own point when plotted on the grid formed by the two functions.

11.10 The Number of Functions

When there are more than two groups in a discriminant analysis, more than one discriminant function can be calculated. If the number of groups is K, then $K - 1$ discriminant functions can be computed. Thus with three groups, two discriminant functions can be calculated. With four groups, three discriminant functions can be calculated, and so on.

The first function has the maximum ratio of between-groups variance to within-groups sums of squares. The second function will be uncorrelated with the first function and will maximize the remaining between-groups variance to within-groups sums of squares, subject to the constraint that the functions are uncorrelated.

The output from the multigroup discriminant analysis will include an analysis of variance for each function. We may decide to use in the analysis only those functions that have a substantial between-groups F ratio. To limit the number of functions used in the analysis, use the **FUNCTIONS** subcommand as illustrated (indented at least one space if it begins a line):

```
FUNCTIONS=1
```

Note that the number of functions to be used is specified after the equals sign. In our example it is 1.

11.11 Summary

In a discriminant analysis we are concerned with predicting correctly to which of two or more groups each case belongs.

Information in the DISCRIMINANT output lets us know

- the percentage of cases we predict correctly
- how much better our model is than random assignment (this relationship must be calculated)
- how much of the variance in the predicting variables is accounted for by each function, and whether this amount is statistically significant

DISCRIMINANT does not directly provide a statistic showing how much each predictor variable contributes to our ability to classify correctly and whether this contribution is statistically significant. We can, however, approximate the contribution of an individual variable by repeating the analysis without the variable and noting the change in the percentage of cases classified correctly and the change in the statistical significance of the analysis.

11.12 Where to Look in the *SPSS Reference Guide*

DISCRIMINANT is discussed on pages 127–140.

RESEARCH PROJECT WORK FOR CHAPTER 11

1.   For your research project data set, do a discriminant function analysis of
      HAPPY using AGE, EDUC, HEALTH, INCOME, MARITAL, and SEX as
      predictor variables.

2.   Discuss the possibility of spuriousness (when a variable appears to
      cause something but does not) for each of the predictor variables in
      Problem 1. That is, might they be affected by HAPPY instead of, or in
      addition to, affecting HAPPY? Might both HAPPY and the predictor vari-
      able be affected by a third variable and hence be associated without being
      causally related?

REVIEW QUESTIONS FOR CHAPTER 11

(Answers to Review Questions are given at the back of the book.)

11.1   Write the SPSS command necessary to produce a discriminant analysis
       with CLASS as the group (dependent) variable and SEX, RACE, AGE, IN-
       COME, EDUC, DEFENSE, and SPEND as predictor variables.

11.2   Using the SPSS system file NORC90, write all the SPSS commands nec-
       essary to access the file and produce the following discriminant analysis.
       Create the group variable FAMWORK, a combination of family status
       (CHILDS) and work status (WRKSTAT). Code FAMWORK 1 for nonwork-
       ing women without children, 2 for nonworking women with children, 3
       for working women without children, 4 for working women with chil-
       dren. Do the analysis for women only. Use as predictor variables RACE,
       EDUC, INCOME, AGE, MAWORK, and CLASS.

11.3   How can you evaluate whether a discriminant analysis was effective?

11.4   How can you determine the number of cases that would be mis-
       classified by random assignment?

11.5   How can you determine whether a discriminant analysis is statistically
       significant?

11.6   How can you determine how much an individual function adds to your
       ability to classify cases correctly?

11.7   How do you determine the statistical significance of a particular
       function?

11.8   How do you determine the contribution of a particular variable to the correct classification of cases?

11.9   How do you determine the statistical significance of a particular variable?

11.10   Once you have the final discriminant function (or functions) to use for classifying new cases, how do you use it (or them) to classify new cases?

ASSIGNMENT QUESTIONS FOR CHAPTER 11

(Solutions to the Assignment Questions are provided in the *Instructor's Manual.*)

11.1   Write the SPSS commands necessary to access the file NORC90 and to do a discriminant analysis using UNEMP as the group variable and SEX, AGE, MARITAL, RACE, CHILDS, HEALTH, and HAPPY as the predictor variables.

11.2   What subcommand would you need to add following the VARIABLES= subcommand if the probability of being unemployed was not equal to the probability of being employed? (Let the probability of being unemployed equal .1 and the probability of being employed equal .9.)

11.3   If you ran two discriminant analyses, one with SEX and the other without SEX, in order to determine the importance of SEX in predicting unemployment correctly, how would you interpret the following results?

Percentage unemployed classified correctly with SEX: 15 percent

Percentage unemployed classified correctly without SEX: 12 percent

Statistical significance with SEX = .003

Statistical significance without SEX = .060

11.4   How much did the variable SEX affect the statistical significance of the discriminant analysis in Assignment Question 11.3? In other words, how much did the variable SEX reduce the likelihood that the predictions were due to sampling probability error?

11.5   How would you evaluate how much the discriminant functions improved your ability to predict whether a person would be unemployed in Assignment Question 11.3?

TABLE 11.5 Pearson Correlation Coefficient Matrix for Assignment Question 11.6

	TRAINING	AGE	SEX	MARITAL	EDUC	DIPLOMA	RACE	EMPLOY
TRAINING	1.00							
AGE	− .31	1.00						
SEX	.20	.05	1.00					
MARITAL	.70	.85	.20	1.00				
EDUC	.75	.25	.25	− .20	1.00			
DIPLOMA	.80	.15	.30	− .35	.90	1.00		
RACE	− .15	− .15	.15	− .15	.30	.10	1.00	
EMPLOY	.40	.55	− .10	.60	.40	.55	− .30	1.00

11.6 Looking at Table 11.5, how would you evaluate the decision to include all these hypothetical variables in a discriminant analysis of being employed versus being unemployed? (Assume that they have all been coded as interval or dichotomous variables, and focus your evaluation on the correlation coefficients.)

TABLE 11.6 Complete Output from Commands:

```
RECODE MARITAL (2 THRU 5=0)
DISCRIMINANT   GROUPS=HAPPY(1,3) /
               VARIABLES=SEX AGE EDUC INCOME HEALTH MARITAL CHILDS/
               PRIORS=SIZE/
               STATISTICS TABLE
```

                    D I S C R I M I N A N T   A N A L Y S I S

ON GROUPS DEFINED BY HAPPY   IS RESPONDENT HAPPY

1372 (UNWEIGHTED) CASES WERE PROCESSED.
542 OF THESE WERE EXCLUDED FROM THE ANALYSIS.
    2 HAD MISSING OR OUT-OF-RANGE GROUP CODES.
  531 HAD AT LEAST ONE MISSING DISCRIMINATING VARIABLE.
    9 HAD BOTH.
  830 (UNWEIGHTED) CASES WILL BE USED IN THE ANALYSIS.

NUMBER OF CASES BY GROUP

            NUMBER OF CASES
HAPPY   UNWEIGHTED   WEIGHTED   LABEL

   1   275   275.0   VERY HAPPY
   2   469   469.0   PRETTY HAPPY
   3   86   86.0   NOT TOO HAPPY

   TOTAL   830   830.0

ON GROUPS DEFINED BY HAPPY   IS RESPONDENT HAPPY

ANALYSIS NUMBER   1
DIRECT METHOD: ALL VARIABLES PASSING THE TOLERANCE TEST ARE ENTERED.
    MINIMUM TOLERANCE LEVEL................   0.00100
```
```

TABLE 11.6 *Continued*

CANONICAL DISCRIMINANT FUNCTIONS

```
MAXIMUM NUMBER OF FUNCTIONS............     2
MINIMUM CUMULATIVE PERCENT OF VARIANCE.....  100.00
MAXIMUM SIGNIFICANCE OF WILKS' LAMBDA.......  1.0000
```

PRIOR PROBABILITIES

GROUP	PRIOR	LABEL
1	.33133	VERY HAPPY
2	.56506	PRETTY HAPPY
3	.10361	NOT TOO HAPPY
TOTAL	1.00000	

CANONICAL DISCRIMINANT FUNCTIONS

FCN	EIGENVALUE	PERCENT OF VARIANCE	CUMULATIVE PERCENT	CANONICAL CORRELATION		AFTER FUNCTION	WILKS' LAMBDA	CHI-SQUARED	D.F.	SIGNIFICANCE
					:	0	0.8632	121.187	14	0.0000
1*	0.1561	98.72	98.72	0.3675	:	1	0.9980	1.663	6	0.9479
2*	0.0020	1.28	100.00	0.0449	:					

* MARKS THE 2 CANONICAL DISCRIMINANT FUNCTIONS REMAINING IN THE ANALYSIS.

STANDARDIZED CANONICAL DISCRIMINANT FUNCTION COEFFICIENTS

	FUNC 1	FUNC 2
SEX	.12607	.37290
AGE	.18120	.17656
EDUC	.13949	-.28485
INCOME	.00390	-.47651
HEALTH	-.66062	.31277
MARITAL	.72845	.75866
CHILDS	-.19809	-.54487

STRUCTURE MATRIX:

POOLED WITHIN-GROUPS CORRELATIONS BETWEEN DISCRIMINATING VARIABLES
AND CANONICAL DISCRIMINANT FUNCTIONS

(VARIABLES ORDERED BY SIZE OF CORRELATION WITHIN FUNCTION)

	FUNC 1	FUNC 2
MARITAL	.70321*	.37120
HEALTH	-.69063*	.48315
INCOME	.46116*	-.37771
EDUC	.31552	-.46565*
SEX	-.03120	.30314*
AGE	-.10041	.21800*
CHILDS	-.03946	-.18924*

CANONICAL DISCRIMINANT FUNCTIONS EVALUATED AT GROUP MEANS (GROUP CENTROIDS)

GROUP	FUNC 1	FUNC 2
1	.48322	.03226
2	-.13491	-.03625
3	-.80945	.09452

CLASSIFICATION RESULTS -

ACTUAL GROUP	NUMBER OF CASES	PREDICTED GROUP MEMBERSHIP		
		1	2	3
GROUP 1 VERY HAPPY	275	90 32.7%	185 67.3%	0 .0%
GROUP 2 PRETTY HAPPY	469	69 14.7%	400 85.3%	0 .0%
GROUP 3 NOT TOO HAPPY	86	5 5.8%	80 93.0%	1 1.2%
UNGROUPED CASES	2	0 .0%	2 100.0%	0 .0%

PERCENTAGE OF "GROUPED" CASES CORRECTLY CLASSIFIED: 59.16%

CLASSIFICATION PROCESSING SUMMARY
1372 CASES WERE PROCESSED.
  0 CASES WERE EXCLUDED FOR MISSING OR OUT-OF-RANGE GROUP CODES.
540 CASES HAD AT LEAST ONE MISSING DISCRIMINATING VARIABLE.
832 CASES WERE USED FOR PRINTED OUTPUT.

12

LOG-LINEAR MODELS

New SPSS Command:

`HILOGLINEAR`

We have seen that happiness is affected by income. We have questioned whether the effects of income are the same for all groups. For example, perhaps income is more important for men than for women in affecting happiness. Perhaps income is more important at some ages than at others. Maybe the effects of age are not the same for men as for women. Answers to these questions may be found in crosstabulation tables, but the tables are so complex and have so many cells that it is a tedious task to evaluate all the possible interactions among the variables.

The log-linear analyses that can be done with the SPSS command HILOGLINEAR swiftly untangle the information in a crosstabulation table. The output reveals which associations are most important and whether they are statistically significant. With a little additional work, we can state very precisely how interactions among certain variables affect the likelihood that a subject will be in a particular category on another variable.

12.1 When to Use HILOGLINEAR

The program produced by the HILOGLINEAR command is a way of summarizing and highlighting the associations in a complex crosstabulation table. Loglinear models such as HILOGLINEAR are called for when (1) your analysis involves three or more variables and (2) the variables are nominal, highly skewed in their distribution, or nonlinear in their effects.*

Often nominal variables are dummy coded and treated as interval variables in regression or analysis of variance. The more skewed the variable is to one category, the more this practice leads to biased coefficients. For example, if over 80% of the labor force is employed, married, and nonmigrant, dummy coding any of these variables in a study of worker satisfaction in the United States could distort the results.

The greatest disadvantage of log-linear models is that they need a large number of cases. A rough rule of thumb is that your sample size should be at least five times the number of cells in the table.

One way researchers reduce the number of cells in the analysis (and hence the number of cases they need) is by collapsing categories of ordinal or interval variables that are being used in a log-linear model. For example, instead of having the exact age of each respondent, one can code age into ten-year intervals. In recoding the categories some precision is lost, and we assume that the effects of the variable do not differ significantly within these categories. Collapsing of categories is a practice to be adopted only from necessity.

12.2 How to Use HILOGLINEAR

As with other advanced techniques, begin a HILOGLINEAR analysis by checking the frequency distribution of all the variables you intend to use to ensure they are coded correctly and to familiarize yourself with their distribution. Because we have already done this initial work with the NORC90 data file in earlier chapters, we can move on to an actual log-linear analysis.

Let's see what more can be learned about happiness using the log-linear analysis produced by the HILOGLINEAR command. (Other log-linear techniques are available with SPSS; however, HILOGLINEAR is the simplest to use,

---

*For a more complete discussion of log-linear analysis see David Knoke and Peter J. Burke's *Log-Linear Models* (Beverly Hills, CA: Sage Publications, 1980) and H. T. Reynolds' *Analysis of Nominal Data* (Beverly Hills, CA: Sage Publications, 1977).

requires less computer time, and uses less CPU memory space.) To use HI-LOGLINEAR, you must assume that the log-linear effects are hierarchical. This means that if a variable is in the model as a third-order effect, it must be in the model as a second-order effect. (A second-order effect involves the interaction of two variables, a third-order effect involves the interaction of three variables, and so on.) In most analyses this assumption is not bothersome, because the researcher would not conceptualize a variable as having important higher-order effects unless the lower-order effects were also important.

We have reason to believe that happiness is affected by a person's sex and age. Perhaps the effects of age will be different for males than for females. Further along in the analysis, we will be adding more variables (and thus more cells), so we will recode age into ten-year intervals to ensure that we have enough cases. (98 and 99 are missing value codes. Therefore, we cannot use the keyword HI in our RECODE command.) Likewise, we can consider the interactions of INCOME with the other variables, but we need to recode it into a smaller number of categories. Our RECODE statements will be

```
RECODE    AGE (18 THRU 29=1) (30 THRU 39=2) (40 THRU 49=3)
              (50 THRU 59=4) (60 THRU 69=5) (70 THRU 89=6)
RECODE    INCOME (3,4=3) (5,6=4)
              (7=5)
```

This recoding of variables leaves us with 180 cells in our crosstabulation table. We find this number by multiplying together the number of categories in each variable (HAPPY $*$ SEX $*$ AGE $*$ INCOME $= 3 * 2 * 6 * 5 = 180$). Our NORC90 sample size of 1372 is far more than $5 * 120 = 900$. (Recall that the sample size should be at least five times the number of cells.)

The simplest approach to using the HILOGLINEAR command in SPSS is with the subcommand **PRINT ALL.** This subcommand produces a table that shows the chi-square and probabilities of each order effect. Recall that a chi-square statistic is based on the difference between what you would expect to find in each cell, if there were no associations, versus what was actually found.

The first-order effects test the assumption that each category of a variable has the same number of cases. This assumption is rarely true, and, because it tells us nothing about associations among the variables, we are not very interested in this statistic.

The two-way, or second-order, effects test the assumption that the variables are independent. The likelihood ratio chi-square for this model can be treated as a total error term that can be partitioned into parts associated with each variable. These effects are the bivariate associations controlling for the effects of the other variables.

The three-way and higher-order effects are interaction effects. These effects are usually small and difficult to interpret. Essentially, an interaction effect means that a variable has one effect for one group but a different effect for another group. For example, if the effects of age on the likelihood of being happy were different for men than for women, this effect would be third order.

The HILOGLINEAR command and accompanying PRINT ALL subcommand needed for our analysis of the effects on happiness of age controlling for sex and income are

```
HILOGLINEAR   SEX (1,2)  AGE (1,6)  INCOME (1,5)
              HAPPY (1,3) /
              PRINT ALL
```

Note that the PRINT subcommand is preceded by a slash indicating the variable specifications have ended. The printout is easier to read if the dependent variable is listed last. When placed in the context of the SPSS commands needed to recode AGE and INCOME, our set of commands is

```
RECODE    AGE (18 THRU 29=1) (30 THRU 39=2) (40 THRU 49=3)
              (50 THRU 59=4) (60 THRU 69=5) (70 THRU 97=6)
RECODE    INCOME (3,4=3) (5,6=4)
              (7=5)
HILOGLINEAR   SEX (1,2)  AGE (1,6)  INCOME (1,5)
              HAPPY (1,3) /
              PRINT ALL
```

12.3 Interpreting HILOGLINEAR Output

The output from the preceding set of commands will include the information given in Table 12.1. (An example of the complete output is given in Table 12.4 at the end of this chapter.) In the first row of the table, the 1 indicates that this row contains the information on the first-order effects. This information tests the hypothesis that the cases are equally distributed throughout the cells. We are not interested in testing this hypothesis because we do not expect to have the same number of males as females or the same number of older people as younger people in our sample.

In the second row, the 2 indicates that these effects are second order. These effects are of interest because we want to know whether the variables SEX, AGE, and INCOME are associated with HAPPY. The 49 in the DF column

TABLE 12.1 Partial Output from HILOGLINEAR

TESTS THAT K-WAY EFFECTS ARE ZERO.

K	DF	L.R. CHISQ	PROB
1	12	753.9	.000
2	49	221.2	.000
3	78	97.4	.068
4	40	30.2	.869

indicates that there are 49 degrees of freedom when all the second-order effects are considered. The next number to the right, 221.2 in the L.R. CHISQ column, is the likelihood ratio chi-square for the second-order effects. If there were no associations among the variables, this measure would be 0.0. The next number to the right, .000 in the PROB column, is the probability that the chi-square for this row differs from 0.0 because of sampling error. We can see that it is unlikely–less than 1 time out of 1000–that the associations we find in this row are due to sampling error.

The row beginning with a 3 in the K column pertains to third-order effects. The probability of .068 tells us that the third-order effects this size would be the result of sampling error only 68 times out of 1000.

The final row regards the fourth-order effects. These effects have a sampling error probability, .869. So in our example fourth order effects are not statistically significant. Significant fourth-order effects might indicate that the effects of income on happiness for older males are different from the effects of income for older females or that the effects of age on happiness are different for wealthy males than for poor males. It is helpful to know when there are significant fourth-order effects in our analysis, but we would still face the task of ransacking a crosstabulation table to locate them precisely.

The next table of special interest in the output is entitled TESTS OF PARTIAL ASSOCIATIONS (see Table 12.2). This table gives the partial chi-square and the probabilities for all the associations except the highest-order association. (Information for the highest-order association was given in the preceding table.)

Examine Table 12.2 carefully. The left column, entitled EFFECT NAME, designates each association examined in the analysis. The top row, SEX*AGE* INCOME, shows the association between sex, age, and income. In that row, we can see the following statistics: there are 20 degrees of freedom in this association, the partial chi-square is 36.0, and the probability that an association

TABLE 12.2 Partial Output from HILOGLINEAR

TESTS OF PARTIAL ASSOCIATIONS.

EFFECT NAME	DF	PARTIAL CHISQ	PROB
SEX*AGE*INCOME	20	36.0	.015
SEX*AGE*HAPPY	10	7.7	.660
SEX*INCOME*HAPPY	8	5.7	.681
AGE*INCOME*HAPPY	40	48.0	.180
SEX*AGE	5	7.4	.190
SEX*INCOME	4	17.4	.002
AGE*INCOME	20	137.6	.000
SEX*HAPPY	2	.1	.949
AGE*HAPPY	10	16.0	.101
INCOME*HAPPY	8	49.8	.000
SEX	1	15.4	.000
AGE	5	129.0	.000
INCOME	4	134.3	.000
HAPPY	2	475.3	.000

this large could occur by sampling error is .015. The third-order effect that is most statistically significant is AGE*INCOME*HAPPY, which has a probability of .180 resulting from sampling error. This suggests that the effects of income differ by age, or the effects of age differ by income, or both.

The second-order effects are significant, below the .05 level for sex and income, age and income, and income and happy.

The chi-squares for the single variables are all significant; however, this result merely means that there was not an equal number of cases in each of the cells. It tells us nothing about associations between the variables.

We return to our original question of whether the effects of age on happiness differ for men and women. The SEX*AGE*HAPPY row shows that the differences are so small that 660 times out of 1000 they could result from sampling error.

Are the effects of income on happiness different for men than for women? The SEX*INCOME*HAPPY row indicates that the differences are so small that 681 times out of 1000 they would occur from sampling error.

The output from HILOGLINEAR includes an initial portion entitled OBSERVED, EXPECTED FREQUENCIES AND RESIDUALS (see Table 12.3). We can use this table to describe each association more precisely. For example, we can compare the odds of a male over age 70 with less than $10,000 family income reporting being very happy with the odds of a male under age 30 with the same income being very happy. (Recall that very happy respondents were coded 1 on HAPPY.) To make this comparison, we examine the OBS. COUNT (observed count) column of the table. In Table 12.3 the numbers for the 4 middle-age categories are omitted for brevity. It is necessary to subtract .5 from each count.

We can see that 5 out of 19, or 26 percent, of the under-30 males report being very happy. (19 is the total of the observed counts 5 + 13 + 1.) For the males over age 70, 8 out of 23, or 35 percent, report being very happy. Thus, in this income range the likelihood that a male over age 70 will be very happy is one-third greater than the likelihood for a male under age 30.

The HILOGLINEAR output gives a staggering amount of information. A sensible approach is to look at the summary statistics on the associations to see which are most important. Then dig into the table of observed counts to see the details of the association.

One also has the option of printing out coefficients and significance levels for each cell. Unfortunately, the present form of HILOGLINEAR output for these statistics is not easy to interpret. As Reynolds notes, researchers will probably use log-linear models to detect the presence or absence of a model. Afterwards, "it may be easier to measure the strength of association with other statistics" (H. T. Reynolds, 1977, p. 65). For example, doing a crosstabulation of HAPPY by AGE controlling for SEX and INCOME would allow us to see easily the percentage of men who were very happy compared to the percentage of women who were very happy in each income group. (See Chapter 5 for a discussion of crosstabulations.)

TABLE 12.3 Partial Output of HILOGLINEAR

OBSERVED, EXPECTED FREQUENCIES AND RESIDUALS

FACTOR	CODE	OBS. COUNT
SEX	1	
AGE	1	
INCOME	1	
HAPPY	1	5.5
HAPPY	2	13.5
HAPPY	3	1.5
⋮		
AGE	6	
INCOME	1	
HAPPY	1	8.5
HAPPY	2	13.5
HAPPY	3	2.5

12.4 Summary

Log-linear models are a way of summarizing and highlighting the associations in a complex crosstabulation table. Log-linear models such as HILOGLINEAR are called for when your analysis involves three or more variables, all of which are either nominal, highly skewed in their distribution, or nonlinear in their effects.

The greatest disadvantage of log-linear models is that they require a large number of cases. A rough rule of thumb is that your sample size should be at least five times the number of cells in the table.

12.5 Where to Look in the *SPSS Reference Guide*

- HILOGLINEAR is discussed on pages 277–283.

RESEARCH PROJECT WORK FOR CHAPTER 12

For your research project data file, replicate the example analysis of this chapter. Describe any differences between the outcome of your analysis and the outcome of our example, and discuss the possible causes of these differences.

REVIEW QUESTIONS FOR CHAPTER 12

(Answers to Review Questions are given at the back of the book.)

12.1   What assumptions are made for regression analysis that are not required for log-linear models?

12.2   What advantages are there to doing a log-linear analysis instead of a crosstabulation?

12.3   How many cases would normally be required to do a log-linear analysis of health (four categories) by marital (five categories) by religion (five categories)?

12.4   Write the SPSS commands that would produce a hierarchical log-linear analysis of the variables HEALTH, MARITAL, and RELIGION. Treat HEALTH as the dependent variable. Include the subcommand necessary to produce a printout of associations.

12.5   What would the first-order effects in the analysis of Review Question 12.4 indicate?

12.6 What would the second-order effects from Review Question 12.4 indicate?

12.7 What would the third-order effects from Review Question 12.4 indicate?

12.8 The chi-square and probability of the highest-order effects are omitted from the HILOGLINEAR output for TESTS OF PARTIAL ASSOCIATIONS. How can these statistics be found?

12.9 How would you interpret a probability of .023 for the partial chi-square of the effect HEALTH*MARITAL?

12.10 If the output from HILOGLINEAR indicates that a particular association is significant, what is the simplest way to determine the strength of the association?

ASSIGNMENT QUESTIONS FOR CHAPTER 12

(Solutions to the Assignment Questions are provided in the *Instructor's Manual.*)

12.1 What assumptions are made in analysis of variance that are not required in log-linear analysis?

12.2 Write the HILOGLINEAR command and subcommands needed to analyze SEX by RELIGION by MARITAL by SATFAM in the NORC90 file making SATFAM the dependent variable.

12.3 If the following table resulted from the commands in Assignment Question 12.2, what would these statistics mean?

TESTS THAT K-WAY AND HIGHER ORDER EFFECTS ARE ZERO.

K	DF	L.R. CHISQ	PROB
4	14	5.4	.452
3	26	8.2	.220
2	37	40.7	.043
1	45	607.7	.000

12.4 What would the following portion of output from Assignment Question 12.2 indicate?

TESTS OF PARTIAL ASSOCIATIONS.

EFFECT NAME	DF	PARTIAL CHISQ	PROB
SEX*RELIG*SATJOB	24	13.654	.354
SEX*MARITAL*RELIG	16	34.234	.463
SEX*MARITAL*SATJOB	70	73.004	.453
SEX*MARITAL	5	5.929	.312
SEX*RELIG	2	2.141	.343
SEX*SATJOB	24	13.654	.050
MARITAL*RELIG	16	34.234	.463
MARITAL*SATJOB	70	73.004	.003
SATJOB*RELIG	5	5.929	.312
SEX	10	2.141	.343
MARITAL	1	33.433	.000
RELIG	5	129.233	.000
SATJOB	2	404.293	.000

12.5   What would the following portion of output from Assignment Question 12.2 indicate?

OBSERVED, EXPECTED FREQUENCIES AND RESIDUALS.

FACTOR	CODE	OBS. COUNT & PCT.
SEX	1	
MARITAL	1	
RELIGION	1	
SATJOB	1	11.00
SATJOB	2	25.00
SATJOB	3	33.00
SATJOB	4	24.00
SATJOB	5	23.00
SATJOB	6	33.00
SATJOB	7	23.00
SEX	2	
MARITAL	1	
RELIGION	1	
SATJOB	1	22.00
SATJOB	2	50.00
SATJOB	3	66.00
SATJOB	4	48.00
SATJOB	5	46.00
SATJOB	6	66.00
SATJOB	7	46.00

TABLE 12.4 More Complete Output from Commands:

HILOGLINEAR SEX(1,2) AGE(1,6) INCOME(1,4) HAPPY(1,3) /
    PRINT ALL

********************* H I E R A R C H I C A L L O G L I N E A R *********************

DATA INFORMATION
  1319 UNWEIGHTED CASES ACCEPTED.
     0 CASES REJECTED BECAUSE OF OUT-OF-RANGE FACTOR VALUES.
   154 CASES REJECTED BECAUSE OF MISSING DATA.
  1319 WEIGHTED CASES WILL BE USED IN THE ANALYSIS.

FACTOR INFORMATION
  FACTOR   LEVEL   LABEL
  SEX   2   RESPONDENT'S SEX
  AGE   6   AGE OF RESPONDENT
  INCOME   5   TOTAL FAMILY INCOME
  HAPPY   3   GENERAL HAPPINESS

DESIGN 1 HAS GENERATING CLASS

  NOTE: FOR SATURATED MODELS .500 HAS BEEN ADDED TO ALL OBSERVED CELLS.
  THIS VALUE MAY BE CHANGED BY USING THE CRITERIA = DELTA SUBCOMMAND.

    SEX*AGE*INCOME*HAPPY

THE ITERATIVE PROPORTIONAL FIT ALGORITHM CONVERGED AT ITERATION 1.
THE MAXIMUM DIFFERENCE BETWEEN OBSERVED AND FITTED MARGINAL TOTALS IS   .000
AND THE CONVERGENCE CRITERION IS   .250

TABLE 12.4 Continued

OBSERVED, EXPECTED FREQUENCIES AND RESIDUALS.

FACTOR	CODE	OBS. COUNT	EXP. COUNT	RESIDUAL	STD. RESID.
SEX	MALE				
	1				
AGE	1				
INCOME	1				
HAPPY	1	5.5	5.5	.000	.000
HAPPY	2	13.5	13.5	.000	.000
HAPPY	3	1.5	1.5	.000	.000
INCOME	2				
HAPPY	1	9.5	9.5	.000	.000
HAPPY	2	14.5	14.5	.000	.000
HAPPY	3	5.5	5.5	.000	.000
INCOME	3				
HAPPY	1	14.5	14.5	.000	.000
HAPPY	2	30.5	30.5	.000	.000
HAPPY	3	3.5	3.5	.000	.000
INCOME	4				
HAPPY	1	4.5	4.5	.000	.000
HAPPY	2	7.5	7.5	.000	.000
HAPPY	3	.5	.5	.000	.000
INCOME	5				
HAPPY	1	2.5	2.5	.000	.000
HAPPY	2	6.5	6.5	.000	.000
HAPPY	3	.5	.5	.000	.000
AGE	2				
INCOME	1				
HAPPY	1	2.5	2.5	.000	.000
HAPPY	2	6.5	6.5	.000	.000
HAPPY	3	2.5	2.5	.000	.000
INCOME	2				
HAPPY	1	8.5	8.5	.000	.000

. . .

GOODNESS-OF-FIT TEST STATISTICS

LIKELIHOOD RATIO CHI SQUARE = .00000   DF = 0   P = 1.000
PEARSON CHI SQUARE = .00000   DF = 0   P = 1.000

TESTS THAT K-WAY AND HIGHER ORDER EFFECTS ARE ZERO.

K	DF	L.R. CHISQ	PROB	PEARSON CHISQ	PRCB	ITERATION
4	40	30.21	.869	24.19	.977	4
3	118	127.57	.258	124.86	.315	4
2	167	348.73	.000	348.58	.000	2
1	179	1102.66	.000	1206.48	.000	0

TESTS THAT K-WAY EFFECTS ARE ZERO.

K	DF	L.R. CHISQ	PROB	PEARSON CHISQ	PROB	ITERATION
1	12	753.94	.000	857.91	.000	0
2	49	221.16	.000	223.71	.000	0
3	78	97.36	.068	100.67	.043	0
4	40	30.21	.869	24.19	.977	0

TESTS OF PARTIAL ASSOCIATIONS.

EFFECT NAME	DF	PARTIAL CHISQ	PROB	ITER
SEX*AGE*INCOME	20	36.02	.015	4
SEX*AGE*HAPPY	10	7.68	.660	4
SEX*INCOME*HAPPY	8	5.70	.681	3
AGE*INCOME*HAPPY	40	48.00	.180	4
SEX*AGE	5	7.44	.190	4
SEX*INCOME	4	17.39	.002	4
AGE*INCOME	20	137.56	.000	4
SEX*HAPPY	2	.10	.950	4
AGE*HAPPY	10	15.96	.100	2
INCOME*HAPPY	8	49.81	.000	2
SEX	1	15.38	.000	2
AGE	5	129.03	.000	2
INCOME	4	134.26	.000	
HAPPY	2	475.27	.000	

13

FACTOR ANALYSIS

New SPSS Command.

FACTOR

Looking at the variables in the NORC90 file, we can see many that may affect happiness that are not yet in our analysis, including SIBS, CHILDS, HELPFUL, FAIR, CONEDUC, CONPRESS, CONLEGIS, SATFAM, SATFRND, SATJOB. On closer inspection, some of these variables together appear to be measuring a more general variable. For example, HELPFUL, FAIR, CONEDUC, CONPRESS, and CONLEGIS may all measure trust in others. SATFAM, SATFRND, and SATJOB may all be indicators of satisfaction with one's social position. SIBS, CHILDS, and MARITAL (which is already in our analysis) may be measures of the extensiveness of one's family network.

Working with a large number of variables is tedious. If the variables are really just different measures of another more general variable, we can facilitate and simplify our work by constructing a measure of the general variable and using that measure in our analysis. **Factor analysis** is a way of measuring a general variable, or **factor**, underlying a large set of variables. This method also helps in dealing with the problem of multicollinearity, discussed in earlier chapters.*

13.1 What Factor Analysis Is and When to Use It

Often a researcher has several variables that appear to be related to one another because they are different ways of measuring one general variable or factor.

Factor analysis is a technique for condensing many variables into a few underlying constructs. For example, we might have a 100-item test that we think measures three distinct abilities: verbal, mathematical, and analytical. Using factor analysis we could try to obtain a "factor score" for each of these abilities. Our analysis would reveal whether there were less or more than three distinct factors. Our analysis would also reveal which variables were most closely associated with each factor and would weigh those variables most heavily in calculating the factor scores.

Factor analysis is not necessary when one already knows (1) which variables measure each factor and (2) the variables' relative importance—for example, one may have predetermined that all the variables will be weighted equally.

Before doing a factor analysis, you should examine a correlation matrix of the variables. Because you are assuming that underlying factors account for the variance in all the variables, it is questionable to include any variable whose correlations with the other variables are all below 0.4 in absolute value.

Factor analysis is sometimes used when the researcher has a large set of variables and suspects that they could be summarized more concisely by a few underlying factors but is not certain what these factors would be. This use of factor analysis would be termed *exploratory*.

13.2 How to Use FACTOR

To do a factor analysis for the variables mentioned at the beginning of this chapter as possible influences on happiness, we would use the following commands:

---

*For a more complete discussion of factor analysis see Jae-On Kim and Charles W. Mueller's *Introduction to Factor Analysis: What It Is and How to Do It* (Beverly Hills, CA: Sage Publications, 1978).

```
FACTOR  VARIABLES=SIBS MARITAL CHILDS HELPFUL FAIR
                   CONEDUC CONPRESS CONLEGIS SATFAM
                   SATFRND SATJOB
```

By default, FACTOR in SPSS uses a technique called **principal components** to extract factors. Several other extraction techniques are available; however, principal components is the most frequently used. (See the *SPSS Reference Guide,* page 191, for a list of the other SPSS extraction techniques available and the subcommands used to initiate them.)

First the principal-components method calculates a factor that will explain the maximum variance in all the variables. Then a second factor is calculated that explains the maximum amount of the remaining variance. However, the second factor has the restriction that it cannot be correlated with the first factor. Another way of stating that two factors are not correlated with each other is to say they are **orthogonal.**

The process can be continued until all the variance in the variables has been explained. Normally this point is reached when the number of factors equals the number of variables. Such a solution is not helpful, however, because we are striving for greater simplicity. Having as many factors as there are variables does not simplify anything! Most researchers use the eigenvalue statistic, discussed in the next section, to decide how many factors to use in their analysis.

13.3 Output from FACTOR

The first part of the factor analysis output will be a table entitled INITIAL STATISTICS. Part of this output is given in Table 13.1. (Table 13.7 at the end of the chapter presents complete output.) The far left column gives the names of all variables used in the factor analysis. To the right of the names is a column of COMMUNALITY statistics. The **communality** statistic for each variable is the proportion of variance in the variable explained by all the factors. The communality of a variable can range from 0.0, indicating absolutely no association, to 1.0, indicating a perfect association. When a principal-components extraction is done, the communality of each variable in the initial statistics will be 1.0, which results from the initial analysis having as many factors as there are variables.

The third column gives the factor numbers. All the statistics to the right of the factor number apply to that factor number—not to the variable named on the far left. Accordingly, the column of eigenvalue statistics pertains to the factors, not the variables. For example, the eigenvalue 1.98 in the first row indicates the amount of variance underlying all the variables associated with factor

TABLE 13.1 Partial Output of FACTOR

INITIAL STATISTICS:

VARIABLE	COMMUNALITY	*	FACTOR	EIGEN-VALUE	PERCENT OF VARIANCE	CUMULATIVE PERCENT
		*				
SIBS	1.0	*	1	1.98	18.0	18.0
MARITAL	1.0	*	2	1.52	13.9	31.9
CHILDS	1.0	*	3	1.37	12.5	44.4
HELPFUL	1.0	*	4	1.13	10.3	54.7
FAIR	1.0	*	5	.95	8.7	63.4
CONEDUC	1.0	*	6	.81	7.4	70.9
CONPRESS	1.0	*	7	.80	7.3	78.2
CONLEGIS	1.0	*	8	.75	6.9	85.1
SATFAM	1.0	*	9	.64	5.9	91.0
SATFRND	1.0	*	10	.59	5.4	96.4
SATJOB	1.0	*	11	.40	3.6	100.0

TABLE 13.2 Partial Output of FACTOR

FACTOR MATRIX:

	FACTOR 1	FACTOR 2	FACTOR 3	FACTOR 4
SIBS	.24	.18	-.50	.16
MARITAL	.44	-.63	.27	.00
CHILDS	-.10	.67	-.43	.13
HELPFUL	.39	.06	-.21	-.59
FAIR	-.34	-.01	.30	.63
CONEDUC	.20	.32	.52	-.26
CONPRESS	.08	.45	.45	.19
CONLEGIS	.26	.51	.44	-.17
SATFAM	.76	-.13	.03	.27
SATFRND	.67	.14	-.18	.27
SATJOB	.52	.06	-.02	.20

1. The sum of the eigenvalues equals the number of variables; hence, an eigen-value of 1.98 in an analysis of 11 variables shows that the proportion of the variance explained by factor 1 is 1.98 divided by 11, or 18.0 percent, as indicated in the PCT OF VAR (percent of variance) column on the right.

Following the initial statistics is a table entitled FACTOR MATRIX that gives more information about the first extraction (see Table 13.2). In the factor matrix are the loadings of each variable on each factor. The **factor loading** is the correlation of a variable with a factor. For example, the factor loading of

TABLE 13.3 Partial Output of FACTOR

FINAL STATISTICS:

VARIABLE	COMMUNALITY	*	FACTOR	EIGEN-VALUE	PERCENT OF VARIANCE	CUMULATIVE PERCENT
		*				
SIBS	.38	*	1	1.98	18.0	18.0
MARITAL	.66	*	2	1.52	13.9	31.9
CHILDS	.67	*	3	1.37	12.5	44.4
HELPFUL	.55	*	4	1.13	10.3	54.7
FAIR	.61	*				
CONEDUC	.48	*				
CONPRESS	.46	*				
CONLEGI	.57	*				
SATFAM	.68	*				
SATFRND	.59	*				
SATJOB	.31	*				

SIBS on factor 1 is .24. The factor loadings of SIBS on factor 2, factor 3, and factor 4 are .18, .50, and .16, respectively. A factor loading of .24 means that $(.24)^2$ or 5.7 percent of the variance in SIBS is accounted for by factor 1.

The next portion of FACTOR output is a table entitled FINAL STATISTICS (see Table 13.3). Note that the communalities no longer equal 1. The final statistics are based only on factors with an eigenvalue greater than 1. In our example, only the first four factors had an eigenvalue greater than 1 (see Table 13.1). Although the communalities no longer equal 1, meaning that not all the variance in the variables is accounted for, we have simplified our data from 11 variables to 4 factors.

For example, with SIBS we have accounted for $(.38)^2$ or 14 percent of its variance using the first four factors.

13.4 Rotating Factors

Rotating factors is a method of simplifying factors so that each variable tends to load highly on only one factor. Remember that the first factor was calculated to maximize the total amount of variance it could explain. In using this procedure, the factor may have distorted somewhat in order to accommodate some of the variance of variables that are not really part of the factor. Rotating the factors helps correct this distortion.

An important decision we have to make is whether to do an **orthogonal rotation,** which means that the factors will remain uncorrelated, or an **oblique rotation,** which means that the factors will be allowed to correlate with one

TABLE 13.4 Partial Output for FACTOR: Orthogonal Rotation

ROTATED FACTOR MATRIX:

	FACTOR 1	FACTOR 2	FACTOR 3	FACTOR 4
SIBS	.39	.39	−.23	.12
MARITAL	.31	−.74	−.08	.06
CHILDS	.07	.81	.04	.01
HELPFUL	.10	−.00	.07	.73
FAIR	−.06	−.01	.02	−.78
CONEDUC	−.02	−.11	.67	.13
CONPRESS	.10	.11	.59	−.28
CONLEGI	.09	.07	.73	.10
SATFAM	.78	−.25	.05	.04
SATFRND	.75	.10	.04	.08
SATJOB	.55	−.02	.09	.03

another. The choice is up to the researcher. If we thought the factors were truly distinct and unassociated with one another, we would do an orthogonal rotation. For example, we might be doing a profile of consumers in which one factor is rustic preferences and a second factor is luxury designer preferences. If we decide that these two factors are not associated with each other, we can do an orthogonal rotation.

As another example, we might be doing a profile of diet preferences that has a sweet food factor and a fatty food factor. If we decide these two factors are associated, we will want to do an oblique rotation.

A varimax orthogonal rotation is produced by default, so no additional commands are needed. In a **varimax rotation,** the calculations are done to maximize the tendency of each variable to load highly on only one factor. Other orthogonal rotation techniques are available; however, the varimax is the most frequently used. (See the *SPSS Reference Guide,* pp. 191–192, for a list of other rotation techniques available.)

The final portion of output from the FACTOR command would be the ROTATED FACTOR MATRIX presented in Table 13.4. In this factor matrix after the rotation, the variables tend to be more extreme in their loadings. Interpretation of the results is simplified because each factor is more clearly identified by a subset of variables that load high on it but low on other factors. Note, for example, that MARITAL loads .31 on factor 1 and −.74 on factor 2. Before the rotation, its loading was .44 on factor 1 and −.63 on factor 2 (see Table 13.2).

An orthogonal rotation does not change the communalities of the variables. Just as much variance is explained after the rotation as before. Likewise, an orthogonal rotation does not change the eigenvalues of the factors. Each factor explains the same proportion of the variance as it did before the rotation. Furthermore, after an orthogonal rotation, the correlation between the factors remains 0.0, as it was before the rotation.

Now let's do an oblique rotation of the same data. An oblique rotation allows for some correlation between factors. To do an oblique rotation, we must add the subcommand **ROTATION=OBLIQUE** preceded by a slash. The SPSS commands for our example will now be

```
FACTOR   VARIABLES=SIBS MARITAL CHILDS HELPFUL FAIR
                CONEDUC CONPRESS CONLEGIS SATFAM
                SATFRND SATJOB/
         ROTATION=OBLIQUE
```

The default method of oblique rotation employed by SPSS is called **oblimin.** When an oblique rotation is done, the output differs somewhat from an orthogonal rotation. Instead of a factor matrix, an oblique rotation produces both a *factor pattern* matrix and a *factor structure* matrix.

The **factor pattern matrix** contains the regression coefficients of each variable for each factor produced when the variable is regressed on the factors (see Chapter 9 for a discussion of regression). These regression coefficients are not the same as the correlations of the variables with the factors, because a regression coefficient is affected by intercorrelations among the factors. On the other hand, a correlation between a variable and a factor is not affected by inter-correlations among the variables. This distinction is not necessary prior to rotation or after an orthogonal rotation, because there are zero correlations among all the factors until we do an oblique rotation.

As an example of a factor pattern matrix coefficient, look at the first variable, SIBS, in the left-hand column of Table 13.5. To the right of this variable, in the FACTOR 1 column, is the coefficient .38, which is the regression coefficient, or factor loading, of SIBS on factor 1. The loadings of SIBS on factor 2, factor 3, and factor 4, respectively, are .39, −.24, and −.10. These loadings indicate the relative importance of the factors in accounting for variance in SIBS.

Looking at the factors, we can see that factor 1 has high pattern matrix coefficients for satisfaction with family (.78) and friends (.75) and a moderate coefficient for marital status (.32). We might label this the good relationships factor. Factor 2 has two of its higher loadings on SIBS (.39) and CHILDS (.81) and might be labeled the relative factor. Factor 3 has high loadings for CONEDUC (.68), CONPRESS (.58), and CONLEGIS (.74) and might be labeled the confidence in public institutions factor. Factor 4 has high coefficients for HELPFUL (−.73) and FAIR (.78) and could be labeled the trust factor. We will discuss in Secton 13.6 how these factors can be used as variables in further analyses.

The second half of Table 13.5 is the **factor structure matrix.** The coeffi-

TABLE 13.5 Partial Output for FACTOR: Oblique Rotation

PATTERN MATRIX:

	FACTOR 1	FACTOR 2	FACTOR 3	FACTOR 4
SIBS	.38	.39	-.24	-.10
MARITAL	.32	-.74	-.10	-.03
CHILDS	.06	.81	.04	-.00
HELPFUL	.03	-.00	.09	-.73
FAIR	.01	-.01	.00	.78
CONEDUC	-.04	-.10	.68	-.14
CONPRESS	.12	.12	.58	.28
CONLEGI	.07	.08	.74	-.11
SATFAM	.78	-.25	.03	.00
SATFRND	.75	.09	.02	-.03
SATJOB	.55	-.02	.08	.00

STRUCTURE MATRIX:

	FACTOR 1	FACTOR 2	FACTOR 3	FACTOR 4
SIBS	.39	.40	-.23	-.16
MARITAL	.30	-.74	-.07	-.09
CHILDS	.08	.81	.03	-.01
HELPFUL	.16	-.00	.06	-.73
FAIR	-.11	-.01	.03	.78
CONEDUC	.00	-.11	.67	-.11
CONPRESS	.10	.11	.60	.28
CONLEGI	.12	.07	.73	-.09
SATFAM	.78	-.24	.07	-.11
SATFRND	.76	.11	.05	-.15
SATJOB	.55	-.01	.10	-.08

cients in this matrix are the correlations of each variable with each factor. The correlation of SIBS with factor 1 is .39. SIBS' correlations with factor 2, factor 3, and factor 4 are .40, -.23, and -.16, respectively. These correlation coefficients differ from the regression coefficients in the factor pattern matrix because they do not adjust for correlations among the factors.

13.5 Factor Correlation Matrix

The factor correlation matrix printed only after an oblique rotation shows the correlation of the factors with one another (see Table 13.6). Prior to rotation, the factors are orthogonal; that is, their correlation with one another is 0.0. Low correlations indicate that the factors are distinct.

TABLE 13.6 Partial Output of FACTOR

FACTOR CORRELATION MATRIX:

	FACTOR 1	FACTOR 2	FACTOR 3	FACTOR 4
FACTOR 1	1.00			
FACTOR 2	.02	1.00		
FACTOR 3	.03	-.01	1.00	
FACTOR 4	-.16	.00	.03	1.00

13.6 Factor Score Coefficients

We are now faced with the task of calculating the score for each case on each factor. (Remember, the factor pattern coefficients and the factor structure coefficients concerned the association between *variables* and factors, not *cases* and factors.) To calculate the factor score of each case for each factor, we use yet another type of coefficient—**factor score coefficients.**

The score on a particular variable is multiplied by the factor score coefficient of that variable for that factor. We do this multiplication for each score of the case on each variable and then sum the products.

The factor scores for each case can be saved. Each set of factor scores can then be treated as a new variable. For example, suppose we extracted four factors and wanted to save the factor scores for all four. We would decide on a variable name and then use the subcommand SAVE. (Although we have seen SAVE as a command in earlier chapters, in this context it is a subcommand that must begin after column 1.) For our example, let's use the name FACTVAR. The indented SAVE subcommand would be

SAVE   (ALL FACTVAR)

The first factor's scores would be saved under the variable name FACTVAR1, the second factor's scores under the name FACTVAR2, and so on. Be careful to allow space for the digits at the end of the variable name; you must not exceed the 8-character limit.

Once the variables based on factor scores are saved, we can do other analyses that include these factors as variables. For example, to use FACTVAR1 (our good relationships factor), FACTVAR2 (our relatives factor), FACTVAR3 (our trust-in-others factor), and FACTVAR4 (our confidence in public institutions factor), the complete commands to calculate the factors and do a regression with HAPPY as the dependent variable are

```
FACTOR   VARIABLES=SIBS MARITAL CHILDS HELPFUL FAIR
                   CONEDUC CONPRESS CONLEGIS SATFAM
                   SATFRND SATJOB/
         ROTATION=OBLIQUE/
         SAVE   (ALL FACTVAR) /
REGRESSION   VARIABLES=HAPPY FACTVAR1 FACTVAR2 FACTVAR3
             FACTVAR4/
             DEPENDENT=HAPPY/
             METHOD=ENTER/
```

If we wanted, we could include other variables from our file as independent variables in the regression along with the four factors.

Factor analysis has many variations. The SPSS program contains seven extraction techniques, four rotation techniques, and three possible calculations of factor scores. We have presented the most commonly used approaches. The *SPSS Reference Guide,* gives the commands for the other methods but without much discussion of the various assumptions and advantages of each method. To understand better the various methods of factor analysis, you will need to study articles by statisticians on the subject.

13.7 Summary

A factor is a composite variable underlying the variance in a set of variables.

A factor loading is a measure of the association between a variable and the factor of which it is a component. Factor loadings range from -1.0 to 1.0. Zero would indicate no association; 1 would indicate a perfect association. The sign of the loading indicates whether the association is positive or negative.

The eigenvalue is a measure of variance in the set of variables in the factor analysis. The total eigenvalue is equal to the number of variables in the analysis.

The communality of a variable is the proportion of its variance accounted for by the variables in the analysis. The communality is 0.0 for no association and 1.0 for a perfect association. The communality of all the variables will be 1.0 when the number of factors equals the number of variables.

A factor score is the value of the factor for a particular case.

In an orthogonal rotation, the correlation between the factors in the analysis is kept at 0.0. In an oblique rotation, some correlation is permitted among the factors in the analysis.

13.8 Where to Look in the *SPSS Reference Guide*

- FACTOR is discussed on pages 182–196.

RESEARCH PROJECT WORK FOR CHAPTER 13

Do an exploratory factor analysis on your research data set, including all the variables except ID. Before you execute the analysis, hypothesize which variables you think will cluster together. If your hypotheses prove incorrect, discuss why the findings were different from what you expected.

REVIEW QUESTIONS FOR CHAPTER 13

(Answers to Review Questions are given at the back of the book.)

13.1   What is a factor?

13.2   What is a factor loading?

13.3   What is the eigenvalue in factor analysis?

13.4   What is the communality of a variable in factor analysis?

13.5   What is a factor score?

13.6   How is an orthogonal rotation different from an oblique rotation?

13.7   What is the factor extraction technique used by default in FACTOR?

13.8   What is the default rotation done by FACTOR if no technique is specified?

13.9   What type of oblique rotation is done by FACTOR if the ROTATION= OBLIQUE subcommand is given without specifying a technique?

13.10 What command would be needed to produce a factor analysis with an orthogonal rotation of the 13 variables CONFINA through CONARMY in the SPSS system file NORC90, described in Appendix B?

ASSIGNMENT QUESTIONS FOR CHAPTER 13

(Solutions to the Assignment Questions are provided in the *Instructor's Manual.*)

13.1   What does the following output indicate about the factors produced by the command in Review Question 13.10?

INITIAL STATISTICS:

VARIABLE	COMMUNALITY	*	FACTOR	EIGENVALUE	PERCENT OF VARIANCE
CONFINAN	1.0	*	1	3.93	30.2
CONBUS	1.0	*	2	1.32	10.2
CONCLER	1.0	*	3	1.18	9.1
CONEDUC	1.0	*	4	.99	7.6
CONFED	1.0	*	5	.84	6.4
CONLABOR	1.0	*	6	.78	6.0
CONPRESS	1.0	*	7	.74	5.7
CONMEDI	1.0	*	8	.69	5.3
CONTV	1.0	*	9	.61	4.7
CONJUDG	1.0	*	10	.53	4.1
CONSCI	1.0	*	11	.52	4.0
CONLEGI	1.0	*	12	.47	3.6
CONARMY	1.0	*	13	.42	3.2

13.2 What does the following output indicate about the factors produced by the command in Review Question 13.10?

FACTOR MATRIX:

	FACTOR 1	FACTOR 2	FACTOR 3
CONFINAN	.63	-.03	.35
CONBUS	.50	-.21	.26
CONCLER	.43	-.21	.43
CONEDUC	.51	.00	.14
CONFED	.61	-.02	-.36
CONLABOR	.48	.44	-.20
CONPRESS	.44	.55	.01
CONMEDI	.58	-.36	.19
CONTV	.45	.59	.23
CONJUDG	.60	-.21	-.52
CONSCI	.57	-.46	-.15
CONLEGI	.69	.09	-.40
CONARMY	.61	.06	.26

13.3   What does the following output indicate about the factors produced by the command in Review Question 13.10?

FINAL STATISTICS:

VARIABLE	COMMUNALITY	*	FACTOR	EIGENVALUE	PERCENT OF VARIANCE
		*			
CONFINAN	.51	*	1	3.93	30.2
CONBUS	.36	*	2	1.32	10.2
CONCLER	.41	*	3	1.18	9.1
CONEDUC	.28	*			
CONFED	.50	*			
CONLABOR	.46	*			
CONPRESS	.49	*			
CONMEDI	.50	*			
CONTV	.60	*			
CONJUDG	.67	*			
CONSCI	.55	*			
CONLEGI	.64	*			
CONARMY	.44	*			

13.4   What does the following output indicate about the factors produced by the command in Review Question 13.10?

PATTERN MATRIX:

	FACTOR 1	FACTOR 2	FACTOR 3
CONFINAN	.66	.19	.01
CONBUS	.59	-.03	-.05
CONCLER	.69	-.04	.14
CONEDUC	.40	.17	-.12
CONFED	.05	.13	-.64
CONLABOR	-.07	.56	-.31
CONPRESS	.03	.67	-.08
CONMEDI	.62	-.16	-.19
CONTV	.21	.74	.13
CONJUDG	-.02	-.07	-.84
CONSCI	.37	-.29	-.54
CONLEGI	.01	.26	-.70
CONARMY	.54	.27	-.04

STRUCTURE MATRIX:

	FACTOR 1	FACTOR 2	FACTOR 3
CONFINAN	.69	.32	−.28
CONBUS	.60	.09	−.27
CONCLER	.63	.07	−.11
CONEDUC	.48	.27	−.30
CONFED	.32	.28	−.69
CONLABOR	.16	.61	−.41
CONPRESS	.20	.69	−.23
CONMEDI	.67	.00	−.40
CONTV	.31	.75	−.10
CONJUDG	.28	.09	−.82
CONSCI	.52	.10	−.62
CONLEGI	.33	.41	−.76
CONARMY	.61	.39	−.30

13.5   What does the following output indicate about the factors produced by the command in Review Question 13.10?

FACTOR CORRELATION MATRIX

	FACTOR 1	FACTOR 2	FACTOR 3
FACTOR 1	1.00		
FACTOR 2	.05	1.00	
FACTOR 3	−.25	−.04	1.00

TABLE 13.7 Output from command FACTOR   VARIABLES=SIBS MARITAL CHILDS HELPFUL FAIR CONEDUC CONPRESS CONLEGIS SATFAM SATFRND SATJOB

F A C T O R   A N A L Y S I S

ANALYSIS NUMBER   1 LISTWISE DELETION OF CASES WITH MISSING VALUES

EXTRACTION   1 FOR ANALYSIS   1, PRINCIPAL-COMPONENTS ANALYSIS (PC)

INITIAL STATISTICS:

VARIABLE	COMMUNALITY	*	FACTOR	EIGENVALUE	PERCENT OF VARIANCE	CUMULATIVE PERCENTAGE
SIBS	1.00000	*	1	1.98339	18.0	18.0
MARITAL	1.00000	*	2	1.52608	13.9	31.9
CHILDS	1.00000	*	3	1.37503	12.5	44.4
HELPFUL	1.00000	*	4	1.13457	10.3	54.7
FAIR	1.00000	*	5	.95954	8.7	63.4
CONEDUC	1.00000	*	6	.81941	7.4	70.9
CONPRESS	1.00000	*	7	.80416	7.3	78.2
CONLEGI	1.00000	*	8	.75807	6.9	85.1
SATFAM	1.00000	*	9	.64510	5.9	91.0
SATFRND	1.00000	*	10	.59327	5.4	96.4
SATJOB	1.00000	*	11	.40137	3.6	100.0

TABLE 13.7 Continued

PC EXTRACTED   4 FACTORS.

FACTOR MATRIX:

	FACTOR 1	FACTOR 2	FACTOR 3	FACTOR 4
SIBS	.24998	.18936	-.50887	.16985
MARITAL	.44214	-.63140	.27060	.00282
CHILDS	-.10221	.67946	-.43443	.13084
HELPFUL	.39452	.06027	-.21198	-.59460
FAIR	-.34553	-.01328	.30618	.63297
CONEDUC	.20227	.32658	.52005	-.26635
CONPRESS	.08718	.45599	.45695	.19153
CONLEGI	.26832	.51912	.44838	-.17599
SATFAM	.76544	-.13358	.03223	.27590
SATFRND	.67959	.14086	-.18299	.27996
SATJOB	.52124	.06586	-.02506	.20322

FACTOR ANALYSIS

FINAL STATISTICS:

VARIABLE	COMMUNALITY	*	FACTOR	EIGENVALUE	PCT OF VAR	CUM PCT
		*				
SIBS	.38615	*	1	1.98339	18.0	18.0
MARITAL	.66738	*	2	1.52608	13.9	31.9
CHILDS	.67796	*	3	1.37503	12.5	44.4
HELPFUL	.55776	*	4	1.13457	10.3	54.7
FAIR	.61397	*				
CONEDUC	.48897	*				
CONPRESS	.46101	*				
CONLEGI	.57349	*				
SATFAM	.68089	*				
SATFRND	.59354	*				
SATJOB	.31795	*				

14

ANALYZING CENSUS DATA WITH SPSS

New SPSS Command:

FILE TYPE

The U.S. Bureau of the Census does not ask any attitudinal questions in its decennial census nor in its current population surveys. Therefore, we cannot extend our analysis of reported happiness to the data gathered by the Bureau of the Census. On the other hand, SPSS is well equipped to cope with some of the difficulties posed by census data files. You may very likely want to use one of these files someday.

An introduction to the many variables in the census data files is beyond the scope of this book, but we will describe the two basic types of files and the requirements for working with them. These files are the PUMS files (Public-Use Microdata Sample) and the STF files (Summary Tape File).

Also beyond the scope of this book, and simply impossible, is a description of the operating system commands or hardware limitations of the numerous types of computer installations around the country. In this chapter we describe the necessary SPSS commands.

14.1 Individual Level Census Data: PUMS Files

The distinguishing characteristic of the PUMS files is that the basic case units are individuals. With over 250 million individuals in the United States, even computer technology does not enable the typical user to work with every individual, so the Bureau of the Census releases samples (on tape) from its decennial census for the public to use. Useful documentation available about census data includes the following:

- *1990 Census of Population and Housing Tabulation and Publication Guide* (available from the U.S. Government Printing Office)
- *Telephone Contacts for Data Users* (available from the Bureau of the Census)
- *Data User News* (available from the Bureau of the Census)
- *Directory of Data Files* (available from the Bureau of the Census)

The smallest of these documents, and often the most useful, is the *Telephone Contacts for Data Users,* a free four-page brochure.

State data centers with regional branches provide the census data tapes and CD-ROM disks at nominal cost and are also a convenient source of expertise on how to use them. If you are having trouble locating a state data center or an office of the Bureau of the Census to help you, call the Bureau's Data User Services at (301) 763-4100.

The major difficulty with the PUMS files is that household information is on one record, followed by one or more records containing the information on the persons living in the household—one record for each individual. If you simply want to use household information, there is no problem. Simply give a SELECT IF command that specifies 'H' (in single quotes) for the variable RECTYPE. This alphanumeric variable, in the same location for both types of records, is coded P for individuals and H for households. Likewise, if you want to use individual information, use a SELECT IF command that specifies 'P' for the record type variable.

More likely you will want to use information from both the household and the individual records so that each individual is connected with the attributes of his or her household. In this case, you will be dealing with what is called a *nested hierarchical file* and will need to use the command **FILE TYPE.** For example, to do an analysis using the variable FAMINCOM from the household records and linking it with the variables SEX, MARITAL, and AGE from the individual records for each household, we would use the following set of SPSS commands:

```
FILE TYPE   NESTED   FILE=PUMS80   RECORD=RECTYPE 1  (A)
RECORD TYPE  'H'
DATA LIST   FAMINCOM 112-116
RECORD TYPE  'P'
DATA LIST   SEX 7   MARITAL 11   AGE 33-34
END FILE TYPE
```

This example uses the PUMS 1980 data columns because PUMS 1990 was not available at the time this book went to press. Note that several other commands and subcommands must accompany the FILE TYPE command. First is the subcommand **NESTED,** which indicates that we want the data from the first record type "spread" to the records of the second record type. In our example, the data from each record of type H will be spread to each P record that follows it, until the next H record is encountered.

The next subcommand in the FILE TYPE command is **FILE = PUMS80,** which specifies the name we gave to the file in our operating system commands (which are not shown here). On the same line is the subcommand **RECORD = RECTYPE 1 (A),** which indicates that the record type will be identified by the variable RECTYPE, which is in column 1. [The (A) indicates that this variable is alphanumeric.]

RECORD TYPE 'H' indicates that the first record type is identified by having the value H for the variable and location specified by the RECORD= subcommand on the first line. So, if the value in column 1 for the variable REC-TYPE is H, then the DATA LIST command following RECORD TYPE 'H' applies.

DATA LIST FAMINCOM 112–116 applies to the type H records, because this command follows the RECORD TYPE 'H' command. Likewise RECORD TYPE 'P' indicates that the DATA LIST following it applies to records with the value P in column 1.

END FILE TYPE indicates that the set of commands specifying the file type has been concluded.

After the more complicated set of commands surrounding the DATA LIST phase of your data definition process, you can proceed as usual with other SPSS commands.

The Bureau of the Census Current Population Survey (CPS) data tapes are also hierarchical nested files and require a FILE TYPE set of commands to combine household and individual data. The Current Population Survey samples approximately 50,000 households monthly. The data items are similar to those in the decennial census, so the CPS allows you to update census data for states and large metropolitan areas.

In the STF data files, however, the units of analysis are geographic units and the data are aggregate statistics. These files present a different set of challenges, which we discuss in the next section.

14.2 Aggregate Data by Geographic Area: STF Files

The STF files are tables of data organized by geographic units. Each case is a geographic area, but the areas might be anything from a neighborhood block group to a state. The geographic level is specified by the value of SUMRYLV, a variable whose location varies depending on which type of STF file you are using. You'll need to check your codebook to locate SUMRYLV and to learn the values that correspond to each level. You do not have to treat these files as nested for most analyses because the same variables are used for each geographic level.

   A simple DATA LIST command will suffice to define your data. Often, however, you will want to print out the information for just some of the levels. You can do so by using a SELECT IF command with the SUMRYLV variable after the DATA LIST command. There is also a variable RECOIND for some of the STF files that indicates whether the aggregated statistics are for the total population or a particular ethnic/racial group within it. Using a SELECT IF command with RECOIND enables you to select out the total population or just those subgroups of the total that you wish to examine.

   A tricky aspect of STF files is that each cell in a table must be thought of as a variable. If you have the population by age in five-year intervals, each of those five-year intervals must be given a variable name. (The SPSS convention of defining a set of variables with the same prefix by using the keyword **TO** is most useful. With it we can define 18 variables by using the words AGE1 TO AGE18 on the DATA LIST command followed by the columns these adjacent variables span.) For example:

```
DATA LIST AGE1 TO AGE18 20-109
```

   To produce a table when each cell has its own variable name, use a LIST command that specifies each variable name. Use the VARIABLE LABELS command to identify the cell to which each variable label corresponds. If you make AREANAME (a variable containing the first name of each geographic unit) the first variable named on the LIST command, the output will indicate which area the table is for.

   Another problem in working with the STF file is that a 0 sometimes indicates that the information is being suppressed, whereas other times a 0 is a legitimate value. (The Bureau of the Census suppresses some information when there are so few cases that confidentiality would be jeopardized.) To solve this problem, certain variables indicate whether the information for another variable is being suppressed. For example, the first **suppression variable** on one of the STF files is coded 1 when the total population count is being suppressed because fewer than 30 persons live in the area. For this file you would need to use an IF command to change values of the total population variable from 0 to a missing value when the suppressor variable has a value of 1.

There are four STF file types (STF1, STF2, STF3, and STF4), and for each type there are either three or four files (A, B, C, and D) which cover different levels of geography.

14.3 Summary

The PUMS files (Public-Use Microdata Samples) have households and individuals as the basic case units.

The major difficulty with the PUMS files is that household information is on one record, followed by one or more records containing the information on the persons living in the household—one record for each individual. If you want to use information from both the household and the individual records such that each individual is connected with the attributes of his or her household, you need to use the FILE TYPE command.

The STF files (Summary Tape Files) consist of tables of data organized by geographic units. Each case is a geographic area, but the areas might be anything from a block group to a standard metropolitan statistical area (SMSA). (By the 1990 census SMSAs had been renamed SMAs, that is, Standard Metropolitan Areas.) The geographic level is specified by the value of SUMRYLV, a variable whose location varies depending on which type of STF file you are using.

For STF files each cell in a table must be thought of as a variable.

Another problem in working with the STF files is that a 0 may indicate either suppressed information or a legitimate value. To solve this problem, certain variables indicate whether the information for another variable is being suppressed.

An excellent discussion of how to choose which census data file to use is presented by Dowell Meyers in *Analysis with Local Census Data: Portraits of Change* (San Diego: Academic Press, 1992), pp. 73–83. This book is the best introduction I have found to the methods and issues involved in using census data.

14.4 Where to Look in the
SPSS Reference Guide

The *SPSS Reference Guide* does not discuss using census data tapes. A sophisticated discussion can be found in *SPSS Processing of U.S. Census Data* (Chicago, Ill.: SPSS Inc., 1984).

- The FILE TYPE command is discussed on pages 199–211, *SPSS Reference Guide.*

REVIEW QUESTIONS FOR CHAPTER 14

14.1   What is the basic difference between PUMS files and STF files?

14.2   Could you use a PUMS file if you wanted to determine the correlation among individuals between family income and educational attainment?

14.3   Could you use an STF file if you wanted to determine the correlation among individuals between family income and educational attainment?

14.4   When is it necessary to use a FILE TYPE command with a PUMS file?

14.5   In using an STF file, if you wanted to produce tables for the county geographic level only, what would you do?

14.6   In using an STF file, if you wanted to produce tables for the total population and for the Spanish-origin populations only, what would you do?

14.7   Suppose that using an STF file you want to produce for SMSAs the table of number of households in each household-value category. Why would you need a variable name for each category in the distribution of household values?

14.8   Why are the 0 values in an STF file problematic?

ASSIGNMENT QUESTIONS FOR CHAPTER 14

14.1   For the PUMS80 file used in the example in Section 14.1, what SPSS commands would be necessary to produce a FREQUENCIES run of the variable MARITAL for individuals only?

14.2   For the PUMS80 file, what SPSS commands would be necessary to produce a FREQUENCIES run of the variable FAMINCOM for households only?

14.3 For the PUMS80 file, what SPSS commands would be necessary to produce a CROSSTABS of FAMINCOM by MARITAL?

14.4 Assuming that the following commands are correct and that no information has been suppressed, what additional SPSS commands would be needed to produce a table showing the name and total population size (POPSIZE) for each county?

(The VALUE LABEL information in the following commands shows how SUMRYLV and RECOIND are coded.)

```
DATA LIST   FILE=STF   RECORDS=6
 /1 SUMRYLV 10-11   RECOIND 16-17  (A)   POPSIZE 107-108
     AREANAME 145-174  (A)
VALUE LABELS   SUMRYLV  8 'SMSA'   17 'COUNTY'   24 'CENSUS
               TRACT'
VALUE LABELS   RECOIND  0 'TOTAL'  1 'WHITE'  2 'BLACK'
               3 'HISPANIC'
```

14.5 What SPSS commands would you need to add to produce a table of the total population, the black population, and the area name for SMSAs?

15

DOING SPSS WITH A PERSONAL COMPUTER

There are nuisances involved with using a mainframe computer that is part of a complex installation: You need to master the operating system. Turnaround time can be slow when usage is heavy. The system can be down due to part failures or maintenance needs. You or your department may be charged for services. Or you may have to submit several jobs with annoying interruptions before you are able to debug all the errors in your program. One solution to these problems is SPSS/PC+, a version of SPSS designed for personal computers (PCs).*

15.1 Is SPSS/PC+ Right for You?

Even aside from the problems with learning to use and relying on a mainframe system, SPSS/PC+ has some nifty advantages over SPSS. A HELP command enables you to ask for help with commands, subcommands, and options while you are entering the program. A REVIEW command activates an editor program that enables you to change your latest output using the top part of the screen,

---

*References to the user manual in this chapter are to *SPSS/PC+ for the IBM PC/XT/AT* by Marija J. Norušis (Chicago: SPSS Inc., 1986).

while at the bottom of the screen you can make changes in the set of commands that produced the output.

If you want to do part of your work on a personal computer and part of your work on a mainframe, and be able to ship data and command files back and forth, SPSS/PC+ provides for this purpose a communication package called *Kermit,* developed at Columbia University.

An important consideration, however, before you rush out and purchase SPSS/PC+ is the computer hardware requirements. Our discussion in this paragraph presumes you have a basic knowledge of PC hardware. If you don't, take the information here to whoever advises you on these matters. You need not understand the following terminology to operate SPSS/PC+, but you must be sure that your system will support SPSS/PC+ before you purchase it. Use of SPSS/PC+ requires what is by today's standards a modest personal computer system. You will need a RAM (random access memory) of at least 640K and a hard disk with at least 20 megabytes of storage space. To ensure adequate RAM when using the more demanding procedures, a RAM of 640K (the maximum manageable by DOS) is recommended, as is a math coprocessor to provide greater speed.

The SPSS/PC+ software is extensive and somewhat expensive. In 1992 the basic package cost $195. The Advanced Statistics, Harvard Graphics, and Tables enhancements cost an additional $295 each. The Advanced Statistics enhancement has the following procedures: FACTOR, DISCRIMINANT, MANOVA, CLUSTER, QUICK CLUSTER, and HILOGLINEAR. The Harvard Graphics module allows you to link with the popular Harvard Graphics program, if you have the latter installed. The Tables package enables you to customize tables, a feature also available in mainframe SPSS by using the TABLES command. There are several other modules and new ones are created periodically. The prices of the enhancements change over time. There are volume discounts and, for academic institutions, site-licensing contracts and student software that reduce the software costs.

A nice feature is that the number of cases for most procedures is not limited. You are, however, limited to using 500 variables when operating SPSS/PC+. Larger data files would have to be split into smaller files to run with SPSS/PC+.

Despite these requirements and limitations, the typical user of SPSS will want to use SPSS/PC+ because of the HELP and REVIEW features and, perhaps most of all, because of the psychological boost of feeling in control of the entire process.

15.2 Entering the SPSS/PC+ Program

There are two approaches for entering data and commands: one is the Review editor program and the other is the Menu mode. As you become proficient, you will use both of these approaches, switching from one to the other in the same session. This chapter assumes that SPSS/PC+ Version 2.0 or Version 3.0 has been installed on your machine.

A preliminary step before using SPSS/PC+ is to create a separate directory for your work apart from the directory containing the SPSS/PC+ command files. (A **directory** is assigned work space in your disk memory.) We will name the directory YOURID to remind you that you should make a directory for your own work to keep it apart from that of other users.

For most PC systems, once you turn the machine on, it runs through about a minute of system checks. Then the DOS prompt C⟩ appears with the cursor next to it. At that point, type the command

```
md  yourid
```

Then press the Enter key (on some keyboards this will be labeled Return or ↵). These actions create a new directory named YOURID. The name we've used is arbitrary; choose one that is easy to remember and easy to type. Change to this new directory by executing the command

```
cd  yourid
```

Normally, YOURID directory would be used to store your data files, command files, and output files. Your instructor, however, may have you store these files on your own diskette to save space on the systems hard disk. If this is the case, you would add a designator of where this diskette is when saving or retrieving files. Most likely it will be in a disk drive called A. To refer to a diskette on that drive, add A: as a prefix to the file name. In this case, to save the file project you would use the command

```
save  file 'a:project'.
```

Once in the YOURID (or whatever you've named it) directory, you start the SPSS/PC+ program by entering the command

```
spsspc
```

In the SPSS/PC+ program there is more than one way to enter commands. Our next section describes using the Review editor in its Edit mode.

15.3 Using SPSS/PC+ through the Review Editor

When you first enter the SPSS/PC+ program, a box titled Main Menu (see Figure 15.1) appears at the top left of your screen. On the top right is a box titled Orientation. The bottom half of the screen is a blank space that is identified as "scratch.pad" by a title along the bottom.

At this time you are in Menu mode (we'll explain this mode later in this chapter) and even though the cursor is in scratch.pad, if you try to type characters there, unexpected menu commands can occur.

Shift into the Review program Edit mode by holding down the Alt key while you press the M key. Do that now.

FIGURE 15.1 REVIEW Editor Program Main Menu

```
┌──────────────────────────────────────────────────────────────────┐
│ ┌──── MAIN MENU ─────────────────┬─────── orientation ─────────┐   │
│ │ orientation                    │ The "orientation" section provides a brief │
│ │ read or write data             │ explanation of how the SPSS/PC+ Menu and   │
│ │ modify data or files           │ Help system works.  If you have not used the │
│ │ graph data                     │ Menu and Help system before,  you may want to │
│ │ analyze data                   │ read through the screens in the orientation. │
│ │ session control & info         │                                            │
│ │ run DOS or other pgms          │ To do so, press ◄─┘ (Enter).               │
│ │ - extended menus —             │                                            │
│ │ - SPSS/PC+ options -           │ Part A of the SPSS/PC+ V2.0 manual contains a │
│ │ FINISH                         │ more complete introduction to the Menu and │
│ │                                │ Help system.                               │
│ │                                │                                            │
│ │                                │ ── F1= Help  Alt-E=Edit  Alt-M=Menus On/Off── │
│ │                                                                  │
│ │                                                                  │
│ └──────────────────── Ins ─────────────────────── Std Menus ──────┘   │
│                           scratch.pad                              │
└──────────────────────────────────────────────────────────────────┘
```

In Edit mode, the Main Menu is gone from the top of your screen. The top part of the screen is now a display area for the listing or output of your commands. "Edit mode—press Esc to resume menu mode" should appear at the bottom of your screen. This indicates that you are in the Edit mode. Although pressing the Escape key will resume the Menu mode, we recommend that you develop the habit of using the Alt-M key combination to move back and forth between the Menu mode and the Edit mode. The advantage of Alt-M is that it will shift you either way between the Review modes.

Now you can enter numbers and letters on the line where the cursor is positioned simply by typing what you want. This enables you to type into scratch.pad (we'll call this the scratch pad) the commands, variable names, and data you wish to use. Press the F10 key and then the Enter key to run the commands from the cursor line on.

What if you make a typing mistake? While in the Review editor, use the Backspace key to move the cursor back over the error—this will cause it to be erased.

The Review editor can be used in two modes: Insert and Replace. In the Insert mode, what you type will be inserted to the left of the cursor. In the Replace mode, what you type will replace or type over the character indicated by the cursor. When Review is in Insert mode, the word *Ins* appears at the bottom right of the screen. If you press the Insert key, the editor shifts from Insert mode to Replace mode and the word *Ins* disappears. Press the Insert key again, and the editor goes back into Insert mode.

15.4 Using the Review Editor to Perform a Run and Save the Output

Once into SPSS/PC+ you are ready to begin your own program. You can perform a run by typing data definition commands, BEGIN DATA, the data, END DATA, and the control commands into the scratch pad.

Use the Review editor to enter the following lines.

```
data list /
    id        1—2
    educ      3—4
    sex       5
    happy     6.
begin data.
010912
021223
```

```
031521
041222
050611
061612
071522
081612
091821
101412
111321
121611
130922
141212
151221
161821
170821
181222
191613
20142
end data.
missing values
     educ      (-9)
     happy
     sex       (0).
list.
```
save file 'project'.

To run this program, place the cursor on the line of the first command that you want entered (DATA LIST), and then press the F10 key. SPSS/PC+ will print a prompt asking whether you want to "Run from the cursor" or "Exit to prompt". "Run from the cursor" is highlighted, indicating that this action will be performed if you press the Enter key. This is what we want to happen continuing until the last line in the scratch pad. (If you had wanted the other option, you would need to move the highlight to "Exit to prompt" with the LeftArrow key.)

As the commands are executed, the output will appear on the screen; at the same time the output is stored in a file named SPSS.LIS. When the output from your commands is printed on the screen, the MORE is displayed in the upper-right corner to indicate that there is more output to follow. Press the Enter key to print further output on the screen. Until all the lines have printed once, you cannot scroll back to previous screens.

Once the commands have run, you will no longer be in Edit mode. You will be in Menu mode with the submitted commands in the scratch pad. By reentering Edit mode (hold down the Alt key and press the M key), you can view your program's output on the top half of the screen. Press the F2 key and SPSS/PC+ will give you a Switch window's prompt. Press the Enter key and you will enter the upper part of the screen where your output is. You can use the Arrow, Page-Up, and PageDown keys to move through the output. You can insert, delete, and perform other word-processing functions in this screen just as you can in the scratch pad.

Your output should show the variable names and entries for each case in your file. You can save it by pressing the F9 key and responding to prompts. Do this now, and name the listing OUT1. If your instructor wants you to save the output on your own diskette, call the file to be saved A:OUT1. The A: indicates that the file is to be saved on a diskette in your computer's A drive.

The reason for saving the output in the SPSS.LIS file to a different file is that SPSS.LIS will be erased the next time you enter the SPSS/PC+ program.

To print the output, press the F9 key and follow the prompts. If you are content with the output, you may also want to save the file that created it. Switch back to the scratch pad by pressing the F2 key. Then press the F9 key and follow the prompts to indicate that you want to save the file and name it PROG1. That way you will know which program file produced the output, and you will be able to reuse it.

To retrieve files that you have saved back into the Review editor, press the F3 key. A prompt will ask you to enter the name of the file you want to retrieve. (If your file is on a diskette in the A drive you will have to add the A: prefix to the file name.) If you do not remember the file name, before pressing the F3 key, hold down the Alt key and press F.

If there is a command error in a run, SPSS/PC+ will give an error message and then return you to the menu concerning the command in which there was an error. Go to the Review editor mode (hold down the Alt key and press M). Then correct the errors and resubmit the commands by positioning the cursor on the line of the first command you want to run and press F10.

If it was a large output with more errors than you can easily note in the listing, enter the Review editor mode and submit the command REVIEW LOG. This will bring up on the screen the submitted commands and SPSS/PC+'s responses to the commands including error messages; it omits the procedure output. You can correct the errors in this file. Then resubmit the run by placing the cursor on the line of the first command you want run and pressing F10. The bracketed comments will be ignored, so you do not have to delete them.

The SPSS.LOG file is deleted when you reenter the SPSS/PC+ program. To save this file, press the F9 key, highlight that you wish to save the whole file, and press the Enter key. Then following the prompt, enter the name you want the saved file to have. (Remember to add the A: prefix if the file is to be saved on a diskette in the A drive.)

The Alt-E key combination will take you out of the SPSS.LOG and back to the Review editor.

15.5 Review Editor Line and Block Commands

Review also allows you to perform more complicated operations. If you press the F1 key while in the editor, it will change the bottom line of the screen and highlight the choice "Review Help". Since at the bottom of this screen the words *Review Help* are highlighted, pressing the enter key will summon up the Review Help screen. In this screen, shown in Figure 15.2, you can see the function keys to press to perform various operations. Reading down the left col-

---

FIGURE 15.2 REVIEW Editor Program Help Screen

```
┌──────────────────────Guide to Review Function Keys──────────────────────┐
│                                                                          │
│  Information         F1   Review Help and Menus, Variable and File Lists, Glossary │
│  Windows             F2   Switch Window, Change Window Size              │
│  Input Files         F3   Insert File, Edit Different File               │
│  Lines               F4   Insert, Delete, Undelete                       │
│  Search & Replace    F5   Search for Text, Replace Text                  │
│  Go To               F6   Area, Output Page, Line in Error, After Last Line Executed │
│  Define Area         F7   Mark/Unmark Lines, Rectangle, or Command       │
│  Area Actions        F8   Copy, Move, Delete, Round Numbers, Copy Glossary Entry │
│  Output File         F9   Write Area or File, Delete File                │
│  Run                 F1Ø  Run Commands from Cursor or Marked Area, Exit to Prompt │
│                                                                          │
│  ┌────────────────── Guide To Menu Commands ──────────────────────┐      │
│  │  Enter (◄──┘)         Paste Selection & Move Down One Level in Menu │  │
│  │  Tab or (──►)         Temporarily Paste Selection & Move Down One Level │ │
│  │  ESC or (◄── )        Remove Last Temporary Paste & Move Up One Level │ │
│  │  Alt-ESC              Jump To Main Menu (Also Ctrl-ESC)          │      │
│  │  Alt-K                Kill All Temporary Pastes                 │      │
│  │  Alt-T                Get Typing Window                         │      │
│  │  Alt-E                Switch to Edit Mode                       │      │
│  │  Alt-M                Remove Menus                              │      │
│  │  Alt-X                Switch between Standard and Extended Menus │     │
│  │  Alt-Cursor Pad       Scroll Help Windows and Glossary (if NumLock Off) │ │
│  └─────────────────────────────────────────────────────────────────┘     │
│                                                                          │
│        Enter Command or Press F1 for More Help or Escape to Continue     │
└──────────────────────────────────────────────────────────────────────────┘
```

FIGURE 15.3 REVIEW Editor Program Cursor Control Help Screen

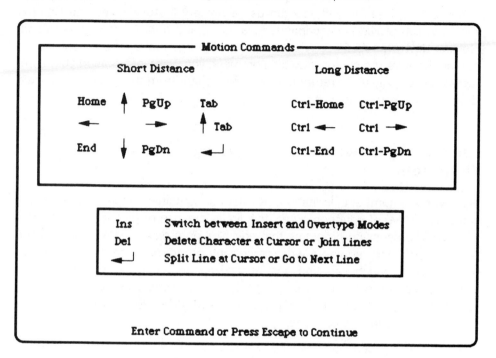

umn, you see that you have choices ranging from "Information" to "Run". The fourth choice down from the top is "Lines". To the right appears *F4;* this indicates that the F4 function key allows you to perform line operations. To the right of F4 are the words *Insert, Delete, Undelete;* these are the operations that can be performed on lines.

The F7 key marks blocks of lines for moving, copying, and deleting; the F8 key executes these operations. Blocks of lines from SPSS.LOG can also be run or saved. Use the F7 key and the prompts that follow to indicate the line beginning the block and the line ending the block.

At the bottom of the screen appears a message indicating that you can obtain more information about using the Review editor by pressing the F1 key. Press the F1 key. The screen reproduced in Figure 15.3 will appear. This information indicates how you can move the cursor around the scratch pad when you are in the Edit mode.

15.6 Review Editor Context Menu

When editing a command you can use a Review feature called the Context menu, which provides descriptions, examples, and options of the command. Holding down the ALT key while pressing M brings the Context menu to the screen. Be sure the cursor is on the command you want information about, before you press Alt-M. To return to the Review editor from the Menu mode, hold down the Alt key while pressing M.

15.7 Using Other Word-Processing Programs

Review has a number of limitations. Its files are contained in the random access memory (RAM) of your computer; this limits the size of files it can edit more than word-processing programs that edit files on a disk. It lacks some of the functions of more powerful word-processing programs such as WordStar or WordPerfect, which can find and replace words, or allow you to undo a command entered by mistake. These other programs can be used in their nondocument or ASCII mode for compiling SPSS/PC+ files. In using other editors *note the following cautions:*

- Line length cannot exceed 80 characters.
- Line wrap-around features cannot be used. End each line with a carriage return keystroke.
- Special features such as boldface or underline cannot be used.
- See the *SPSS/PC+ V2.0 Base Manual* pages, G3–G4, for a more detailed description of the use of other editors.

You can exit the SPSS/PC+ program by typing the line FINISH at the end of your scratch pad. Then press the F10 key. The "Run from cursor" option will appear as a highlighted prompt. Press Return and you will be taken out of the SPSS/PC+ program.

15.8 Using the NORC90 File

Let's look at a larger data set and practice using the GET command at the same time. Presuming your instructor has stored the NORC90 data set on the SPSS directory, you can call up this large data set with the GET FILE command and then use the FREQUENCIES command to discover the distribution by education, sex, and happiness. The necessary program would be

```
get file 'norc90'.
frequencies educ
          sex
          happy/
          statistics.
```

Enter those lines now and run them by placing the cursor on the GET FILE NORC90 line and pressing the F10 key. When the output has scrolled by and you are in the Menu mode, press Alt-M to return to the Edit menu. Press F2 and then press the Enter key to switch to the output screen. This output can be edited with the Review editor and then saved by pressing the F9 key followed by the Enter key. Do this now and save it as OUT2. (Remember to include the A: prefix if you are saving it to a diskette in the A drive.)

Return to the scratch pad by pressing the F2 key and then the Enter key. Save the program as PROG2 by pressing the F9 key and entering PROG2 as the file name and pressing the Enter key.

In this and previous sections we have shown you how to enter SPSS/PC+ and use the Review editor to enter commands and data, to save programs and save output. In the next section we explore how the same type of work can be done using the Menu mode.

15.9 Using the SPSS/PC+ Menus and the Review Editor

If you have not exited SPSS/PC+, do so now. Otherwise when you call up the PROJECT file with the SPSS/PC+ Menus mode, you'll receive an error message that the PROJECT file is already the active file.

The Menu mode allows you to "paste" commands into the scratch pad without typing. It's great for those of us with ten thumbs! But it requires some attention, practice, and patience to learn to use this mode.

When you go into SPSS/PC+, the program is in Menu mode. You know you are not in Edit mode because the line "Edit mode—press Escape to resume menu mode" is *not* on a line beneath the top boxes. Using direction arrows or typing the first letter of a command will shift the highlight up and down the column of menu choices. Pressing the Enter key (labeled Return or ↵ on some keyboards) or the RightArrow key will shift the screen to a submenu, and once again you move the highlight to the keyword or specification that you want. Pressing the Enter key when a command is highlighted will "paste" it into the scratch pad. When you enter SPSS/PC+, the box titled Main Menu is in the upper-left portion of the screen.

Do not press any keys until told to do so in this section. Throughout this section if you press keys before instructed to do so you may jump into sub-menus and become hopelessly lost. If this happens, you can press the Escape key a series of times. Each time you press the Escape key you will move further up the submenu hierarchy until eventually you will have returned to the Main Menu screen. (Holding down the Alt key and pressing the Escape key is a one-step method of returning to the Main Menu screen.) But then you will have to retrace your steps to catch up with the text discussion.

If you type a letter that corresponds to the first letter of one of the Main Menu lines, the highlight that is behind Orientation at the beginning will move to that line. Try typing an R (lowercase and uppercase letters will be treated the same by SPSS/PC+). The highlight moves down to the "Read or write data" line and the writing in the Orientation box changes to a description of what the commands in the "Read or write data" section will allow you to do.

The highlight can also be moved by using the Arrow keys. Press the DownArrow key and the highlight will move from the "Read or write data" line to the "Modify data or files" line.

As the highlight moves, the Orientation box contents change so that it contains a description of what is highlighted. Press the UpArrow so that the highlight returns to the "Read or write data" line. Note that there is a right arrow indicator at the end of the line. This means that there is more information available about this topic than is in the Orientation box. You can move further into the "Read or write data" menus in two ways, one in the Menu mode and one in the Edit mode.

First you can simply press the Enter key on your keyboard. Press the Enter key now and see what happens. You should now be looking at a screen that has a box labeled "Read or write data" on the top left. The highlight is behind DE and the box on the top right contains a description of what the DE command does. Type G to move the highlight to GET. Then press the Enter key and note how GET is placed into the scratch pad.

At the same time you are moved to the next GET submenu. The highlight covers !/FILE ' '. The ! indicates that this command is required. Press the Enter key and note that FILE ' ' is added to the GET command. You can see the file names in your directory by striking the Esc key and then holding the Alt key while pressing the Enter key. This brings up a screen which has a list of your directory files. Assuming you have already saved the file PROJECT on your directory, move the highlight with the Arrow keys to PROJECT and press Enter. That file name is placed on the GET FILE line between the single quotation marks. The line should now read

```
get file 'project'.
```

To add a FREQUENCIES command, move the highlight to the "Analyze data" line and press the Enter key. The menu presents a new set of choices. Highlight F and press the Enter key. You are shown examples of FREQUENCIES commands.

If there are errors in your command, shift to the Review editor by holding down the Alt key and pressing the E key. Once in the Review editor, make whatever corrections are necessary. Now pressing the F10 key and Return will run this command.

The alternative to pasting in commands with the Menu mode is to enter the commands using the Review Edit mode as described in Sections 15.2 to 15.7. The Edit mode of entering lines is easier to control and is the best approach for most new users of SPSS/PC+.

15.10 Submitting Commands and Data from a File: INCLUDE and GET

A non-SPSS file containing commands, data, or both can be submitted as a **batch** to be executed all together with the command **INCLUDE.** Follow the command with the name of the file you want submitted enclosed in single quotes. Thus, to submit a file named NORC84, the complete INCLUDE command would be

```
INCLUDE   'NORC84'.
```

If, for the first example in this chapter, the DATA LIST and data were stored in a file named NORC84, our total set of commands for a LIST procedure would be

```
INCLUDE   'NORC84'.
LIST.
```

SPSS/PC+ also has the capability of reading SPSS portable system files from an SPSS mainframe system. A portable file is in a format that can be read by modem programs that can upload a file from a microcomputer to a mainframe or download a file from a mainframe to a microcomputer. Such files are created with the EXPORT command and read with the IMPORT command. An example of the process is given in the next section.

SPSS/PC+ can read files from most editor, spreadsheet, and database programs that use DOS as an operating system. These files are submitted using the INCLUDE command. (See the SPSS/PC+ user manual for an explanation of possibly required alterations to the data files.)

15.11 Downloading from and Uploading to a Mainframe Computer: KERMIT, IMPORT, and EXPORT

With SPSS/PC+ comes a program called *Kermit* that can be used to ship files back and forth between a mainframe computer with SPSS and a microcomputer with SPSS/PC+. Kermit must be present in both the mainframe and the microcomputer systems; it is distributed free of charge to licensed SPSS installations by SPSS Inc. You will want to use Kermit because SPSS portable files contain special characters that are not communicated correctly by other programs.

To use Kermit, following the DOS prompt **C>** enter the command

KERMIT

This command produces the prompt **Kermit-MS>** and the message that you can receive help about what command to enter next by entering a question mark (?). At any point when entering Kermit commands, you can enter a ? and the program will describe your options. To communicate with a mainframe (or another PC computer system), you enter the command **CONNECT.** You will then be connected to the mainframe system, and you can log on in your system's normal manner. The next step is to give the command to run Kermit on your mainframe system. You will receive a **Kermit-__>** prompt (where the last two characters before the > will depend on which system you are using). Use the command **SEND** followed by the file name to send a file. Use the command **RECEIVE** followed by the file name to receive a file. Use the command **CTRL]C** to go from the mainframe to the PC and the command **CONNECT** to go from the PC to the mainframe.

You must first send the file from one system and then move to the other system to receive it. If you take more than 5 seconds, the first part of the transmission will appear garbled, but don't worry—it will be retransmitted. At both the mainframe and the PC, use the command **EXIT** to leave Kermit. An example of using Kermit is provided in the SPSS/PC+ manual on pages F–4 to F–5.

Kermit must be used when you want to transmit SPSS system files. Other microcomputer communication programs such as PC-TALK III and CROSSTALK cannot transfer SPSS/PC+ system files or portable system files. These communication programs can, however, transfer the non-SPSS system files read and written by SPSS/PC+, such as data files, listings of output, or sets of commands.

To access an SPSS portable file from your PC, use the command IMPORT FILE= followed by the name of the file enclosed by apostrophes. To create an SPSS portable file from your PC, use the command EXPORT FILE= followed by the name of the file enclosed by apostrophes.

15.12 Differences between SPSS/PC+ and SPSS

We mentioned earlier that SPSS/PC+ commands must end with a period or be followed by a blank line, that commands need not begin in column 1 and continuations need not begin after column 1, and that SPSS/PC+ cannot handle more than 200 variables. SPSS/PC+ also differs from SPSS in the names of some commands. The following list shows the SPSS command and the corresponding SPSS/PC+ command:

SPSS Command	*Corresponding SPSS/PC+ Command*
N OF CASES	N
MATCH FILES and ADD FILES	JOIN
COMMENT	*

There are also differences between SPSS and SPSS/PC+ in the OPTIONS and STATISTICS of most commands. Use the Menu mode to highlight a command and check what OPTIONS and STATISTICS are available.

15.13 Summary

This chapter introduced the Review editor. The Review editor has many features of word-processing programs. Furthermore, it allows you to

1.   run commands from within SPSS/PC+;

2.   obtain help about a command the cursor is on by holding down the Alt key while pressing the M key;

3.   see the list of variable names in an active file by holding down the Alt key while pressing the V key;

4.   see the list of files in your directory by holding down the Alt key while pressing the F key.

Pressing the F1 key while in Review will bring up a Help menu that explains line and file management function keys. Pressing the F1 key when in the first Help menu will bring up a second Help menu that explains cursor movement function keys.

Commands are executed by moving the cursor to the first command in the run, pressing the F10 key, and then the Enter key.

Commands are stored after execution in the SPSS.LOG file. Output is stored after appearing on the screen in the SPSS.LIS file. To retain the information in these files for use in future sessions you must save them under a different name, because they are erased each time you enter SPSS/PC+.

Differences in syntax between SPSS/PC+ and SPSS include the following:

- SPSS/PC+ can begin commands after column 1 and continuations of commands in column 1.
- The end of a command is signaled with a period or a blank line.
- In SPSS/PC+, certain commands have been renamed:
    BREAKDOWN is replaced by MEANS
    COMMENT is replaced by *
    CONDESCRIPTIVE is replaced by DESCRIPTIVES
    MATCH FILES and ADD FILES are replaced by JOIN
    N OF CASES is replaced by N
    PEARSON CORR is replaced by CORRELATION

15.14 Where to Look in the *SPSS Reference Guide*

There is no explanation of how to use SPSS/PC+ or of translating between SPSS and SPSS/PC+. SPSS/PC+ comes with a 400-page manual entitled *SPSS/PC+ for the IBM PC/XT/AT.* A manual also comes with each of the SPSS/PC+ enhancements—SPSS/PC+ Tables, SPSS/PC+ Advanced Statistics, and others.

RESEARCH PROJECT WORK FOR CHAPTER 15

1. Use the Review editor to enter and store in a permanent file the data you gathered on the questionnaires doing the research project in Chapter 1.

2. Use the Review editor to create a permanent file with the commands you wrote for the research projects in Chapters 2 and 3.

3. Write a LIST ALL and a FREQUENCIES ALL program for your research project data.

REVIEW QUESTIONS FOR CHAPTER 15

15.1 How would you create a directory named YOURID from which to work?

15.2 How would you enter a directory named YOURID?

15.3 How would you enter the SPSS/PC+ program once you were in the YOURID directory?

15.4 How would you enter the Edit mode once you were in the SPSS/PC+ Review editor?

15.5 What key will erase an error? What key will delete an error and move to the left the remaining text?

15.6 How do you find out what the Review editor function keys do?

15.7 How do you find out how to move the cursor more effectively while in the Review editor?

15.8 What key combination will move you to the top of a Review file?

15.9 What key combination will move you to the bottom of a Review file?

15.10 What key will move Review back and forth between the Insert mode and the Replace mode?

15.11 How do you run a program that is in the Review editor?

15.12 What do you have to do when the word *MORE* appears in the upper-right corner of the screen?

15.13 When the commands in your Review program have executed will you be in the Edit mode or the Menu mode?

15.14 How do you move Review back and forth between the Edit mode and the Menu mode?

15.15 On what file is your output stored?

15.16 Will your output file be stored permanently?

15.17 How would you save your output to be used in another SPSS/PC+ session?

15.18 How would you print your output?

15.19 On what file are your commands stored?

15.20 How would you save your commands to be used in another SPSS/PC+ session?

15.21 How would you retrieve a stored file of commands back into Review?

15.22 How would you obtain help concerning a command you were entering or editing?

ASSIGNMENT QUESTIONS FOR CHAPTER 15

15.1 Describe the commands necessary to create and move to a directory named JH.

15.2 Once your computer was turned on and you were at the C⟩ prompt, how would you enter the SPSS/PC+ Review editor mode from an existing directory named JH?

15.3 Once in the Review editor mode, how would you retrieve a program named PROG1 from the MYID directory?

15.4 Having retrieved a file named PROG1 into Review, how would you run it?

15.5 If your program did not run correctly, how would you return to Review's Edit mode?

15.6 If there was an error in your FREQUENCIES command and you wanted to look at an example of a correct FREQUENCIES command in Review, what would you do?

15.7 If you could not remember the name of a file you wanted to retrieve, how could you see a list of the files on your directory?

15.8 If PROG1 ran, how would you scroll through the output.

15.9 If the output was correct, how would you print it?

15.10 How would you save a listing to a permanent file named OUT3?

APPENDIX A
SPECIAL TOPICS

A.1 COUNT

The **COUNT** command allows you to create a new variable by counting the number of times a given value occurs for a set of variables. For example, we could count the number of times a respondent gave the most positive response to the first five questions of the Happiness Questionnaire in Appendix C. We create the new variable SAT#MAX as follows:

```
COUNT    SAT#MAX=HAPPY  HEALTH  SATFAM  SATFRND  SATJOB  (1)
```

More than one value can be used in the COUNT command. We could, therefore, count the number of times a respondent gave one of the two most positive responses on the same questions:

```
COUNT    SAT#POS=HAPPY  HEALTH  SATFAM  SATFRND  SATJOB  (1,2)
```

More than one variable can be created with one COUNT command. Separate the new variables with a slash. For example, we could have created the two variables SAT#MAX and SAT#POS with one command:

```
COUNT    SAT#MAX=HAPPY  HEALTH  SATFAM  SATFRND  SATJOB  (1) /

         SAT#POS=HAPPY  HEALTH  SATFAM  SATFRND  SATJOB  (1,2)
```

If all the data are missing for the variables being used in the COUNT command, the new variable will have a value of 0. If you want to eliminate cases with all missing data, use a SELECT IF command before the COUNT command.

The keywords LO, HI, and THRU can be used with the COUNT within the parentheses to specify the values to be counted.

A.2 DO IF

DO IF instructs SPSS to carry out the operations that follow up to **END IF.** The advantage is that processing time is not wasted on cases that do not meet the initial condition. For example, suppose you want to analyze the traits of immigrants to the United States who are coded 2 on the variable NATIVE. The following commands would recode the variable YRIMMIG for immigrants only; it would not apply to nonimmigrants. These commands also create a new variable, CLASS, that is coded 1 for cases that are coded over 25000 on the variable INCOME. Other cases will have a value of 0. (These variables are from a census public use sample, not NORC90.)

```
DO IF   NATIVE EQ 2
RECODE   YRIMMIG (LO TO 1959=1) (1960 TO 1969=2)
                 (1970 TO 1979=3) (1980 TO HI=4)
COMPUTE   YEARS=YRIMMIG-1986
IF   INCOME GT 25000   CLASS=1
IF   INCOME LE 25000   CLASS=0
END IF
```

Without the DO IF-END IF sequence, the transformations done in the one RECODE command would require four IF commands. In addition to processing time, the DO IF-END IF commands can save the programmer considerable time by doing transformations with fewer commands. When many transformations are involved, this succinctness is a great advantage.

Two commands that can be used within the DO IF-END IF commands are ELSE IF and ELSE. **ELSE IF** refers to another subset of the file not specified by the DO IF specifications. **ELSE** refers to all the remaining cases not specified on the DO IF command or on any ELSE IF commands. You can use only one ELSE command, and it must follow the last ELSE IF command within the DO IF-END IF sequence. The following commands elaborate this section's first example using ELSE IF and ELSE.

```
DO IF   NATIVE EQ 2
RECODE   YRIMMIG (LO TO 1959=1) (1960 TO 1969=2)
                 (1970 TO 1979=3) (1980 TO HI=4)
COMPUTE   YEARS=YRIMMIG-1986
IF   INCOME GT 25000   CLASS=1
```

```
IF   INCOME LE 25000   CLASS=0
ELSE IF   NATIVE EQ 1
RECODE   BIRTHPL  (LO TO  15=1) (16 TO  29=2)
                  (30 TO  40=3) (41 TO HI=4)
ELSE
LIST ID
END IF
```

In the elaborated example, the birthplace (BIRTHPL) of cases coded 1 on NATIVE is recoded, and the ID values of cases that are not coded 1 or 2 on NATIVE are listed.

A.3 FREE and LIST Format Statements

In FREE format the user does not need to place the data for each variable in specific columns. All that is necessary is that the data be entered in the correct sequence with one or more blanks between the entries. For example, say we want to enter the income and education of a set of persons and the first person had income of $35,000 and 16 years of education, the second had $9,000 income and 9 years of education, and the third had $130,000 income and 20 years of education. The data entries would be

```
35000  16
9000  9
130000  20
```

The Subcommand FREE or LIST is added to the DATA LIST command before the variable names.

Using string variables in a FREE or LIST format statement requires that you place an A and the maximum number of columns for the variable in parentheses after the variable name. For example, to access a variable NAME—a string variable—and a variable INCOME—not a string variable—with a **FREE** format, the following command could be used:

```
DATA LIST  FREE/ NAME  (A23)   INCOME
```

The greatest advantage of the FREE format is that you do not have to pay attention to column position when entering data. The greatest disadvantage is that you may not notice when you omit the data for a variable.

LIST format is similar to FREE format, except each record begins a new case. Therefore, one cannot use LIST format with multirecord files. However, if data are omitted for one variable, only one case would have data out of sequence, whereas with the FREE format all the subsequent cases would have data out of sequence. To use the LIST format for our example, the DATA LIST command would read:

```
DATA LIST  LIST/ NAME (A23)   INCOME
```

A.4 Multiple Record Files

If the data are spread over more than one record, we need a RECORDS subcommand in the DATA LIST command to indicate how many records each case has. The following example shows the placement of the RECORDS subcommand in the DATA LIST command:

```
DATA LIST  RECORDS=2/1 ID 1-4  SEX 6
                      /2 MARITAL 5
```

Beginning in column one is the task command DATA LIST. This command is followed by RECORDS=2, which tells the program that each case will have two records. The 1 after the slash indicates that the first variable being referred to will be on the first record. ID indicates the name of the first variable we will use. We are assigning the variable name through this command and could name it whatever we want. The 1-4 indicates that the data for this variable are stored in columns 1, 2, 3, and 4. SEX indicates that we will use another variable named SEX. The 6 indicates that the data for SEX are in column 6.

The next line, which begins with /2, is a continuation of the DATA LIST command. *In SPSS all continued commands must begin after column 1.* We indented the line quite a bit to make it more apparent that this line is a continuation of the one above.

Suppose the next variable, marital status, is located in column 5 of the second record. /2 indicates that the next variable will be on the second record. MARITAL indicates our name for the third variable. The 5 indicates that the data for this variable are found in column 5 of the second record. A bit complex? Yes, it is. You may want to read this paragraph a few times to be sure you understand it completely.

A.5 String Variables

String variables may contain nonnumeric characters. To indicate that a variable is a string variable, on the DATA LIST command place an A in parentheses after the column numbers for the variable. For example, if we had a string variable called NAME on columns 1–20 of a single record file, the following DATA LIST command would allow us to access NAME:

```
DATA LIST   NAME 1-20  (A)
```

A string variable cannot be used if multiplication, division, or other arithmetic operations will be performed. A string variable can be used as the variable in MEANS for which other variable means are calculated. For example, one could use MEANS INCOME BY SECTION, where INCOME is not a string variable but SECTION is.

When using FREE or LIST formats, the A in parentheses is followed by the maximum number of columns the variable uses (see Section A.3).

A.6 The Keyword TO

The keyword TO enables you to refer easily to a large number of adjoining variables on your DATA LIST command. For example, suppose you have a data file corresponding to that of the Happiness Questionnaire in Appendix C, in which ID is the first variable, HAPPY is the second, and, after several other variables, AGE is the last. If you want to refer to the variables from HAPPY through AGE on a FREQUENCIES command, you can give the command FREQUENCIES VARIABLES=HAPPY TO AGE instead of specifying each variable separately.

New variables created through IF and COMPUTE commands are added to the end of the variable list in the order that they are created. So, in the preceding example, if you create a new variable called CLASS before the FREQUENCIES command, it will not be included in the specification HAPPY TO AGE. You will have to specify HAPPY TO CLASS to include it.

APPENDIX B
THE SPSS SYSTEM FILES
NORC84 AND NORC90

Codebook for the SPSS System Files NORC84 and NORC90

The SPSS system files NORC84 and NORC90 contain data from the 1984 and 1990 General Social Survey. The General Social Survey is an annual survey conducted by the National Opinion Research Center. Probability samples of 1473 persons in 1984 and 1372 persons in 1990 were taken using multistage cluster sampling. Following is a list of the variable names in alphabetical order and then a list of the variables by column number. On the same line as the variable name is a more descriptive variable label, the question number of the variable, and the column number(s) of the variable in the file. Use the question number to look up more complete information in the questionnaire that follows the lists. In the questionnaire the column numbers of the variable are given in parentheses under the variable name, and the question number appears to the right at the beginning of the question. With the questionnaire is printed the frequency of responses for each value from both the 1984 and 1990 surveys.

Alphabetical Listing of Variables

Variable Name	Variable Label	Question Number	Column Number
ABDEFECT	Abortion if birth defect likely	61	67
ABHLTH	Abortion if mother's health in danger	62	68
ABNOMORE	Abortion if no more children wanted	63	69
ABPOOR	Abortion if family is poor	64	70

Variable Name	Variable Label	Question Number	Column Number
ABRAPE	Abortion if pregnancy from rape	65	71
ABSINGLE	Abortion if unmarried	66	72
AGE	Age of respondent	1	1–2
ANOMIA1	Conditions getting worse	56	62
ANOMIA2	Not fair to bring child into world	57	63
ANOMIA3	Officials neglect average man	58	64
ATTEND	Frequency of religious attendance	17	23
CAPPUN	Feelings about capital punishment	26	32
CHILDS	Number of children	9	15
CLASS	Social class identification	18	24
COMMUN	Feelings about Communism	29	35
CONFINAN	Confidence in banks	41	47
CONBUS	Confidence in major companies	42	48
CONCLER	Confidence in organized religion	43	49
CONEDUC	Confidence in educational institutions	44	50
CONFED	Confidence in presidency	45	51
CONLABOR	Confidence in organized labor	46	52
CONPRESS	Confidence in press	47	53
CONMEDI	Confidence in medicine	48	54
CONTV	Confidence in television	49	55
CONJUDG	Confidence in Supreme Court	50	56
CONSCI	Confidence in scientific community	51	57
CONLEGI	Confidence in congress	52	58
CONARMY	Confidence in military	53	59
DEGREE	Highest school degree of respondent	10	16
DRUNK	Sometimes drink too much	54	60
EDUC	Years of education of respondent	4	7–8
FAIR	Fairness of people	35	41
FINALTER	Changes in financial situation	59	65
GETAHEAD	Get ahead by hard work	60	66
GRASS	Favor legalizing marijuana	28	34

Variable Name	Variable Label	Question Number	Column Number
GUNLAW	Favor gun permits	27	33
HAPPY	Is respondent happy	30	36
HEALTH	Respondent's health	31	37
HELPFUL	Helpfulness of people	34	40
INCOME	Family income	3	5–6
MARITAL	Current marital status	8	14
MAWORK	Was your mother employed	13	19
NATEDUC	Nation spending enough on education	20	26
NATFARE	Nation spending enough on welfare	21	27
PARTYID	Political party identification	32	38
POLVIEWS	Political ideology	33	39
PRESTIGE	Prestige of occupation	6	11–12
RACE	Race of respondent	12	18
REGION	Region of interview	14	20
RELIG	Religious preference	16	22
SATCITY	Satisfaction with city	36	42
SATFAM	Satisfaction with family	37	43
SATFRND	Satisfaction with friendships	38	44
SATJOB	Satisfaction with job	39	45
SATHEALT	Satisfaction with health	40	46
SEX	Sex of respondent	11	17
SIBS	Number of siblings	2	3–4
SMOKE	Do you smoke	55	61
SPKATH	Allow speakers against churches	23	29
SPKCOM	Allow Communists to speak	24	30
SPKHOMO	Allow homosexuals to speak	25	31
SRCBELT	Size of residential city	15	21
TAX	Paying fair federal income tax	22	28
TVHOURS	Average daily TV watching	5	9–10
UNEMP	Ever unemployed in past ten years	19	25
WRKSTAT	Employment status currently	7	13
YEAR	Year of survey	67	73–74

Variables by Column Number

AGE 1–2	SIBS 3–4	INCOME 5–6	EDUC 7–8
TVHOURS 9–10	PRESTIGE 11–12	WRKSTAT 13	MARITAL 14
CHILDS 15	DEGREE 16	SEX 17	RACE 18
MAWORK 19	REGION 20	SRCBELT 21	RELIG 22
ATTEND 23	CLASS 24	UNEMP 25	NATEDUC 26
NATFARE 27	TAX 28	SPKATH 29	SPKCOM 30
SPKHOMO 31	CAPPUN 32	GUNLAW 33	GRASS 34
COMMUN 35	HAPPY 36	HEALTH 37	PARTYID 38
POLVIEWS 39	HELPFUL 40	FAIR 41	SATCITY 42
SATFAM 43	SATFRND 44	SATJOB 45	SATHEALT 46
CONFINAN 47	CONBUS 48	CONCLER 49	CONEDUC 50
CONFED 51	CONLABOR 52	CONPRESS 53	CONMEDI 54
CONTV 55	CONJUDG 56	CONSCI 57	CONLEGI 58
CONARMY 59	DRUNK 60	SMOKE 61	ANOMIA1 62
ANOMIA2 63	ANOMIA3 64	FINALTER 65	GETAHEAD 66
ABDEFECT 67	ABNOMORE 68	ABHLTH 69	ABPOOR 70
ABRAPE 71	ABSINGLE 72	YEAR 73–74	

Questions by Column Number with Frequencies of Responses.

AGE
(1–2)

1. Age (determined by asking date of birth)
   18–90. Actual age
   98. Don't know
   99. No answer

   The actual data are in single year intervals. Grouped into larger categories, the frequencies are as follows:

	1984	1990
18–19	22	19
20–29	371	257
30–39	334	338
40–49	222	254
50–59	173	141

	1984	1990
60–69	185	172
70–79	111	134
80–88	42	47
89+	7	10
99	6	0

SIBS
(3–4)

2. How many brothers and sisters did you have? Please count those born alive but no longer living, as well as those alive now. Also include stepbrothers and stepsisters and children adopted by your parents.

0–24. Actual number
99. No answer

	1984	1990
0	64	64
1	222	224
2	266	261
3	234	243
4	158	164
5	122	119
6	90	88
7	92	60
8	63	49
9	46	31
10	36	23
11	28	22
12	14	10
13	17	4
14	5	5
15	2	1
16	1	0
17	1	2
18	2	0
19	0	1
20	1	0
24	1	0
99	16	1

INCOME
(5–6)

3. Into which of the following groups did your total FAMILY income, from ALL sources, fall last year—before taxes, that is?

	1984		**1990**
1. Under $5,000	127	1. Under $10,000	201
2. $5,000 to $9,999	173	2. $10,000 to $19,999	259
3. $10,000 to $14,999	201	3. $20,000 to $29,999	211
4. $15,000 to $19,999	154	4. $30,000 to $39,999	195
5. $20,000 to $24,999	193	5. $40,000 to $49,999	109
6. $25,000 to $34,999	206	6. $50,000 to $59,999	82
7. $35,000 to $49,999	168	7. $60,000+	172
8. $50,000+	120	97. Refused	73
97. Refused	0	98. Don't know	58
98. Don't know	0	99. No answer	12
99. No answer	180		

EDUC
(7–8)

4. Number of years of formal education.
   0–20. Actual number
   99. No answer.

	1984	**1990**
0	3	4
1	3	1
2	4	5
3	9	1
4	11	9
5	11	5
6	19	19
7	26	14
8	77	58
9	58	52
10	99	53
11	91	81
12	491	436
13	108	106
14	121	167
15	74	62
16	149	163
17	40	44
18	31	49

	1984	1990
19	20	13
20	25	28
99	3	2

TVHOURS
(9–10)

5. On the average day, about how many hours do you personally watch television? (Not asked in 1984.)
   Actual hours.
   97. Not asked
   98. Don't know
   99. No answer

	1990
0	29
1	200
2	261
3	172
4	115
5	67
6	36
7	12
8	14
9	2
10	10
12	5
15	1
17	1
97	444
98	1
99	2

PRESTIGE
(11–12)

6. Hodge/Siegel/Rossi prestige scale score for respondent's occupation.
   12–89. Prestige scale score for job
   99.   No answer

The actual data are by exact score. Grouped into larger categories the frequencies are as follows.

	1984	1990
10–19	150	109
20–29	212	165
30–39	362	370

	1984	**1990**
40–49	311	290
50–59	193	210
60–69	126	105
70–79	20	47
80–89	5	4
99	94	72

WRKSTAT
(13)

7. Last week were you working full-time, working part-time, going to school, keeping house, or what?

	1984	**1990**
1. Working full-time	717	704
2. Working part-time	162	147
3. With a job, but temporarily not at work	34	26
4. Unemployed	49	33
5. Retired	154	194
6. In school	41	48
7. Keeping house	302	199
8. Other	14	21

MARITAL
(14)

8. Are you currently married, widowed, divorced, separated, or have you never been married?

	1984	**1990**
1. Married	829	727
2. Widowed	154	171
3. Divorced	166	171
4. Separated	42	37
5. Never married	282	265
9. No Answer	0	1

CHILDS
(15)

9. How many children have you ever had? Please count all that were born alive at any time (including any you had from a previous marriage).

	1984	**1990**
0	431	392
1	230	208
2	328	341
3	212	215

		1984	**1990**
	4.	134	117
	5.	55	50
	6.	17	26
	7.	19	14
	8. Eight or more.	30	7
	9. No answer	17	2

DEGREE
(16)

10. Highest degree.

	1984	**1990**
0. Less than high school.	400	282
1. High school	764	726
2. Associate/junior college.	54	75
3. Bachelor's.	175	197
4. Graduate.	77	87
9. No Answer.	3	5

SEX
(17)

11. Sex (coded by interviewer).

	1984	**1990**
1. Male	598	604
2. Female	875	768

RACE
(18)

12. What race do you consider yourself?

	1984	**1990**
1. White	1251	1150
2. Black	170	159
3. Other.	52	63

MAWORK
(19)

13. Did your mother ever work for pay for as long as a year, after she was married?

	1984	**1990**
1. Yes.	802	797
2. No	494	412
7. Not Applicable	0	135
8. Don't know.	148	24
9. No answer	29	4

REGION
(20)

14. Region of interview.

	1984	1990
1. New England	78	73
2. Middle Atlantic	217	200
3. East North Central	282	243
4. West North Central	134	134
5. South Atlantic	249	238
6. East South Central	118	105
7. West South Central	128	115
8. Mountain	86	85
9. Pacific	181	179

SRCBELT
(21)

15. Size/type of residence location.

	1984	1990
1. Central city of one of 12 largest Standard Metropolitan Statistical Areas (SMSAs)	128	106
2. Central city of remainder of the 100 largest SMSAs	211	170
3. Suburbs of one of 12 largest SMSAs	165	165
4. Suburbs of the remainder of the 100 largest SMSAs	285	239
5. Other urban (counties having towns of 10,000 or more)	499	496
6. Other rural (counties having no towns of 10,000 or more)	185	196

RELIG
(22)

16. What is your religious preference? Is it Protestant, Catholic, Jewish, some other religion, or no religion?

	1984	1990
1. Protestant	932	862
2. Catholic	375	327
3. Jewish	27	27
4. None	107	109
5. Other	20	42
9. No answer	12	5

ATTEND
(23)

17. How often do you attend religious services?

	1984	1990
0. Never	190	180
1. Less than once a year	107	114
2. About once or twice a year	173	163
3. Several times a year	206	175
4. About once a month	110	105
5. 2–3 times a month	122	127
6. Nearly every week	71	70
7. Every week	345	306
8. Several times a week	136	93
9. Don't know/No answer	13	39

CLASS
(24)

18. If you were asked to use one of four names for your social class, which would you say you belong in: the lower class, the working class, the middle class, or the upper class?

	1984	1990
1. Lower class	66	57
2. Working class	679	623
3. Middle class	670	640
4. Upper class	47	43
8. Don't know	0	4
9. No answer	11	5

UNEMP
(25)

19. At any time during the last ten years, have you been unemployed and looking for work for as long as a month?

	1984	1990
1. Yes	490	265
2. No	978	632
7. Not asked	0	473
9. No answer	0	2

We are faced with many problems in this country, none of which can be solved easily or inexpensively. I'm going to name some of these problems, and for each one I'd like you to tell me whether you think we're spending too much money on it, too little money, or about the right amount. Are we spending too much, too little, or about the right amount on [19, 20]?

NATEDUC
(26)

20. Improving the nation's educational system?

	1984	**1990**
1. Too little	924	478
2. About right	421	156
3. Too much	77	20
7. Not asked	0	698
8. Don't know	0	17
9. No answer	51	3

NATFARE
(27)

21. Welfare?

	1984	**1990**
1. Too little	746	148
2. About right	390	232
3. Too much	280	255
4. Not asked	0	698
5. Don't know	0	35
6. No answer	57	4

TAX
(28)

22. Do you consider the amount of federal income tax that you have to pay to be too high, about right, or too low?

	1984	**1990**
1. Too little	917	531
2. About right	475	331
3. Too low	8	6
7. Not asked	0	455
8. Don't know	0	34
9. No answer	44	15

SPKATH
(29)

23. If somebody who is against all churches and religion wanted to make a speech in your city/town/community against churches and religion, should he be allowed to speak or not?

	1984	1990
1. Yes, allowed to speak	1002	663
2. Not allowed	459	236
7. Not asked	0	455
8. Don't know	0	15
9. No answer	12	3

SPKCOM
(30)

24. Suppose a man who admits he is a Communist wanted to make a speech in your community. Should he be allowed to speak or not?

	1984	1990
1. Yes, allowed to speak	870	589
2. Not allowed	562	298
7. Not asked	0	455
8. Don't know	0	27
9. No answer	41	3

SPKHOMO
(31)

25. Suppose a man who admits he is a homosexual wanted to make a speech in your community. Should he be allowed to speak or not?

	1984	1990
1. Yes	628	674
2. No	792	206
7. Not asked	0	455
8. Don't know	0	34
9. No answer	53	3

CAPPUN   26. Do you favor or oppose the death penalty for persons
(32)   convicted of murder?

	1984	**1990**
1. Favor	1029	1018
2. Oppose	347	264
8. Don't know	0	84
9. No answer	97	6

GUNLAW   27. Would you favor or oppose a law that would require a per-
(33)   son to obtain a police permit before he or she could buy
                a gun?

	1984	**1990**
1. Favor	1034	719
2. Oppose	396	179
7. Not asked	0	455
8. Don't know	0	16
9. No answer	43	3

GRASS   28. Do you think the use of marijuana should be made legal or
(34)   not?

	1984	**1990**
1. Should	332	146
2. Should not	1074	721
7. Not asked	0	473
8. Don't know	0	27
9. No answer	67	5

COMMUN
(35)

29. Thinking about all the different kinds of government in the world today, which of these statements comes closest to how you feel about Communism as a form of government?

	1984	1990
1. It's the worst kind of all	875	501
2. It's bad, but no worse than some others	373	275
3. It's all right for some countries	155	103
4. It's a good form of government	29	6
7. Not asked	0	455
8. Don't know	0	28
9. No answer	41	4

HAPPY
(36)

30. Taken all together, how would you say things are these days—would you say that you are very happy, pretty happy, or not too happy?

	1984	1990
1. Very happy	502	455
2. Pretty happy	756	784
3. Not too happy	187	122
9. No answer	28	11

HEALTH
(37)

31. Would you say your own health, in general, is excellent, good, fair, or poor?

	1984	1990
1. Excellent	437	285
2. Good	697	419
3. Fair	258	162
4. Poor	69	48
7. Not asked	0	455
8. Don't know	0	2
9. No answer	12	1

PARTYID   32. Generally speaking, do you usually think of yourself as a
(38)   Republican, Democrat, Independent, or what?

	1984	**1990**
0. Strong Democrat.................	265	170
1. Not very strong Democrat.........	280	315
2. Independent, close to Democrat ...	209	133
3. Independent (neither, no response)	163	155
4. Independent, close to Republican	156	143
5. Not very strong Republican........	245	280
6. Strong Republican................	125	160
7. Other party, refused to say	22	12
9. No answer	8	4

POLVIEWS 33. I'm going to show you a seven-point scale on which the
(39)   *political* views that people might hold are arranged from
              extremely liberal—point 1—to extremely conservative—
              point 7. Where would you place yourself on this scale?

	1984	**1990**
1. Extremely liberal	29	36
2. Liberal	133	141
3. Slightly liberal....................	177	179
4. Moderate, middle of the road......	568	476
5. Slightly conservative..............	276	240
6. Conservative	186	192
7. Extremely conservative	41	51
8. Don't know.....................	0	53
9. No answer	63	4

HELPFUL
(40)

34. Would you say that most of the time people try to be help-ful or that they are mostly just looking out for themselves?

	1984	1990
1. Try to be helpful	763	464
2. Just look out for themselves	650	372
3. Depends (volunteered)	54	55
7. Not asked	0	473
8. Don't know	0	7
9. No answer	6	1

FAIR
(41)

35. Do you think most people would try to take advantage of you if they got a chance, or would they try to be fair?

	1984	1990
1. Would take advantage of you	507	325
2. Would try to be fair	913	515
3. Depends (volunteered)	47	53
7. Not asked	0	473
9. No answer	6	6

SATCITY
(42)

36. Tell me the number that shows how much satisfaction you get from the city or place you live in.

	1984	1990
1. A very great deal	288	136
2. A great deal	478	299
3. Quite a bit	256	161
4. A fair amount	262	183
5. Some	85	69
6. A little	72	38
7. None	20	12
8. Not asked	0	473
9. No answer	12	1

SATFAM
(43)

37. Tell me the number that shows how much satisfaction you get from your family life.

	1984	1990
1. Very great deal	663	367
2. Great deal	460	305
3. Quite a bit	159	94
4. A fair amount	93	63
5. Some	34	34
6. A little	35	17
7. None	21	17
8. Not asked	0	473
9. No answer	8	1

SATFRND
(44)

38. Tell me the number that shows how much satisfaction you get from your friendships.

	1984	1990
1. Very great deal	534	282
2. Great deal	558	373
3. Quite a bit	179	117
4. A fair amount	134	62
5. Some	27	30
6. A little	26	22
7. None	4	9
8. Not asked		473
9. No answer	11	4

SATJOB
(45)

39. On the whole, how satisfied are you with the work you do—would you say you are very satisfied, moderately satisfied, a little dissatisfied, or very dissatisfied?

	1984	1990
1. Very satisfied	555	481
2. Moderately satisfied	423	413
3. A little dissatisfied	146	109
4. Very dissatisfied	84	38
9. Not applicable due to no job	265	331

SATHEALT
(46)

40. Tell me the number that shows how much satisfaction you get from your health and physical condition.

	1984	**1990**
1. Very great deal	423	225
2. Great deal	500	312
3. Quite a bit	211	137
4. A fair amount	200	130
5. Some	57	47
6. A little	49	31
7. None	23	14
8. Not asked	0	473
9. No answer	10	3

I am going to name some institutions in this country. As far as the *people running* these institutions are concerned, would you say that you have a great deal of confidence, only some confidence, or hardly any confidence at all in them? [40–52]?

CONFINAN
(47)

41. Banks and financial institutions

	1984	**1990**
1. A great deal	310	160
2. Only some	538	520
3. Hardly any	520	198
7. Not asked	0	473
9. No answer	0	21

CONBUS
(48)

42. Major companies

	1984	**1990**
1. A great deal	301	223
2. Only some	561	544
3. Hardly any	85	97
7. Not asked	0	473
8. Don't know	0	33
9. No answer	525	2

CONCLER
(49)

43. Organized religion

	1984	1990
1. A great deal	304	203
2. Only some	457	442
3. Hardly any	184	212
7. Not asked		473
8. Don't know		41
9. No answer	528	1

CONEDUC
(50)

44. Education

	1984	1990
1. A great deal	275	241
2. Only some	579	529
3. Hardly any	102	110
7. Not asked		473
8. Don't know	0	15
9. No answer	517	4

CONFED
(51)

45. Executive branch of the federal government

	1984	1990
1. A great deal	181	210
2. Only some	493	451
3. Hardly any	280	208
7. Not asked	0	473
8. Don't know	0	30
9. No answer	519	0

CONLABOR
(52)

46. Organized labor

	1984	1990
1. A great deal	84	96
2. Only some	517	476
3. Hardly any	353	279
7. Not asked	0	473
8. Don't know	0	47
9. No answer	519	1

CONPRESS
(53)

47. Press

	1984	1990
1. A great deal	166	132
2. Only some	574	516
3. Hardly any	219	219
7. Not asked	0	473
8. Don't know	0	31
9. No answer	514	1

CONMEDI
(54)

48. Medicine

	1984	1990
1. A great deal	499	410
2. Only some	407	418
3. Hardly any	62	61
7. Not asked	0	473
8. Don't know	0	9
9. No answer	505	1

CONTV
(55)

49. TV

	1984	1990
1. A great deal	129	123
2. Only some	558	522
3. Hardly any	278	241
7. Not asked	0	473
8. Don't know	0	13
9. No answer	508	0

CONJUDG
(56)

50. U.S. Supreme Court

	1984	1990
1. A great deal	325	315
2. Only some	497	431
3. Hardly any	121	114
7. Not asked	0	473
8. Don't know	0	39
9. No answer	530	0

CONSCI   51. Scientific community
(57)

	1984	**1990**
1. A great deal	436	335
2. Only some	430	425
3. Hardly any	54	59
7. Not asked	0	473
8. Don't know	0	79
9. No answer	553	1

CONLEGI   52. Congress
(58)

	1984	**1990**
1. A great deal	123	137
2. Only some	622	528
3. Hardly any	212	204
7. Not asked		473
8. Don't know	0	28
9. No answer	516	2

CONARMY   53. Military
(59)

	1984	**1990**
1. A great deal	352	293
2. Only some	473	459
3. Hardly any	125	121
7. Not asked	0	473
8. Don't know		26
9. No answer	523	0

DRUNK   54. Do you sometimes drink more than you think you should?
(60)   0. Total abstainer

	1984	**1990**
1. Yes	456	220
2. No	598	404
7. Not asked	0	736
8. Don't know	0	3
9. No answer	419	9

SMOKE   55. Do you smoke?
(61)

	1984	1990
1. Yes	542	285
2. No	925	612
7. Not asked	0	473
9. No answer	6	2

ANOMIA1   56. In spite of what some people say, the lot/situation/condition of the average man is getting worse, not better. Do
(62)   you more or less agree with that, or more or less disagree?

	1984	1990
1. Agree	819	507
2. Disagree	619	374
7. Not asked	0	455
8. Don't know	0	34
9. No answer	35	2

ANOMIA2   57. It's hardly fair to bring a child into the world with the way
(63)   things look for the future.
                 (Same answers as ANOMIA1, #55)

	1984	1990
1. Agree	587	320
2. Disagree	861	566
7. Not asked	0	455
8. Don't know	0	27
9. No answer	25	4

ANOMIA3   58. Most public officials (people in public office) are not really
(64)   interested in the problems of the average man.

	1984	1990
1. Agree	997	613
2. Disagree	434	275
7. Not asked	0	455
8. Don't know	0	26
9. No answer	42	3

FINALTER
(65)

59. During the last few years, has your financial situation been getting better or getting worse, or has it stayed the same?

	1984	1990
1. Getting better	568	527
2. Getting worse	316	282
3. Stayed the same	577	558
8. Don't know	0	3
9. No answer	12	2

GETAHEAD
(66)

60. Some people say that people get ahead by their own hard work; others say that lucky breaks or help from other people are more important. Which do you think is most important?

	1984	1990
1. Hard work most important	976	598
2. Hard work, luck equally important	264	190
3. Luck most important	219	122
7. Not asked	0	455
8. Don't know	0	5
9. No answer	14	2

Please tell me whether or not *you* think it should be possible for a pregnant woman to obtain a *legal* abortion [60–65].

ABDEFECT
(67)

61. If there is a strong chance of serious defect in the baby.

	1984	1990
1. Yes	1140	715
2. No	281	165
7. Not asked	0	455
8. Don't know	0	35
9. No answer	52	2

ABNOMORE
(68)

62. If she is married and does not want any more children.

	1984	1990
1. Yes	606	396
2. No	814	483
7. Not asked	0	455
8. Don't know	0	33
9. No answer	53	5

ABHLTH
(69)

63. If the woman's health is seriously endangered by the pregnancy.

	1984	1990
1. Yes	1281	814
2. No	150	73
7. Not asked	0	455
8. Don't know	0	27
9. No answer	42	3

ABPOOR
(70)

64. If the family has a very low income and cannot afford any more children.

	1984	1990
1. Yes	654	416
2. No	760	449
7. Not asked	0	455
8. Don't know	0	47
9. No answer	59	5

ABRAPE
(71)

65. If she became pregnant as a result of rape.

	1984	1990
1. Yes	1130	740
2. No	276	133
7. Not asked	0	455
8. Don't know	0	39
9. No answer	67	5

ABSINGLE
(72)

66. If she is not married and does not want to marry the man.

	1984	1990
1. Yes	628	395
2. No	792	477
7. Not asked	0	455
8. Don't know	0	41
9. No answer	53	4

YEAR
(73–74)

67. Year of survey

1984	1990
1473	0
0	1372

APPENDIX C
A COURSE RESEARCH
PROJECT

Completing a research project on your own is much more challenging than using the data we provide in Chapter 2 or in the SPSS system file NORC90. In this appendix we outline a class research project. The subject of this research is happiness, and the questions on this survey come from the SPSS system file NORC90. This similarity will allow you to compare your results with those of a representative national sample.

Following is a questionnaire you can photocopy and use in an interview. The questionnaire is designed so that the interviewer can record in the boxes on the right the numbers that correspond to the respondent's answers. The numbers under the boxes designate the columns in which these data are to be stored when the information is placed in a computer file.

Let us suppose that you are going to administer this questionnaire to 20 people. The obvious question is which 20? One choice would be to go to a store and hand out questionnaires to people leaving the store.

Another choice would be to go to a random selection of households and interview the individuals in these households.

Or you could randomly dial telephone numbers and interview individuals over the phone.

Each of these sampling methods is reasonably good, although there are always problems with biases that might make your sample different from the general population. The store may attract people from one social class or ethnic group more than others. You may be biased in which shoppers you approach to question and which ones you let pass by. Households with many members are more likely to have someone home when you knock on the door or call on the phone; hence you may undersample single people. Households with ferocious guard dogs are judiciously skipped by prudent interviewers. People without phones will not be netted in a telephone survey.

The fact that it is nearly impossible to obtain a perfect random sample does not mean that research is impossible. Our burden as researchers is to do work that is as free from bias as we can make it, and yet humbly admit that some small distortion still creeps in. An analogy is radio reception from a distant station: Occasionally there may be static distortion, but normally you can distinguish the music and lyrics. Accepted survey practices are accepted because experience has shown that they provide reasonably accurate data about the population being sampled.

You need to consider the purpose of your research. Are there special reasons why, given that purpose, a particular sampling method is desirable or undesirable? For example, if you wanted to study homeless people, a phone survey or a household survey of a middle-class neighborhood would not be efficient or appropriate. If you wanted to survey wealthy people, passing out questionnaires at a fast-food outlet would not be the best approach. There is no substitute for careful thinking. Consider first who is in the population you want to sample, and second what would be the most efficient means of obtaining a sample of these people that is approximately random.

Once you have gathered your data, the next step is to code it. All but one of the questions in the Happiness Questionnaire are precoded; that is, all possible responses for each question have already been given a number, and columns have been designated for the responses for each variable. Precoding saves time; however, it does require painstaking forethought and pretesting of the questionnaire. Precoding usually restricts you to multiple-choice questions. The choices may help the respondents answer as they consider the alternatives, but the set of answers may not allow some respondents to express their position precisely.

The last question on the questionnaire was deliberately left open-ended to provide the option of dealing with less structured data. If you want to have a quick and easy coding experience stop at question 12.

Question 13—"What do you think you could do to be happier five years from now than you are today?" will result in a plethora of answers. Come coding time you will have to decide whether you are going to categorize these responses into numbered groups for quantitative analysis or simply keep the verbal responses as material to quote when illustrating your findings in the coded questions. Open-ended questions can be eye openers for the researcher in illustrating factors that he or she may have overlooked or in pointing out that assumptions are unfounded.

Follow your instructor's guidelines for administering the Happiness Questionnaire to a sample of people.

The DATA LIST command for questions 1 through 12 of the questionnaire will be

DATA LIST / ID 1–4   HAPPY 5   HEALTH 6   SATFAM 7
           SATFRND 8   SATJOB 9
           EDUC 10–11   MARITAL 12   CHILDS 13
           INCOME 14   TVHOURS 15–16   SEX 17   AGE 18

Happiness Questionnaire

(Interviewer: Record the answer to each question in the boxes at right.)

ID

Columns 1–4

As a class exercise we are doing a study of what affects happiness. Will you please answer thirteen questions for us?

1.   Taken all together, would you say that you are very happy, pretty happy, or not too happy?
      1. Very happy
      2. Pretty happy
      3. Not too happy
      8. Don't know (DK)
      9. No answer (NA)

HAPPY

Column 5

2.   Would you say your own health, in general, is excellent, good, fair, or poor?
      1. Excellent
      2. Good
      3. Fair
      4. Poor
      8. DK
      9. NA

HEALTH

Column 6

3.   Tell me the number that shows how much satisfaction you get from your family life.
      1. A very great deal
      2. A great deal
      3. Quite a bit
      4. A fair amount
      5. Some
      6. A little
      7. None
      8. DK
      9. NA

SATFAM

Column 7

4. Tell me the number that shows how much
    satisfaction you get from your friendships.
    (Use the same choices as for Question 3)

SATFRND

Column 8

5. On the whole, how satisfied are you with the
    work you do? Would you say you are very
    satisfied, moderately satisfied, a little dissat-
    isfied, or very dissatisfied.
    0. Not applicable due to no job
    1. Very satisfied
    2. Moderately satisfied
    3. A little dissatisfied
    4. Very dissatisfied
    8. DK
    9. NA

SATJOB

Column 9

6. How many years of formal education have
    you completed? (Enter number of years.)
    98. DK
    99. NA

EDUC

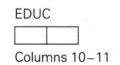

Columns 10–11

7. Are you currently married, widowed, di-
    vorced, or separated, or have you never been
    married?
    1. Married
    2. Widowed
    3. Divorced
    4. Separated
    5. Never married

MARITAL

Column 12

8. How many children have you ever had?
    Please count all that were born alive at any
    time (including any you had from a previous
    marriage).
    0–7. Actual number
    8.   Eight or more
    9.   NA

CHILDS

Column 13

9. Into which of the following groups did your total family income, from all sources, fall last year before taxes?
    1. Under $10,000
    2. $10,000 to $19,999
    3. $20,000 to $29,999
    4. $30,000 to $39,999
    5. $40,000 to $49,999
    6. $50,000 to $59,999
    7. $60,000+
    98. Don't know
    99. No answer

INCOME

Columns 14–15

10. On the average day, about how many hours do you personally watch television?
    0–24. Actual number
    98.   DK
    99.   NA

TVHOURS

Columns 16–17

11. Sex.
    1. Male
    2. Female

SEX

Column 18

12. What is your age?
    0–97. Actual age
    98.   DK
    99.   NA

AGE

Columns 19–20

13. This is the last question. What do you think you could do to be happier five years from now than you are today?

Thank you for your cooperation.

GLOSSARY OF SPSS COMMANDS

COMPUTE examples:

Mathematical operators—

+	plus
−	minus
*	multiplication
/	division
**	exponention
SQRT	square root

```
COMPUTE   ANSWER1=450+200

COMPUTE   ANSWER2=450-200

COMPUTE   ANSWER3=450*2

COMPUTE   ANSWER4=450/50

COMPUTE   ANSWER5=5**3

COMPUTE   ANSWER6=SQRT(81)

COMPUTE   TINC=WINC+HINC

COMPUTE   RETIRE=65-AGE

COMPUTE   TPAY=DSALARY*DAYS

COMPUTE   AVESAL=PAYROLL/NEMPLOYS

COMPUTE   DEVIAT=(INC-MINC)**2

COMPUTE   SD=SQRT(SUMDEV)
```

CROSSTABS examples:

```
DATA LIST   ID 1-2   EDUC 3-4   SEX 5   HAPPY 6
BEGIN DATA
    .
    .
    .
END DATA
MISSING VALUES   EDUC(-9,99)   HAPPY SEX(0)
RECODE   EDUC  (0 THRU 11=1)(12 THRU 15=2)(16 THRU 30=3)
CROSSTABS   EDUC BY SEX /
            CELLS=COLUMNS


GET  FILE=NORC90
CROSSTABS   SATFAM SATFRND SATJOB BY INCOME /
            CELLS=COUNT, COLUMNS /
            STATISTICS=CHISQ PHI
```

DATA LIST examples:

Single record file—

```
DATA LIST   ID 1-2   EDUC 3-4   SEX 5   HAPPY 6
```

Multiple record file—

```
DATA LIST / RECORDS=2/1 ID 1-4   SEX 6
                       /2 MARITAL 5
```

FREQUENCIES examples:

```
GET  FILE=NORC90
FREQUENCIES            ALL/
            STATISTICS


GET  FILE=NORC84
FREQUENCIES                 ABDEFECT ABNOMORE ABHLTH ABPOOR
                            ABRAPE ABSINGLE/
            STATISTICS
```

(The variable specifications could also be written ABDEFECT TO ABSINGLE.)

IF examples:

EQ	equal
NE	not equal
LT	less than
GT	greater than
LE	less than or equal to
GE	greater than or equal to

```
IF  AGE  LE  9   AGEGROUP=1
IF  AGE  GT  9   AND   AGE  LE  19   AGEGROUP=2
IF  AGE  GT  19   AND   AGE  LE  29   AGEGROUP=3
IF  AGE  GT  29   AND   AGE  LE  39   AGEGROUP=4
IF  AGE  GT  39   AND   AGE  LE  49   AGEGROUP=5
IF  AGE  GT  49   AND   AGE  LE  59   AGEGROUP=6
IF  AGE  GT  59   AND   AGE  LE  69   AGEGROUP=7
IF  AGE  GT  69   AND   AGE  LE  79   AGEGROUP=8
IF  AGE  GT  79   AGEGROUP=9


IF   TENURE  LT  12   NEWEXEC=1

IF   FAMINCOM  GT  AVEINCOM   INCOME=1
```

LIST examples:

```
LIST   ALL
       CASES=15

LIST   INCOME
       CASES=ALL

DATA LIST / ID 1-2   EDUC 3-4   SEX 5   HAPPY 6
BEGIN DATA
   .
   .
   .
END DATA
SELECT IF   SEX NE 1   OR   SEX NE 2
LIST   ALL
```

MEANS examples:

```
DATA LIST / ID 1-2   EDUC 3-4   SEX 5   HAPPY 6
BEGIN DATA
   .
   .
   .
END DATA
MISSING VALUES  EDUC(-9,99)   HAPPY SEX(0)
MEANS HAPPY BY SEX


GET  FILE=NORC90
MEANS  HAPPY BY HEALTH =
       STATISTICS ALL
```

MISSING VALUES examples:

```
MISSING VALUES   EDUC(-9)

MISSING VALUES   INCOME(-8,-9)

MISSING VALUES   SEX RELIGION PARTY(0)

MISSING VALUES   EDUC(-9,99)   HAPPY SEX(0)


DATA LIST / ID 1-2   EDUC 3-4   SEX 5   HAPPY 6
BEGIN DATA
   .
   .
   .
END DATA
MISSING VALUES   EDUC(-9,99)   HAPPY,SEX(0)
FREQUENCIES              ALL
```

RECODE examples:

```
RECODE   MARITAL  (2 THRU 4=1)

RECODE   HEIGHT  (LOW THRU 59=1)(60 THRU 70=2)
             (71 THRU HI=3)

RECODE   CARS  (3 THRU HI=2)

RECODE   AGE  (LO THRU 15=1)(16 THRU 65=2)(66 THRU HI=3)
```

SELECT IF examples:

EQ   equal

NE   not equal

LT   less than

GT   greater than

LE   less than or equal to

GE   greater than or equal to

SELECT IF   EDUC GT 15

SELECT IF   SEX EQ 1

SELECT IF   AGE GT 15   OR   AGE LT 66

SELECT IF   EDUC GT 16   OR   INCOME GT 30000

SELECT IF   EDUC GT 12   AND   SEX EQ 2

SELECT IF   SEX EQ 2   AND   (AGE GT 14   AND   AGE LT 45)

(The parentheses in this command are not necessary, but they do make it easier to read. The same cases could be selected by using two SELECT IF commands—one for SEX and one for AGE.)

SELECT IF   SEX EQ 2
SELECT IF   AGE GT 14   AND   AGE LT 45

DATA LIST / ID 1−2   EDUC 3−4   SEX 5   HAPPY 6
BEGIN DATA
   .
   .
   .
END DATA
SELECT IF   SEX EQ 1
FREQUENCIES   EDUC SEX HAPPY/
                STATISTICS

TEMPORARY examples:

```
DATA LIST / ID 1—2   EDUC 3—4   SEX 5   HAPPY 6
BEGIN DATA
    .
    .
    .
END DATA
TEMPORARY
SELECT IF   SEX EQ 1
FREQUENCIES   ALL/
              STATISTICS
TEMPORARY
SELECT IF   SEX EQ 2
FREQUENCIES   ALL/
              STATISTICS


GET   FILE=NORC90
TEMPORARY
SELECT IF   AGE GT 49
FREQUENCIES   EDUC/
              STATISTICS
TEMPORARY
SELECT IF   AGE GT 24   AND   AGE LT 50
FREQUENCIES   EDUC/
              STATISTICS
```

ANSWERS TO
REVIEW QUESTIONS

Chapter 1

1.1 Column 1

1.2 Any column after column 1 and before column 72

1.3 Column 72

1.4 Column 80

1.5 Column 72

1.6 No. Computer installations do not all use the same operating system language. Even if they did, the components of the system and the names given to accounts, printers, tapes, disks, and so on, would differ.

1.7 Yes

1.8 Tapes, disks, and memory core

1.9 Most likely not. It will probably be one of many terminals communicating with a mainframe central processing unit and its accompanying set of input devices, storage devices, and output devices.

1.10 Program commands instruct the computer about how to obtain, process, and store information about cases in your study. The data are the actual information about the cases.

Chapter 2

2.1 The Hedderson case would be coded 25 in the first two columns to indicate his identification number. The third and fourth columns would be coded 21 to indicate the 21 years of formal education, the fifth column would be coded 1 to indicate his sex, and the sixth column would be coded 1 to indicate that he stated he felt very happy. Thus, the record line for Hedderson would read:

252111

2.2   To code age, researchers usually simply record the respondent's age in years in two columns. Someone who is 19 years old would be given a value of 19. Someone who is 45 years old would be given a value of 45. Grouped intervals could also be used. For example:

AGE	*Code*
Under 10	1
10–19	2
20–29	3
30–39	4
40–49	5
50–59	6
60–70	7
Over 70	8

2.3   In the United States, political party affiliation might be coded as follows:

Party	*Code*
Democrat	1
Republican	2
Independent (no affiliation)	3
Other affiliation	4

The code numbers used to indicate the categories of a variable are an arbitrary choice of the researcher. In this example, Republican could just as well be coded 1, and Democrat 2. The code numbers are merely short labels used to save space.

2.4   The simplest way to code annual salary would be to use two columns and code the case's income in thousands of dollars. Thus, someone with an income of $20,000 would be given a value of 20. A value of 99 could be used for people whose annual income is $99,000 or more.

2.5   DATA LIST / EDUC 3-4

2.6   DATA LIST commands are not used with SPSS system files. The variable location information is already saved with the file.

2.7   DATA LIST / INCOME 13
                     SEX 16

2.8   MISSING VALUES   EDUC (-9)

2.9   MISSING VALUES   INCOME (-9, -8)

2.10 MISSING VALUES   SEX
                           RELIGION
                           PARTY (0)

2.11 Nothing. It is treated as missing automatically by the program.

Chapter 3

3.1   DATA LIST / ID 1-2
                     EDUC 3-4
                     SEX 5
                     HAPPY 6
          BEGIN DATA
          010912
          021223
          031521
          041222
          050611
          061612
          071522
          081612
          091821
          101412
          111321
          121611
          130922
          141212
          151221
          161821
          170821

```
181222
191613
201421
END DATA
LIST
```

3.2   GET   FILE=NORC90
LIST   ALL
CASES=20

3.3   GET   FILE=NORC90
LIST   INCOME
CASES=ALL

Your commands would be the same as 3.1 except ALL would replace LIST.

3.4   FREQUENCIES   ZIPCODE

3.5   FREQUENCIES   AGE SEX MARITAL

3.6   You would need to recode INCOME into a manageable number of categories. Otherwise there would be almost as many income categories in the frequencies table as there are cases, because most people would have a unique income.

3.7   This output indicates that a variable named NEIGHBOR has three categories coded 1, 2, and 3. Category 1 has three cases, or 30.0 percent of the total number of cases for which there are data. Category 2 has five cases, or 50.0 percent of the total number of cases for which there are data. Category 3 has two cases, or 20.0 percent of the total number of cases for which there are data. There is one "missing case," which means there is one case for which we do not have the NEIGHBOR information.

3.8   GET   FILE=NORC90
FREQUENCIES   ALL/
STATISTICS

3.9   GET   FILE=NORC90
FREQUENCIES   ABDEFECT ABNOMORE ABHLTH
ABPOOR ABRAPE ABSINGLE/
STATISTICS

3.10   GET   FILE=NORC90
FREQUENCIES   EDUC HEALTH HAPPY/
STATISTICS

3.11   SELECT IF   SEX EQ 1

3.12   SELECT IF   AGE GT 65

3.13   SELECT IF   EDUC GT 16   OR   INCOME GT 30000

3.14   SELECT IF   AGE GT 15   OR   AGE LT 66

3.15   SELECT IF   SEX EQ 2   AND   (AGE GT 14 AND AGE LT 45)

The parentheses in this command are not necessary, but they do make it easier to read. The same cases could also be selected by using two SELECT IF commands: one for SEX and one for AGE:

```
SELECT IF   SEX EQ 2
SELECT IF   AGE GT 14   AND   AGE LT 45
```

3.16   SELECT IF   EDUC GT 15   AND   SEX EQ 2
      LIST   ALL
          CASES=25

Chapter 4

4.1   RECODE   MARITAL   (3,4=2)

4.2   RECODE   HEIGHT   (LOW THRU 59=1) (60 THRU 70=2)
                    (71 THRU HI=3)

4.3   RECODE   CARS   (2 THRU HI=2)

    or

    RECODE   CARS   (3 THRU HI=2)

4.4   RECODE   AGE   (0 THRU 15=1) (16 THRU 65=2)
               (66 THRU HI=3)

4.5   COMPUTE   FAMILY$=WIFE$+HUSBAND$

4.6   COMPUTE   HOURLY$=SALARY/160

4.7   IF   TENURE LT 12   NEWEXEC=1
    IF   TENURE GT 11   NEWEXEC=0

4.8   IF   FAMINCOM GT AVEINCOM   INCOME=1
    IF   FAMINCOM LT AVEINCOM   INCOME=0

4.9   GET FILE=NORC90
            TEMPORARY
            SELECT IF SEX EQ 1
            FREQUENCIES INCOME/
                    STATISTICS
            TEMPORARY
            SELECT IF SEX EQ 2
            FREQUENCIES INCOME/
                    STATISTICS

4.10   GET FILE=NORC90
            SELECT IF AGE GT 49
            FREQUENCIES EDUC/
                    STATISTICS
            TEMPORARY
            SELECT IF AGE GT 24 AND AGE LT 50
            FREQUENCIES EDUC/
                    STATISTICS

4.11   VARIABLE LABEL CHILDS 'NUMBER OF CHILDREN'

4.12   VARIABLE LABEL INCOME 'GROSS INCOME'
                        NET 'NET INCOME'

4.13   VALUE LABELS POLVIEWS 1'LIBERAL'
                           2'MIDDLE OF THE ROAD'
                           3'CONSERVATIVE'

4.14   VALUE LABELS OVERDUE 1'LESS THAN 60 DAYS'
                           2'MORE THAN 60 DAYS'/
                MILITARY 1'MILITARY PERSONNEL'
                         2'CIVILIAN PERSONNEL'

Chapter 5

5.1   CROSSTABS INCOME BY SEX/
                  CELLS=COLUMN

(You might also add COUNT to the CELLS subcommand if you want to print the number of cases in each cell.)

5.2   CROSSTABS SALES BY DAY/
                  CELLS=COLUMN/
                  STATISTICS ALL

5.3   DATA LIST / ID 1-2
                   EDUC 3-4
                   SEX 5
                   HAPPY 6
    BEGIN DATA
    010912
    021223
    031521
    041222
    050611
    061612
    071522
    081612
    091821
    101412
    111321
    121611
    130922
    141212
    151221
    161821
    170821
    181222
    191613
    201421
    END DATA
    MISSING VALUES   EDUC(-9,99)
                       HAPPY
                       SEX(0)
    RECODE EDUC (0 THRU 11=1)(12 THRU 15=2) (16 THRU 30=3)
    CROSSTABS   EDUC BY SEX/
    CELLS=COLUMN/
    STATISTICS=CHISQ PHI

5.4   GET   FILE=NORC90
    CROSSTABS   POLVIEWS BY RELIGION/
                      CELLS=COLUMN/
                      STATISTICS=CHISQ PHI

5.5   GET   FILE=NORC84
    CROSSTABS   HAPPY HEALTH INCOME BY EDUC
                      CELLS=COLUMN/
                      STATISTICS=CHISQ PHI

5.6   GET   FILE=NORC90
            CROSSTABS   HAPPY BY MARITAL BY SEX
                        CELLS=COLUMN/

5.7   STATISTICS=CHISQ PHI

5.8   Cramer's *V* is a transformation of chi-square that ranges from 0.0 for no association to 1.0 for a perfect association. Unlike chi-square, the size of Cramer's *V* is not affected by the number of cases or cells. It is, however, affected by the percentage of cases in each category of the variables being used. For example, if one sample had 20 percent females and a second sample had 60 percent females, this in itself would alter Cramer's *V* involving sex as a variable—even if the associations between sex and the other variables were the same.

Chapter 6

6.1   MEANS   INCOME BY SEX

6.2   MEANS   HEALTH BY EDUC INCOME

6.3   DATA LIST / ID 1-2
                          EDUC 3-4
                          SEX 5
                          HAPPY 6
            BEGIN DATA
            010912
            021223
            031521
            041222
            050611
            061612
            071522
            081612
            091821
            101412
            111321
            121611
            130922
            141212
            151221
            161821
            170821

```
          181222
          191613
          201421
          END DATA
          MISSING VALUES   EDUC (-9,99)
                           HAPPY
                           SEX(0)
          MEANS   HAPPY BY EDUC
```

6.4   GET   FILE=NORC90
        MEANS   HAPPY BY HEALTH

6.5   The criterion variable in a MEANS output is the variable whose mean score is given for each category of another variable.

6.6   In a MEANS command, the dependent variable is placed before the BY.

6.7   MEANS   INCOME BY SEX BY EDUC

6.8   MEANS   INCOME BY EDUC/
        ALL
        STATISTICS

6.9   SELECT IF   EDUC EQ 12   OR   EDUC EQ 15
        MEANS   INCOME BY EDUC/
        ALL
        STATISTICS

Chapter 7

7.1   PLOT/PLOT=INCOME WITH EDUC

7.2   PLOT/PLOT=INCOME EDUC WITH AGE

7.3   CORR   HAPPY HEALTH

7.4   CORR   INCOME AGE FAMSIZE CARSIZE/
        FORMAT SERIAL

7.5   No, there would not be enough variance in the number of cars per family to produce a revealing plot. Too many cases would be clustered in the 1-to-3 range.

7.6   There would be too many cases per point in the plot. The problem could be solved by using the SAMPLE command to select out a suitable proportion of the cases. (See the discussion of SAMPLE in Section 7.2.)

7.7   Technically, the Pearson correlation coefficient is meant for interval variables that are linearly associated. The technique is robust, however, and will usually produce reasonably accurate estimates for ordinal variables. Nominal variables with only two categories may also be used with the Pearson correlation coefficient. Nominal variables with more than two categories are absolutely inappropriate and produce nonsensical coefficients.

7.8   The Pearson correlation coefficient presumes a linear relationship; therefore, an exponential negative relationship would not be measured accurately. Using a COMPUTE statement to create a new variable, the log of the infant death rate, and then doing the correlation analysis with the new variable would be appropriate. (See the discussion of the COMPUTE statement in Section 4.2.)

7.9   The negative coefficient indicates that, as one variable increases in value, the other variable tends to decrease in value. The positive coefficient indicates that, as one variable increases in value, the other variable tends to increase in value.

7.10 The Pearson correlation coefficient squared is the true measure of the strength of the association; thus, the relative strengths would be $(.20)^2$ to $(.30)^2$, or .04 to .09. The association between HEALTH and EDUC is only four ninths as strong as the association between HEALTH and INCOME. (The associations in this question are purely hypothetical.)

Chapter 8

8.1
```
GET FILE NORTH
COMPUTE REGION=1
SAVE OUTFILE=NORTH
```

8.2
```
ADD FILE /   FILE=NORTH/
             FILE=SOUTH/
             FILE=EAST/
             FILE=WEST
```

8.3
```
ADD FILE /   FILE=*/
             FILE=BRITAIN
```

8.4
```
CROSSTABS   HAPPY BY REGION/
            CELLS=COUNT, COLUMN
            STATISTICS=CHISQ PHI
```

8.5   MEANS   INCOME BY REGION BY EDUC /
                    STATISTICS ALL

Chapter 9

9.1   Theoretically, the dependent and independent variables in a multiple regression analysis should be interval variables. In practice, ordinal variables are often used. Two-category nominal variables, also called dichotomous variables, can be used as well, if neither category has fewer than 20 percent of the cases.

9.2   REGRESSION   VARIABLES=HEALTH INCOME EDUC HAPPY
                        AGE SEX /
                        DEPENDENT=HEALTH /
                        METHOD=ENTER

9.3   IF   RELIG EQ 1   D1=1
           IF   RELIG NE 1   D1=0
           IF   RELIG EQ 2   D2=1
           IF   RELIG NE 2   D2=0
           IF   RELIG EQ 3   D3=1
           IF   RELIG NE 3   D3=0
           IF   RELIG EQ 4   D4=1
           IF   RELIG NE 4   D4=0
           REGRESSION
                VARIABLES=HAPPY INCOME HEALTH D1 D2 D3 D4 /
                DEPENDENT=HAPPY /
                METHOD=ENTER

9.4   The multiple R is the correlation between the dependent variable and the entire set of independent variables. The multiple R squared is the proportion of variance in the dependent variable associated with variance in the independent variables.

9.5   Multicollinearity problems exist when there are high intercorrelations among the independent variables. Multicollinearity causes unreliable estimates of beta—that is, estimates that fluctuate greatly from one sample to another. The problem can be resolved by dropping one of two highly correlated variables from the set of independent variables or combining them into a composite variable. There is no problem when more than one independent variable is highly correlated with the dependent variable. Only when two or more independent variables are highly correlated with each other do we have multicollinearity problems.

9.6   When the plot of the standardized residuals by the standardized predicted values is not random, the association between the dependent variable and the set of independent variables is not linear. Either the dependent variable or one or more of the independent variables needs to be transformed.

9.7   REGRESSION VARIABLES=HEALTH INCOME EDUC HAPPY
                                AGE SEX/
                           DEPENDENT=HEALTH/
                           METHOD=ENTER/
                           SCATTERPLOT (*RES,*PRE)/

Chapter 10

10.1   MANOVA will enable the reader to use a covariate, to obtain significance tests for multiple predictor variables, and to analyze group differences on a set of dependent variables. Other techniques would do a separate analysis for each dependent variable.

10.2   When there is only one dependent variable, MANOVA assumes its variance within each of the groups is normal and the same. For more than one dependent variable, MANOVA requires the additional assumption that the joint distribution of the dependent variables is multivariate normal. The variances of the dependent variables need not equal one another, but the distribution of scores on one dependent variable for all the cases with a particular score on another dependent variable should be normal.

10.3   MANOVA EDUC BY MARITAL (1,5) BY SEX (1,2)

10.4   Yes, MANOVA assumes that there are some cases for each value in the range indicated.

10.5   MANOVA EDUC BY MARITAL(1,5) SEX(1,2) WITH INCOME

10.6   MANOVA CONFINAN TO CONARMY BY RELIG(1,5) SEX(1,2)

10.7   It would mean that the differences between MARITAL groups, controlling for SEX, would occur from sampling error only 2 times out of 1000.

10.8   It would mean that the differences between the sexes in the effects of marital status would occur less than 1 time out of 1000 owing to sampling error.

10.9 Marital status would be a significant variable in the analysis because of the way it influenced the differences in scores by sex. It would not matter that the effects of marital status alone were not significant.

10.10 Pillai's trace

Chapter 11

11.1 DISCRIMINANT GROUPS=CLASS(1,4) /
      VARIABLES=SEX RACE AGE INCOME EDUC DEFENSE SPEND

11.2 GET FILE=NORC90
     SELECT IF SEX EQ 2
     IF CHILDS EQ 0 AND WRKSTAT GE 4 FAMWORK=1
     IF CHILDS NE 0 AND WRKSTAT GE 4 FAMWORK=2
     IF CHILDS EQ 0 AND WRKSTAT LT 4 FAMWORK=3
     IF CHILDS NE 0 AND WRKSTAT LT 4 FAMWORK=4
     DISCRIMINANT GROUPS=FAMWORK#
     VARIABLES=RACE EDUC INCOME AGE MEMPLOY CLASS

11.3 The primary purpose of a discriminant analysis is to improve our ability to classify cases. Compare the percent of cases that were misclassified by the discriminant analysis to the percent that would be misclassified by chance. The proportion improvement is equal to

$$\frac{\text{Random error proportion} - \text{Discriminant model-error proportion}}{\text{Random error proportion}}$$

11.4 The expected percentage of correct classifications is equal to the sum of the squared proportion in each group.

11.5 The statistical significance of a discriminant analysis is produced for the Wilks' lambda statistic in the Canonical Discriminant Functions table of the output.

11.6 Compare the percentage of cases classified correctly with that function in the analysis to the percentage classified correctly when that function is not in the analysis. This procedure can be done with the FUNCTIONS subcommand. FUNCTIONS 1 will include only the first and most powerful function; FUNCTIONS 2 will include the two most powerful functions, and so forth. The difference between the percentage of cases classified correctly with function 2 and with function 1 is the improvement made by the second function. The difference between the percentage of cases classified correctly with function 3 and with function 2 is the improvement made by the third function.

11.7 The statistical significance of individual functions can be assessed from the output in the Canonical Discriminant Functions table. The statistical significance is approximated by the drop in the statistical significance after the function's effects are removed. The statistical significance for Wilks' lambda (the ratio of the within-groups sum of squares to the total sum of squares) is used.

11.8 To determine the contribution of a particular variable to the discriminant analysis classification accuracy, redo the analysis, dropping the variable in question from the VARIABLES subcommand. The change in the percentage of cases classified correctly when the variable is dropped represents the variable's contribution.

$$\text{Contribution} = \%\text{ correct with variable} - \%\text{ correct without variable}$$

11.9 To approximate the contribution of a particular variable to the statistical significance of a discriminant analysis, drop the variable in question from the analysis and compare the statistical significance of the analysis using the variable to the statistical significance without the variable. Letting P^2 equal the statistical significance without the variable and P^1 equal the statistical significance with the variable, the formula would be

$$\text{Contribution} = \frac{P^2 - P^1}{P^2}$$

This contribution is the proportionate reduction in the likelihood that the group differences are the result of sampling probability error.

11.10 To classify new cases, use the SELECT subcommand to choose the cases used for calculating the discriminant function, and use the subcommands STATISTICS TABLE PLOT CASES to produce for each of the new cases its predicted group membership.

Chapter 12

12.1 Regression analysis assumes that the dependent variable and the predictor variables are interval and that the dependent variable is normally distributed for each value of the predictor variables.

12.2 When a table has three or more variables and many cells, log-linear analysis with the HILOGLINEAR command will allow the user to see more easily what the significant relationships are.

12.3 A log-linear analysis of health (4 categories) by marital (5 categories) by religion (5 categories) would normally require (4*5*5)*5 = 500 cases.

12.4
```
HILOGLINEAR   HEALTH(1,4) MARITAL(1,5)
                 RELIGION(1,5)/
         PRINT ALL
```

12.5 The first-order effects would indicate whether each cell in the table has the same number of cases. This statistic is uninteresting because we do not expect to have an equal number of cases in each category of these variables.

12.6 The second-order effects would indicate whether any of the bivariate associations controlling for the effects of the third variable were significant—for example, whether the association between HEALTH and MARITAL is significant controlling for the effects of RELIG.

12.7 The third-order effects would indicate interaction effects—for example, whether the association between HEALTH and MARITAL is the same for each value of RELIG.

12.8 The chi-square and probability of the highest-order effects are given in the output in the table entitled TESTS THAT K-WAY AND HIGHER ORDER EFFECTS ARE ZERO.

12.9 The partial chi-square is a measure of the association between HEALTH and MARITAL controlling for the effects of RELIG. A partial chi-square probability of .023 would indicate that an association at least this strong would occur 23 times out of 1000 through sampling error.

12.10 The strength of the association is most easily measured by comparing the observed frequencies in the categories of the dependent variable for the different categories of the predictor variables.

Chapter 13

13.1 A factor is a composite variable underlying the variance in a set of variables.

13.2 A factor loading is a measure of the association between a variable and a factor of which it is one component. Factor loadings range from −1.0 to 1.0. A 0 would indicate no association, and a 1 would indicate a perfect association. The sign of the loading indicates whether the association is positive or negative.

13.3   The eigenvalue is a measure of variance in the set of variables in the factor analysis. The total eigenvalue is equal to the number of variables in the analysis.

13.4   The communality of a variable is the proportion of its variance accounted for by the variables in the analysis. The communality is 0.0 for no association and 1.0 for a perfect association. The communality of all the variables will be 1.0 when the number of factors equals the number of variables.

13.5   A factor score is the value of the factor for a particular case.

13.6   In an orthogonal rotation, the correlation between the factors in the analysis is kept at 0.0. In an oblique rotation, some correlation is permitted among the factors in the analysis. The default level of correlation in an oblique rotation will usually be below an absolute value of 0.30.

13.7   The factor extraction technique used by default for FACTOR is principal components.

13.8   The default rotation technique is a varimax orthogonal rotation.

13.9   The default rotation technique when the ROTATION=OBLIQUE subcommand is given is oblimin.

13.10 `FACTOR   VARIABLES=CONFINAN TO CONARMY/`

Chapter 14

14.1   A PUMS file is a sample of households and individuals. An STF file has as units geographic areas for which aggregate statistics are available.

14.2   Yes

14.3   No. The necessary individual data would be lacking.

14.4   When you want the information on a household record applied to the individuals who reside in the household

14.5   Use a SELECT IF command with the variable SUMRYLV, which indicates geographic level.

14.6   Use a SELECT IF command with the variable RECOIND, which indicates ethnic and racial group.

14.7 There is not a household-value variable for which you can produce a frequencies table. Rather, each cell in the household value distribution is a variable that must be named and included in a LIST command.

14.8 In the STF files a 0 value can indicate that the information was suppressed or it can indicate that the coded value was 0. You need to use an IF statement with the variable that indicates suppression to change 0 to a missing value when suppression is indicated.

Chapter 15

15.1 Use the command MD YOURID. This is not an SPSS/PC+ command and would not be followed by a period.

15.2 Use the command CD YOURID. Again, this is not an SPSS/PC+ command and would not be followed by a period.

15.3 Enter the command SPSSPC. It is not followed by a period and does not have a slash between the SPSS and the PC.

15.4 Hold down the Alt key while pressing the M key.

15.5 The Delete key erases. The Backspace key deletes errors and moves to the left.

15.6 Press the F1 key and then the Enter key.

15.7 When the Help Display is on the screen, press the F1 key.

15.8 Hold down the Ctrl key and press the Home key.

15.9 Hold down the Ctrl key and press the End key.

15.10 The Insert key moves Review between modes.

15.11 Press the F10 key.

15.12 Press the Enter key to see the rest of the output.

15.13 The program will be in Menu mode after it has executed.

15.14 Hold down the Ctrl key and press the M key.

15.15 Output is stored in SPSS.LIS.

15.16 No. Your output file will be written over the next time you execute an SPSS/PC+ program.

15.17 Rename the file.

15.18 Press the F9 key and follow the prompts.

15.19   Commands are stored in SPSS.LOG.

15.20   Press the F9 key and follow the prompts.

15.21   Press the F3 key and follow the prompts.

15.22   Follow prompts while in the Menu mode of the Review editor program.

REFERENCES

Blalock, Hubert. *Social Statistics: Revised Second Edition* (New York: McGraw-Hill, 1979).

Iversen, Gudmund R., and Helmut Norpoth. *Analysis of Variance* (Beverly Hills, CA: Sage, 1976).

Jendrek, Margaret. *Through the Maze: Statistics with Computer Applications* (Belmont, CA: Wadsworth, 1985).

Kim, Jae-On, and Charles W. Mueller. *Introduction to Factor Analysis: What It Is and How to Do It* (Beverly Hills, CA: Sage, 1978).

Klecka, William R. *Discriminant Analysis* (Beverly Hills, CA: Sage, 1980).

Knoke, David, and Peter J. Burke. *Log-Linear Models* (Beverly Hills, CA: Sage, 1980).

Lewis-Beck, Michael S. *Applied Regression: An Introduction* (Beverly Hills, CA: Sage, 1980).

Meyers, Dowell. *Analysis with Local Census Data: Portraits of Change* (San Diego, CA: Academic Press, 1992).

Reynolds, H. T. *Analysis of Nominal Data* (Beverly Hills, CA: Sage, 1977).

Roundtree, Derek. *Statistics Without Tears* (New York: Charles Scribner's Sons, 1981).

SPSS Inc. *Reference Guide* (Chicago, IL: SPSS Inc. 1990).

SPSS Inc. *SPSS Processing of U.S. Census Data* (Chicago, IL: SPSS Inc., 1984).

INDEX

Pages on which definitions appear are *italicized*.